Conversations with
the Cannibals

ALSO BY MICHAEL KRIEGER:

*Tramp: Sagas of High Adventure in the
Vanishing World of the Old Tramp Freighters*

Conversations with

the Cannibals

THE END OF THE

OLD SOUTH PACIFIC

Michael Krieger

THE ECCO PRESS

THE ECCO PRESS
100 West Broad Street
Hopewell, New Jersey 08525
Published simultaneously in Canada by
Penguin Books Canada Ltd., Ontario
Printed in the United States of America

FIRST EDITION

Library of Congress Cataloging-in-Publication Data

Krieger, Michael, 1940-
Conversations with the cannibals : the end of the old South
Pacific / by Michael Krieger.
p.   cm.
1. Ethnology--Polynesia.   2. Ethnology--Melanesia.   3. Polynesia-
-Social life and customs.   4. Melanesia--Social life and customs.
I. Title.
GN670.K75   1994   306'.0995--dc20   93-40011
ISBN   0-88001-360-5

The text of this book is set in Electra

Contents

Introduction

The proposition that the world has changed more in the last two hundred years than in the preceding two thousand certainly rings true for such isolated sections of the globe as the South Pacific, where prior to the early 1800s most indigenous peoples had little or no contact with Europeans or other Westerners. During the last fifty years in particular, modern communication and transportation have brought astonishingly rapid metamorphoses to cultures throughout the region. World War II initiated the process: It sent soldiers, sailors, and airmen cascading over remote areas that had never before felt the footstep of an outsider. After the war, development continued unabated, with roads and landing strips checkerboarding the secluded domains of tribes and villagers still largely innocent of the outside world.

Today, international airports, Hertz rent-a-cars, and the "hamburger culture" have taken over the South Pacific as they have everywhere else. Only isolated outposts of pre–twentieth-century societies still remain today. This book, then, is a modest attempt to capture the flavor of this dying age, of this disappearing way of life, and of the South Pacific's cultures, subcultures, and extraordinary people who represent an epoch on the verge of extinction.

Because my focus has been on those individuals who personify the spirit of the old South Pacific, I have had to neglect hundreds of other people deserving attention, the many brilliant islanders involved in twentieth-century life. For instance, there are Ni Vanuatu entrepreneurs, Tuvaluan statesmen, Cook Islands scientists, and Solomon Islands diplomats, and while I have the highest regard for these Melanesian and Polynesian leaders, this book is not about them. It is about the islanders still living as their ancestors did, and it is about Westerners who bring to mind the faded pictures of the old explorers, plantation owners, missionaries, and rugged individualists who went where most Europeans were afraid to go.

It was not possible to draw stories from every country in the South Pacific, nor would I have wanted to. In most of the South Seas the old cultures have been forgotten. The video parlor has replaced the meeting house; Pepsi, tinned corned beef, and white rice have displaced freshly caught fish and taro. Many countries suffer from grinding poverty, extreme social injustice, and the violence associated with pervasive hopelessness. In any case, this book is not a catalog of traditional life in the South Pacific. Rather, it is a collection of the most fascinating examples I could find from parts of two Melanesian and two Polynesian countries where the old ways have yet to be extinguished.

There are numerous unpalatable aspects of this time-gone-past. The white colonials bestowed inferior status and servitude on many islanders, a legacy of racism that still lingers despite the increased self-respect conferred by recent independence. To ignore or gloss over these colonial vestiges would be grossly misleading. Tribal life was not a bowl of cherries either. The violence and sexual inequities inherent in some of the tribal cultures may lead the reader to judge them harshly. However, I would counsel that before doing so, perhaps we should first examine our own culture for violations in these areas. The stories in this book are true and the characters who appear in them are real people. In order to protect their privacy, I have changed many of their names as well as the names and locations of some of their villages.

While I am critical of the attempts by missionaries to eradicate islanders' cultures, and although I am a strong proponent of efforts to resurrect those cultures, I also respect many of the same missionaries for the good works they have done and continue to do. In most South Pacific countries they were the only ones who stood by the islanders and tried to protect them from injustices and decades of racial abuse at the hands of other Europeans. Missionary organizations still provide the only medical assistance and education throughout large areas of countries too poor to care for their own people. Missionaries furnished me with much valuable information and important contacts without which this book could not have been written.

A great many kind people across the Pacific assisted me in my work and travels. Particularly, I wish to thank Ron Powell, Dawn Neale, Dave (Young Bill) Marsters and his father, Tuakana Marsters, of the Cook Islands; Ray Woosley, Reggie Nalo, Amos Andeng, Mark Yakume, Kirk Huffman, Reece Discomb, and Ken Hutton of Vanuatu; Inspector Uaelesi Taafaki, Vanguna and Sunia Satupa, Geoff and Jenny Jackson, Isa Paeniu, and Tim Gentle of Tuvalu; John Lee, Zina, Gordon Smith, David Kausumae, Rex Inigana, Lysander and Mathew Namo, Silas Wanebeni, Joan Gordon, and Geoff Dennis of the Solomon Islands; and, of course, all the people who are in the stories. I wish also to acknowledge my gratitude to four people who were instrumental in making this book a reality: Mavis Mitten and Jo Ann Gergin, my research assistants; Sue Ann Fazio, who, always with wonderful humor, did most of the transcribing and typing; and Carol Bee, my very fine editor. Finally, I would like to express my appreciation to Susan Krieger, who arrived in time to witness the last and most difficult part of this endeavor.

MIKE KRIEGER

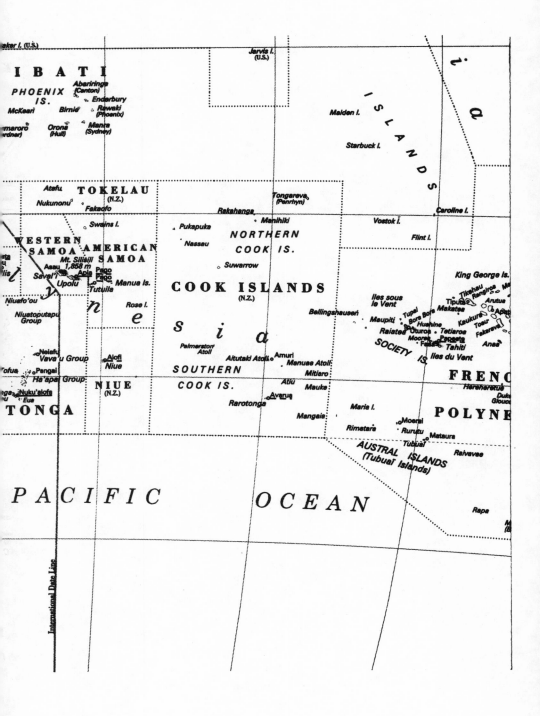

aker I. (U.S.)

IBATI

PHOENIX
IS.

McKean   Birnie   Rawaki
                    (Phoenix)
Abariringa
(Canton)   Enderbury

maroro   Orona   Manra
rdner)   (Hull)   (Sydney)

Jarvis I.
(U.S.)

Maiden I.

Starbuck I.

I S L A N D S

i a

Caroline I.

Atafu   TOKELAU
              (N.Z.)
Nukunonu Fakaofo

Tongareva,
(Penrhyn)

Rakahanga

Manihiki

Vostok I.

Flint I.

Swains I.

Pukapuka

Nassau

NORTHERN
COOK IS.

WESTERN
SAMOA   AMERICAN
              SAMOA
Mt. Silisili
Asau 1,858 m
Savai'i   Aola
Upolu   Pago
              Pago
        Tutuila   Manua Is.

Suwarrow

COOK ISLANDS
(N.Z.)

Iles sous
le Vent

Bellingshausen

King George Is.

Tikehau Rangiroa
Tupai Makatea
Bora Bora
Maupiti Huahine
    Raiatea Tetiaroa
        Oturoa Moorea Papeete
              Fetea Tahiti
              Iles du Vent

Tipuai
Arutua
Kaukura   Toau
        Anaa   Fakarava

SOCIETY IS.

Niuafo'ou

Niuatoputapu
Group

Rose I.

n   e   s   i   a

Neiafu
Vava'u Group

Alofi
Niue

Palmerston
Atoll

SOUTHERN
COOK IS.

Aitutaki Atoll Amuri
        Manuae Atoll
              Mitiaro

Atiu
Mauke

FRENC

Herehere'ue

Duk
Glouce

ofua Pangai
    Ha'apai Group

NIUE
(N.Z.)

Avarua

Rarotonga

Maria I.

Mangaia

Moerai
Rurutu
Rimatara   Mataura

Tubuai

POLYNE

ga Nuku'alofa
    Eua

TONGA

AUSTRAL
ISLANDS
(Tubuai Islands)

Raivavae

PACIFIC   OCEAN

Rapa

M
(B

I

The Cook Islands

TALES FROM

A DISTANT ISLAND

1

WHERE THE FLYING

FISHES PLAY

The *Avarua*, a rusty old tramp, rolls and pitches as she sloshes through a beam sea toward a lonely speck over the horizon. Three hundred miles northwest of Rarotonga and two hundred miles from Aitutake, its closest island neighbor, lies little Palmerston. It is a one-half-mile-long bit of coral, barely three hundred yards wide, and isolated as any island in the Pacific.

The sixty-one Polynesians who live on the tiny atoll see outsiders only a few times a year. The *Avarua* or another interisland freighter stops irregularly to drop off supplies, to load the island's fish and copra, and perhaps to take a few passengers to Samoa or Rarotonga. A passing yacht might stop for a couple of hours, and once every few years, a mini–cruise ship allows its seventy passengers an afternoon there. Since no vessel-size passages cut through the reef into the lagoon and because there are no protected deep-water anchorages, the few captains who do stop at Palmerston usually consider it too dangerous to stay, even overnight. The island also is cut off from air service. With no airstrip and with thousands of coral heads protruding like calcinated sculptures in the beautiful seven-mile-long lagoon, nothing can land there.

I'm on my way to visit this minute outpost of civilization after hearing about the idyllic life there which, purportedly, is much the same today as it was fifty, even a hundred years ago.

So far, my voyage on the *Avarua* has been most colorful. The majority of the thirty or forty passengers returning to their home islands are quartered in a tent erected on the hatch cover, and most of them are presently in their tent suffering greatly from mal de mer. This is a common occurrence on interisland ships, and to many sailors these vessels are affectionately known as "pukers."

Cecil, the ship's captain, has also been indisposed for the better part of the two days since leaving Rarotonga. Cecil is a handsome man, about forty, with curly black hair and limpid brown eyes that most likely have melted many a wahini's heart. However, while age may have slowed his lithe step, his Polynesian jocularity has not deserted him. The few times I see him he is always friendly, conveying some small joke or humorous aside, and he is always helpful. The *Avarua* has been Cecil's one and only command for the last eight years. She is a thirty-year-old, decrepit, 400-tonner registered in the Royal Kingdom of Tonga and carries a general cargo of supplies and building materials, some of which has already been off-loaded at Aitutake. She is now staggering toward the northern island group and Western Samoa to discharge the rest of her cargo and to disembark the vessel's passengers. For U.S. $100 above the normal $50-a-day cabin-and-meal passage, Cecil has agreed to stop at Palmerston, which is roughly en route, to drop me off.

Along with two elderly male proteges, Cecil has been lying low in his cabin. Now he emerges onto the bridge for one of his three or four daily position checks. With his nodding entourage of islanders idling nearby, he makes the simple computations necessary to translate the information from satellite navigator to a position fix. "Ha! We are only four miles off [course]," he proclaims. Cecil jots a penciled position on the chart and carefully connects it by ruled line to the previous position taken at the eight o'clock watch change; then with a broad grin he returns to his cabin. The whole time Cecil has been on the bridge plotting our position, the tall Afro-haired boy at the wheel has been holding an alert posture, carefully watching and adjusting the wheel to the shifting setting on the boxed brass compass in front of him. But as soon as the captain disappears, the young islander slouches back to his normal position. He looks out the side window of the bridge, scratching a leg with his foot, and while absentmindedly steering with one hand, he uses the other, intermittently, to pick his nose. Leaving the vessel on autopilot, he may disappear for ten minutes to get a cup of coffee or to relieve himself. No one takes over the wheel. No one worries. No one cares about anything much at all on the *Avarua*.

This is truly laissez-faire sailing. The first night out I stroll up to the wheelhouse and find it completely untended. This is an unnerving experience; the green revolving glow of the radar repeater forlornly signals a faint sign of civilization, like the proverbial tree falling unheard in the forest. Even more unsettling is coming to the wheelhouse in the midst of a pitch-black, stormy night when visibility is nearly zero to find that no one has bothered even to turn the radar on. The boy at the wheel will be artlessly steering a few degrees off course, totally unconcerned about the possibility of another vessel on a collision course. True, there are few large ships in this part of the Pacific and no reefs or islands to worry about within a day's sailing, but small yachts are not uncommon. I shudder to think of the plight of a sailboat crew if they should find themselves in the path of our unguided missile.

The *Avarua*'s crew consists of seven barefoot outer-island boys, ranging in age from middle teens to early twenties. Most have never been away from their distant islands before joining the vessel and speak only their native Maori, along with maybe a few words of English. They seem displaced, having chosen this alien environment as one of the few avenues of escape from the bare-subsistence living provided by the tiny, culturally comforting but economically stifling coral atolls. Duty on the ship, while long on hours, is not physically demanding. Desultorily the boys clean, paint, tend the engine room, or take their shifts at the wheel. They have, however, retained some prankish adolescent characteristics through this unsettling transition to the adult world. Often their pranks are not in the best of taste. Most of the boys are presently on the boat deck pulling down the pants of their newest and smallest fo'c'sle mate. Finally they disperse, only to come together again to share a box of candy. All the while the *Avarua* plunges, blissfully untended, toward the wave-crested horizon.

I pick my way past the bridge and down to the main deck over thirty years of accumulated crud, rust, and uncounted layers of old paint, heading for the galley, the only place where there is a table and where I can write. Sitting at the galley table is a unique experience. Not only does the nauseating odor of rancid fat overwhelm me, but I have also unwittingly found the cockroach epicenter of the ship. Little brown cockroaches and big black cockroaches crawl up my legs and, worse, throw themselves from the ceiling to land with unerring accuracy on my head or, sensing Valhalla, to plunge down the front of my shirt. These last cockies require careful plucking since I am reluctant to squash out their squirming little bodies against my chest. The hours of darkness, of course, *belong* to the cockroach, so it is no surprise to feel them scurrying over me while I try to sleep. Shipboard nights begin with several incoherent hours defending myself, then finally giving up and either brushing them off in my sleep or simply permitting the little beasts to meander where they will.

The next day I am again in the galley writing. Raui, the chef, is trying to decipher the cooking instructions on two cream-of-asparagus soup cans. This should be an interesting dinner. Raui is a tall, skinny kid and has, I feel, absolutely no instinct for cooking. He does, however, have a great instinct for presenting himself well. His galley attire is a majestic, though slightly tattered, regimental-blue jogging uniform with a royal red stripe. This comes in handy in case there is a young, attractive female passenger on board. Unfortunately, on this trip the effect is wasted. No one on the ship cares in the least if Raui looks either regal or regimental. Perhaps Raui is sulking. He certainly isn't cooking. He putters busily all day, looking most majestic but not accomplishing much, and glances worriedly at anyone entering his domain who might actually call on him to perform some small culinary service not exactly specified in his job description.

Raui's kitchen helper is the yang to Raui's yin. A hard-working, acned adolescent in a "debutante" T-shirt, he diligently attempts to mop the galley floor. His job is difficult because the sea has gotten rougher and the old *Avarua* is really rolling. As each wave hits the weather rail, it sends a torrent of water the length of the ship, burying the fo'c'sle and bridge in spray. In the galley, watching the debutante mop is like watching an ice skater trying to skate on a tilted rink. Amazingly, he is able to maintain his balance and to accomplish his task without crashing down the ladder into the engine room. I feel like giving him a twenty-one-gun salute.

Dinner is not so interesting: fried Spam, taro, and white bread. Perhaps Raui considered the canned asparagus soup too much of a challenge. I take leave for my nocturnal assignation with the cockroach kingdom. Lying in my bunk braced against the roll of the ship and plucking cockroaches with my free hand, I wonder about isolated little Palmerston and its sixty-one residents living totally apart from the rest of the world.

Palmerston's people, finely featured Polynesians, are nearly all descendants of one man, a nineteenth-century English seaman, carpenter, and adventurer. William Marsters was born in England in 1821. He first set sail on a whaling ship when he was still in his teens but did not favor life before the mast. Instead, in 1849, hearing of the discovery of gold in California, he decided to go there to make his fortune. Evidently fortunes were not made as effortlessly as young Marsters had imagined, for he soon moved on, sailing for Australia, where another gold discovery had just been announced. William never reached Australia. Instead, he landed on Penrhyn, the most northeasterly island in the Cook group, where he lived for a time and married a beautiful young Polynesian woman named Akakingaro, the daughter of the local chief. The couple then began moving restlessly from one island to another in search of the perfect home. William and Akakingaro arrived on Palmerston in July of 1863 with their two small children, Joyal and William II.

Though Palmerston had been discovered by Captain James Cook in 1774, there were no indigenous people on the island, nor had any foreigners successfully settled there prior to Marsters. What greeted the new couple could not have been terribly appealing. Only a few scraggly palms poked up from the barren coral. There was no fresh water and little vegetation except for stunted pandanus and au bushes. But the island had a gorgeous untouched lagoon, brim full of fish, and best of all, from Marsters's perspective, no Polynesians living there. That meant William could claim the island as his own kingdom, instead of being under an older chief's thumb.

And claim it he did, founding a dynasty with three women. The records don't reveal when Tepou, the second woman, arrived on Palmerston, though it is known that she was Akakingaro's second cousin. Also from Penrhyn, she had traveled with the Marsterses during their wanderings throughout the island group. In fact, she had left her children with William and Akakingaro while they were on one of the other islands, but these children neither arrived with Tepou nor later came to live with their mother. Tepou settled on Palmerston and became William's second wife, though no official marriage was ever recorded, as indeed it couldn't have been. Polynesians in those days were unconcerned with the Western convention of marriage. They made love with whomever they wished, and no stigma was attached to having a baby by a "married" man. Children were reared communally, and there was always an auntie eager to raise a baby, whether or not she was related to the parents. This is still true today. Many Polynesian children are brought up by a woman whom they call their "second" mama, but who may be only a distant relative or not related to the parents at all.

The woman who would become William's third "wife," Matavia, came to Palmerston from Penrhyn a few years later with family members who arrived to collect bêche-de-mer (sea slugs), considered a delicacy on the Hong Kong market. Evidently Matavia decided to remain on Palmerston, because she was still there some years later when a trading schooner lay to and dropped anchor off the reef. On it was an old shipmate of William's, a Portuguese by the name of John Fanadus, who was working on the vessel. When Fanadus found that his old friend William was king of the island, he jumped ship and settled there, taking Matavia for his woman and subsequently having a daughter with her. John was an expert goldsmith and, as the story goes, William Marsters had brought three jars of gold pieces with him from California. So, using these and pearl shell from the lagoon, John proceeded to make jewelry: rings, brooches, necklaces, and whatnot. While he waited for the arrival of a passing vessel, he would stockpile his wares. Then, when the infrequent schooner stopped, John would take passage to Rarotonga to sell the jewelry. During one of these voyages he was away for more than four months, and when he returned to Palmerston he found that Matavia was pregnant. John undoubtedly suspected he was not the father of the child-to-be, but apparently he waited to see the results of the pregnancy. Unlike its older sister, the baby was blond as the golden sand, as was William Marsters. John and William must have had a great row, for John left Palmerston, forsaking his family, and settled in Rarotonga. So Matavia became William's third "wife."

William seems to have spent his time on Palmerston mainly producing children. With Akakingaro he sired four girls and four boys, with Tepou two girls and four boys, and with Matavia (besides John's daughter) two girls and four boys. On this isolated atoll, visited by ships only once or twice a year, William and his three wives happily (if we are to believe the family legends) tended their vegetable garden, lived off the bounty of the lagoon, and raised their twenty-one children—all speaking the King's English. They also planted more than two hundred thousand palm trees, thereby laying claim to the island. Their claim was accepted by the Crown, which granted William and his family a series of leases on Palmerston that finally expired in 1953.

And William's family has continued to multiply, probably beyond his wildest imagination. Even by 1946, when the New Zealand government published the last census, there were (or had been) more than twenty-five hundred Marsters grandchildren and great grandchildren, plus a further three thousand great-great grandchildren. Everywhere you go in the Cooks and New Zealand, to which many Cook Islanders have emigrated, you will come across members of William's great progeny.

Though Palmerston's population rose to one hundred and twenty in the 1930s, today only half that number live there permanently. It is these remaining Marsters descendants that I am sailing to visit. Little do I know the surprises that this isolated culture will have for me.

On a bright and windy afternoon on our third day out from Rarotonga, Palmerston appears on the horizon as a low-lying smudge off the starboard bow. The *Avarua* creaks around the western tip of the island's encircling reef and surprises a whale cruising in deep water just a quarter mile from shore. In this summer latitude, the slow humpback is on its winter migration from the Antarctic toward the warmer waters nearer the equator. It seems immense:

forty rounded feet of barnacles, enormous dogeared, knobby flippers, and below the surface a great, mystical, unquantified intelligence.

The whale is sandwiched between our vessel and the reef. Realizing it is trapped, it begins swimming faster. Its spouts fill the air with feathery white plumes, alternately blossoming and disappearing in the late afternoon sun. The reef protrudes ahead of us, effectively sealing off the animal's avenue of escape unless it can pass or dive beneath us. It doesn't seem able to overtake the ship, even though we are steaming only at eight knots. Sensing defeat, the whale suddenly reverses course and spouts off toward the horizon, rolling—joyfully, I am convinced—for the open sea.

Two hundred yards off the breaker-lashed reef, the engine telegraph rings the *Avarua* to a stop and she rapidly begins to lose way. Though the *Avarua* is on the lee side of the lagoon, protected from the southeasterly trades, she still lies in an unsheltered seaway subject to the deadly onslaught of a sudden squall that could quickly tear her bottom out on the reef. She is far too large to enter any of the four passages into the lagoon, which at low tide are barely deep enough to admit a small skiff. Judiciously, Captain Cecil decides that she will lay over at Palmerston only a short time.

Even before her rusty anchor has splashed to the bottom, eight silver outboards come screaming through the reef passage at full throttle, converging on the *Avarua* like angry hornets. Bronzed Polynesians hold the skiffs off the rocking freighter as slings of lumber and bags of rice and flour are lowered onto them. Then, wordlessly, the pilots, ranging from teenage boys to white-haired old men, gun their outboards as if fleeing a threatening outer world and escape back to the sanctity of their calm mother-lagoon.

My skiff, filled to the brim with bags of rice, takes off like a shot. It is guided by Aaron, a tousle-haired fifteen-year-old with a broad smile and a physique like a weight lifter. He tells me proudly that he has just been given responsibility for his own outboard-powered fishing skiff. Because the boats and their outboards are Palmerston's most valuable possessions, Aaron has received far more than the Western equivalent of the keys to the family car. With great seriousness he has accepted his new responsibilities, yet a childlike gaiety and naiveté still cling to him like a teddy bear. Skill-fully, as if trying to dispel any doubts about the demise of his resid-ual child, he guides the fourteen-foot aluminum skiff through a baffling labyrinth of channels that lead through the reef to the shel-tered lagoon inside. Bamboo poles protrude like sinister signposts at hidden coral heads and sharp curves. These are the only guides to navigating the half-mile-wide reef, other than the jagged rusting sections of fishing boats and yacht hulks that did not make it: mari-time skulls and carcasses rhythmically covered and uncovered by the waves, warning of the dangers on every side.

Adroitly, Aaron slows the speeding boat to a near halt. The wake wells up to within a few inches of gushing over the transom, as the reef passage funnels to a gap so narrow that we can lean out and touch coral heads on each side. Aaron flexes the throttle again, and off we go, taking a dogleg to the right, then curving around a huge mushroom of coral that springs like a sunburst from the shallow water next to us. He down-throttles and swings us in a sharp turn to the right, and we flash through a straight channel that parallels the outer line of the reef. Another series of curves and turns around pro-truding coral embankments and we glide into a gentle beach of gleaming white sand. Aaron kills the engine, locks it up, and jumps in the water, guiding and breaking our way so that finally, when the bow touches the beach, the crunch is almost imperceptible. Half the island's population—men in shorts and T-shirts, women in sa-rongs, smiling and curious—lines the beach in greeting.

2

THE MARSTERS WORLD

Crotchety old Uncle Carl is shouting, "Care-oh-line, Care-oh-line, where are you? You come here dis minute!" Little ragamuffin Caroline runs up from where she has been playing, her cheeks bulging with food, to stand defiantly before her grandfather, impatiently listening to him scold her for some insignificant breach of behavior. Then with the admonition already forgotten, she dashes off again, totally absorbed in her child's world of the moment. In the distance the rhythmic breaking of the waves on the reef echoes through the quiet tropical morning. The waves play a constant concerto to the daily ritual of Palmerston life.

Sarah, Carl's wife, bends over the cookfire in her faded housecoat. She pokes at the coals, warming up large chunks of leftover fresh tuna for breakfast as she describes to her daughter, Dawn, the comings and goings of a distant relative on Rarotonga. Sarah and Carl are second cousins who have married late in life. Both were raised on Palmerston, then moved to Rarotonga and New Zealand. Sarah's first husband was Tom Neale, the hermit who became a legend in the South Pacific. Her eyes seem to laugh, while her whole face, framed with tight grey curls, dances with warmth. "Sit, sit, sit," she commands me, "and have some breakfast. Come, come, sit down. The children straggle in around a battered wooden table set underneath a big fig tree. It is laden with bowls of taro, potatoes, coconut pudding, and steamed tuna. Besides pretty twenty-nine-year-old Dawn, now the island's schoolteacher, and five-year-old

Caroline, there is lovely Sule, a precocious nine-year-old with the appearance and social awareness of an adult. Sule's parents live on Rarotonga, but she is staying with her grandmother.

Everyone is busy eating—with their hands, as is the custom throughout rural Polynesia. Little Caroline eats with both hands. Her face is a multicolored palette of smeared food. Uncle Carl is after her again, "Care-oh-line, *chew* your food—and don't talk wif your mouth full." A full-blown battle of the wills rages between the bald old man and the feisty, defiant child. She is winning or at least, stubbornly resistant, she isn't losing. Sarah looks on with bemused tolerance. She will criticize neither husband nor granddaughter, though when Caroline's behavior is bad enough, Sarah eventually does get after her, even lightly whopping her bottom.

Already, at nine o'clock, the air is very warm. The family eats outside in front of their modest one-room coral house. Of the eighteen buildings on the island, fourteen are houses, and all but four are made from crushed coral, burned to form lime, then mixed with sand and water to create a good-quality homemade cement. Although the crushing and burning of the coral entails enormous labor, the end product is free, an important consideration in a society where money is scarce and time abundant. Innovation here has been a steady substitute for money. Homemade wheelbarrows constructed from half an oil drum are the only wheeled transport. Large spoked fishing reels, crafted from tamanu wood, Samoan-style rather than costly commercial ones, grace the island's fishing boats. The traditional poverty of the people has dictated that they either make it or do without. Now that the islanders have found a way to ship their fish to a major market for the first time, they are able to buy Western goods, but still they continue to be largely self-sufficient.

Palmerston, called Home Island by most of its inhabitants, looks like an equilateral triangle with rounded corners. It is one of three dozen motus, or tiny islands, some only coral spits with a few lonely palms, scattered around the perimeter of a 120-square-mile diamond-shaped lagoon. All but the main island are uninhabited, used as coconut plantations for the production of copra, the islanders' other major cash crop, and as breeding grounds for one of the delicacies in their limited diet, the bosun-bird or red-tailed tropic-bird.

A short distance from Sarah and Carl's house, Uncle Tuakana is cutting up sections of dried coconut to feed his pigs. He trudges off toward the pigpens behind his house, heralded by an expectant chorus of grunts and squeals. Tuakana moves slowly. Though he is only sixty-two he has the action and appearance of a man fifteen years older. Recently he was hospitalized in New Zealand for a lung disorder, from which he hasn't completely recovered. Tuakana and his wife, Teinano, live with their two youngest daughters in a coral house only a hundred feet from Sarah and Carl's house. Tuakana is a skilled woodworker. Using ancient homemade hand tools, he turns out fragile tamanu bowls and figurines, as well as simple furniture. He is also devoutly religious. When Tuakana is not carving or puttering, he can likely be found praying. At least four times a day he, Aunt Teinano, and their daughters can be seen sitting in a tight circle in their house, heads bowed, praying to their Lord, perhaps asking Him for happier times.

Sarah gazes benevolently at Uncle Tuakana as he shuffles off to feed his pigs. She feels a strong affinity for Tuakana, whose father, Ned, was the son of William Marsters's second child, William II. Sarah is the granddaughter of William's third child, Elizabeth. Sarah and Tuakana and their children are all members of the "middle family." That is, they all come from the union of William and Akakingaro (later called Sarah), the only woman with whom William had an actual marriage ceremony. Collectively, the middle family descendants own the center section of Palmerston Island. They are all entitled to a building site for a home and a share of the family's coconuts. Likewise, the descendants of William's two other wives—the "family of the left" and the "family of the right"—each share their own sections.

Should all of William's progeny return to Palmerston, it would, of course, be impossible to accommodate them. All but these last few families, however, long ago escaped the confines of their remote homeland and the poverty and hardships of day-to-day life there to raise their families in the modern world of Rarotonga or New Zealand.

Depending on how you count, only about ten year-round households still struggle along on Palmerston. Five of them are headed by the island's patriarchs. In addition to Tuakana in the middle family, there's his older brother by two years, Reverend Bill, formerly president and pastor of the largest church in Rarotonga, now returned to his home island.

The family of the left descends from William's union with Tepou, and the family of the right from Matavia, his other "favorite," as the islanders discreetly label the girlfriends. Policeman Bob, the seventy-six-year-old constable without portfolio, reigns over the family of the left. Bob carries a tragicomic sense about him. He wears his resplendent police uniform at every public occasion, yet his single official act was an attempt a few years ago to tax the only vehicular form of transportation on the island, its wheelbarrows, in order to provide himself with a source of revenue. Not only were his efforts unsuccessful, but his constituents threw him in the lagoon for his audacity. Whenever the force of law is needed, it comes from Rarotonga, albeit with true South Seas languor, on the next available tramp steamer. The interval between the commission of a crime and its investigation generally permits the perpetrator to expire from old age rather than incarceration. Fortunately, there have been few serious incidents. Only once has a Palmerstonian gone to jail for a crime committed on the island, and that happened when one young man in a drinking frenzy put out the eye of a cousin for stealing his girlfriend. With few exceptions, other crimes have gone either unreported or unprosecuted.

The family of the right is headed by sixty-one-year-old John, who by edict of the central government has replaced Reverend Bill as Palmerston's chief administrative officer. This action has created some resentment among island factions. Two other older men also belong to the family of the right: Sixty-three-year-old Joseph produces very large sons, including Radio, his twenty-year-old, three-hundred-pound eldest, and the slightly smaller and younger Andrew, both of whom provide most of the island's muscle. Quiet, retiring John Dick and his wife, Tuaine, live outside Palmerston's mainstream, as far from the others as a house can be on the tiny island. There they raise pigs and chickens, which they sell or barter to the other families. Most of their children are grown and have left the island.

Although not as prominent in the island's power structure, four younger, married men also live in their own houses. Taepae, a muscular, reflective thirty-five-year-old, lives on the right with his wife, Mary, and elderly grandmother, Martha. Taepae is the only younger man on the three-person island council. In the center family is shy David, fifty-two, who is the island "dresser," a medical position somewhere between nurse and doctor. David sets broken bones and stitches wounds, but cannot operate. For his aid work he receives a meager stipend from the central government. Another middle-family member is Dave, the thirty-seven-year-old son of Uncle Tuakana. Dave spent two years off the island working for the fisheries department and now earns his living fishing. His wife is presently on Rarotonga caring for a sick baby. Dick, who recently returned to the island with his wife, Teina, fishes and helps his uncle, Reverend Bill—as do many of the younger men—with the elder's private fishing business.

Besides Policeman Bob's house next door, the only other dwelling on the left is occupied by his strapping, handsome twenty-eight-year-old son, George, who is also a fisherman. George and his pretty wife, Tutai, help care for the five children of Bob's other two sons, who have left the island. No one wants to talk about this situation, though in a Polynesian society it is not considered as strange as it would be in other countries.

Until the recent opening of a market for their fish, the Palmerston people had only two sources of income: the dried meat of the coconut (copra) from which coconut oil is extracted, and shell and woven handicrafts—purses, mats, and other items, made by the island women. At most, the islanders could ship twenty tons of copra a year, at an average of U.S. $75.00 a ton, with earnings from handicrafts amounting to perhaps another $1,000. So as late as 1973 the total yearly income of all ten families was no more than U.S. $2,500. In some years income fell to less than $1,000 for the

entire island. A major problem has always been the infrequent, ir-
regular interisland shipping; for decades they saw a supply ship only
once or twice a year. During one three-year period—from July 1935
to November 1938—no vessel stopped at Palmerston at all.

Even in those lean times, however, survival was never a problem except after severe hurricanes, when the islanders had to wait
two or three years for the maturation of a new crop of coconuts,
their main staple besides fish. The islanders have always had as
much fish as they wanted to supplement a diet of taro, eggs, breadfruit, and papaya, along with the occasional chicken, pork, or
bosun-bird. True, their clothes then were rags, darned and re-
darned, but since no one else saw them and since they were all in
the same financial condition, no one minded too much. And they
helped each other; there was real community spirit.

Most of the senior Palmerston people remember the old days
with fondness. Uncle Tuakana says wistfully, "In the past I could
say that even though we had a hard life to live, and getting things
like clothes and food [was difficult], but people worked together as a
family, as *one* family. They shares; they helps each other. The big
days that we have on the island [then], like Christmas Day, New
Year's Day, the Sacrament Sunday, and the Duke's Day [celebrat-
ing the day the Duke of Windsor visited Palmerston], on all these
days we have a feast together. Every home has a table on the road
[in the center of the island] with all good foods made on it, and
when the prayers is finished, so you shout out to others to come
along and enjoy himself in your table, and they calls out to you the
same. Oh, everyone goes 'round, enjoy the day and have a feast.
When the feast is finished, say about two hours, and then we has
singing time and then after the singing time the games go up, different games that the young people plays like volleyball and cricket.
Wonderful time," he adds with a sad look in his eyes.

When I ask whether the Palmerston people still do things together on the island, Uncle Tuakana replies simply, "Not today, I
could tell you, not today." When I ask why, he answers, "I could
tell you, it is because of one man." He refuses to elaborate.

Palmerston still celebrates Duke's Day, an indication of the
depth of loyalty and belonging the people feel for England and the

Crown. In fact, Palmerston is the only island in the Cooks where English, rather than Maori, is the first language. Old William demanded that his wife Akakingaro change her name to Sarah (probably because he couldn't pronounce her given name), but he also insisted that Sarah, Tepou, Matavia, and all their children learn and use English exclusively. During the colonial period in Polynesia, English was revered by the islanders as the language of the educated, the powerful, the in-group that fraternized with the English.

Most of the Palmerston Marsterses understand Maori but do not speak it fluently. Reverend Bill recalls, "When I was a boy on Palmerston I can remember I spoke English with a Gloucestershire accent. When I went to work as a young seaman during the [second] war I could sing the Maori songs and hymns and understand the language, but I couldn't speak it. I spoke English. I was the envy of quite a few people in the upper learning bracket because here I was, somebody who's never gone to secondary school, but he speaks English. And today," Reverend Bill continues, "the people here, you talk to them, you could see this coming out: 'No, we doesn't belong to the Cook Islands; we're English.' And normally, here, when the flag is flown it's the Union Jack."

Dawn, Sarah's daughter, has seen more of the world than her relatives. "Right," she says. "We consider ourselves English descendants, although it's very mixed with Polynesian blood. There's a feeling of superiority here. You see, when the *Britannia*, the queen's royal yacht, is in the South Pacific it always calls to Palmerston. It hardly ever calls at Rarotonga. And in 1972, when the Cook Islands' Prime Minister, Albert Henry, requested the duke to come on a special visit to Rarotonga, the Duke of Windsor first stopped to spend the day here and that started the special holiday. And since then whenever the *Britannia* is here, we are all treated like guests aboard and we're given free rein to go right through the ship. The Palmerston people can't go into the queen's suite, of course, but they can go and look in through the windows and they're given lunch and presents and gifts. The ship people all come on shore and they're given an island welcome. It is just a complete mixing on the same social level. It isn't, you know, 'These are the little colonials.' It's just the cherry on top of the cake as far as our people are concerned. Still, I think that basically we are the same as the Polynesian people from the other [Cook] islands. Our interactions are the same. Most people here, after all, are over ninety percent Polynesian."

.

Early one morning I take a walk around the island to get a better picture of how things are laid out. The long, sandy beach opposite the nearest passage through the reef is the main entrance to the community. Here, with a vestige of English pomp and formality, the islanders receive visitors and VIPs arriving from the occasional interisland freighter or yacht. Long ago, island ancestors planted two rows of palms separated by thirty feet of fine white sand to form a broad avenue leading through the middle of the island and bisecting the middle family's territory. On each side of it sit thatched huts with high peaked roofs used for storing the islanders' fishing boats, and beside them tamanu pigpens hold four or five pigs, most of which are presently sound asleep in the midday heat. Walking toward the middle of the island, I pass the fish-weighing shed. Hanging from the rafters are enormous bunches of green bananas brought from Aitutake by the last cargo boat. Alongside the shed lies a row of old oil drums marked "Rev. Bill Marsters Palm," and half buried in the sand a few feet away, an old tractor, vintage 1950, rusts in the sun. Lumber and other used building materials, piled nearby, await their second, third, or fourth coming. Across the sandy main street a large generator used to power Reverend Bill's fish freezers fouls the air with noise and diesel exhaust. I can certainly understand why the islanders would opt for this technology that has so dramatically improved their finances. Nonetheless, the generator is a dagger in the heart of Palmerston's serenity.

The first house I come to along this avenue of sand belongs to Reverend Bill and Martha. A rectangular cubicle entirely built of galvanized iron sheeting, even to the large openable shutters, it looks as though the only considerations in its design were utility and security. The chief administrative officer's house, across the way, more closely fits the South Pacific stereotype: traditional wooden colonial bungalow with a peaked roof and wide porch on two sides, home for a low-ranking colonial administrator. In fact, the CAO's house was built by the middle family out of materials shipped in following a devastating hurricane that in 1926 destroyed most of the buildings on the island. It fronts on the Palmerston equivalent of Hollywood and Vine, two broad stretches of sand, perhaps fifty feet wide, that cross Palmerston is opposite directions. At this point the island is only about three hundred yards wide. From the veranda of the CAO's house where I am quartered, I can easily see down "Palmerston Avenue." On the left are the Tin House and the church, the two oldest buildings on the island and the only ones to survive the 1926 hurricane.

The little church, one of the loveliest old buildings in the South Pacific, was built entirely of wood from wrecked ships. The exterior timbers and interior floor planking came from the five-masted British windjammer *Thistle*, which crashed on Palmerston's reef in 1900. Much of the original hand-painted interior, including a gorgeous mahogany pulpit and stairway with a brass rail, came from a three-masted barque, the French *La Tour d'Auvergne*, which hit the reef in 1913. Miraculously, the church escaped destruction by numerous hurricanes. During a 1940 cyclone it was pushed intact fifteen feet to the west. The following year a big wave from the worst hurricane of the decade sent it fifteen feet back to the east, where it had started, but nearly demolished it in the process. The islanders then carefully rebuilt it board by board, but it still tilts precariously. Only stout poles propping it up keep it from crashing over.

The small cemetery behind the church holds nearly all the island's history and secrets. The original William Marsters, who died at age 78 on May 22, 1899, lies here under a simple coral tombstone that reads, "Blessed are the dead which die in the Lord." Around William are the remains of his wives, children, and grandchildren in graves inscribed with religious and secular mottoes, such as "A virtuous woman is a crown to her husband," and "Well know [sic] by all that seen her, Europeans and Maories in the South Seas."

The Tin House was built by the first William of massive, clear, vertical-grain fir posts and beams, some eighteen inches thick. It is still securely fastened with the original one-inch-square, hand-forged bolts and spikes that have held it together through an untold number of hurricanes, and it looks as though it could withstand many to come. The islanders have reroofed and patched it with tin, and thus its name, but every other feature dates to William I, including the siding, enormous planks four to six inches thick by fourteen inches wide. To the left of the Tin House is the radio shack containing the island's transmitter, and across from it, next to the CAO's house, is the residence of John and his family. White-haired John operates the radio, and although he is the CAO, he cannot use that house; Reverend Bill, the ousted CAO, still controls it, for reasons I will later discover.

Across "Palmerston Avenue" from the CAO's house stands the island catchment building, a long, tin-roofed, semienclosed structure containing two ten-thousand-gallon concrete water tanks that supply much of the islanders' water. The great deluges common during the rainy season are channeled by means of gutters and downspouts into these tanks from which they provide water during the relatively dry months from May to November. Besides supplying water, the catchment building also serves as the island meeting hall and social center. A large expanse of covered concrete floor allows meetings, dinners, and other activities to be held at any time of year.

At the other end of the seven-hundred-seventy-acre island is the school, where Dawn Neale became the island schoolteacher only by chance. She was born in a Palmerston grass shack with dirt floors after the split-up of her mother, Sarah, and her father, Tom, the legendary hermit who had emigrated from New Zealand to Rarotonga as a young man and lived alone for six years on Suwarrow Island. Dawn's childhood was spent with Sarah, alternating between Rarotonga and Palmerston. She started high school in Rarotonga, then transferred to Church College of New Zealand, a Mormon high school. After that Dawn undertook nurse's training and further studies at Brigham Young University in Utah before traveling to South America on a mission for her church, where she taught and worked in the L.D.S. welfare program in Paraguay. Dawn returned to New Zealand to do graduate work at Auckland University; then, burned out, she spent a year traveling around the United States before returning to the island of her birth.

It was on the wharf at Rarotonga, awaiting the departure of the interisland vessel, that Dawn was approached by the Cook Islands minister of education. Dave's wife, who had been the island teacher, had decided to stay in Raro, where her sick baby had access to better medical facilities. So the island needed a new teacher, and Tara Pae Movate, the minister of education, asked Dawn if she would take over and she agreed. That was four weeks before my arrival.

The schoolhouse, a small, dilapidated limestone box built by the islanders, sits by itself in a dirt clearing at the end of a lovely palm-fringed lane on the west end of the island. Two ramshackle outhouses, one at each end of the playground, lean despondently, the boys' staggering toward the lagoon, the girls' toward an adjacent palm tree. Neither outhouse door will stay closed, and the children must either hold them shut or have helpers hold the doors for them.

It is 9:15 and class has already begun. A disorderly babble of young voices assails the morning peace but does not disturb the scrawny hen pecking in the dirt at the doorway. The noise level inside is deafening, even though there are only sixteen children, ranging in age from four to fourteen. One of the smaller ones cries loudly in the background. Dawn tells a child who has hit another that such behavior is not allowed. "Benjamin," she scolds, "what happens if you hit? What's the rule if you're hitting in class? It's time out, isn't it? You have to sit on the floor. Isn't that right? Okay, so you go. Do that now. Off you go." Seven-year-old Benjamin reluctantly goes off to sit in the corner. Another child has joined the first one, crying. Dawn turns to the perpetrator. "Inano, were you hitting Luke?" Inano's answer is a long and guilty-sounding "Ye-e-s-s." "Okay," Dawn responds, "you both go sit on the floor now. Okay? There's no hitting of anybody. Okay, go on now. Very good."

The kids who have been asked to sit on the floor don't stay there very long. As soon as Dawn turns her back, they are up again. One little girl in a gingham dress with a white cotton turtleneck appears to be in constant difficulty. She is definitely a victim, having already cried three times this morning. The solemn little boy wearing a blue shirt and short pants who has just hit her again is sent back to resume his floor sitting. Dawn systematically maneuvers children into areas out of hitting range from each other on the floor. All the younger children are barefoot. Some of the older ones are, too. The younger ones who have been hitting are mostly eight or nine years old. Dawn spends more than half her time acting as policeman and judge. She must continually repeat requests and instructions. Now there are four kids on the floor out of a total of eight in the younger class. The little boy in the blue shirt is back to his coloring; two other little ones have also been pardoned.

In the other classroom, Dawn chalks math problems on the board and the older kids write the answers in their workbooks, starting with $5.6 + 2.4 + 3.5$. She hardly has started the second problem when a little boy tugs at her dress to show her his drawing. More straggle in from the other room to ask for something, to borrow the scissors, or simply to stand, bored, and see what the older children are doing. Dawn has an impossible job. Sisyphus's rock rolling was simple by comparison.

When I ask her to compare the learning and ability levels of the Palmerston children with their counterparts in Rarotonga and New Zealand, she says, "The children here have a very short attention span. I'll spend time with them setting up their work and then leave to work with the other group. Then I find that the first group has stopped and is standing behind me, just watching me work with the others. I have to be constantly supervising, more than with any other teaching situation I have been in. The ability levels are much different here than they would be in New Zealand or Rarotonga. It is very obvious, especially with Sule [who went to school in Rarotonga before coming here a few months ago] being here. Sule is nine years old. She is obviously an intelligent girl, but she is on a scholastic level of what one would expect for her age. Here she's at the level, can understand and cope with the work that the thirteen- and fourteen-year-olds do—and better than the fourteen-year-old."

I also ask whether the Palmerston children are intellectually lacking or if their education has been deficient. "I think it's their education," she replies, "because when I'm able to get through to them they are intelligent. They do grasp concepts easily. But their work habits are so poor, their attention span is so short; they haven't learned how to. But some of them are quite bright considering that they haven't had any education for three years. The school was closed for that period [and reopened] eighteen months ago." Dawn does not want to elaborate except to say that there was violence associated with the school closing. This and other mysteries surface during conversation with the island people. A strange force is at work here, but it takes time for the pieces to fit together, and so far they haven't. The islanders are still reluctant to air their troubles to an outsider.

The older children begin to work on new projects. They sit at simple, rectangular desks, wooden boxes fastened to legs made of two loops of iron. The desks date back to the 1930s, but the two classrooms with their scarred, chipped, and stained walls look older than that. The children's textbooks are a hodgepodge of New Zealand castoffs, many from the early 1950s. Their math books were published in 1967. Additional school supplies are almost nonexistent. Like most of the small South Pacific nations, the Cook Islands is poor, and Palmerston with its tiny school population does not seem to rate much of the meager monetary assistance available.

The older children are now working on their diaries. Each week they write a story describing one day in their lives. Their work is interrupted when one of the older girls tells another to shut up. Dawn reprimands her. The penalty is to write six times "I will not say 'shut up' in class." Twelve-year-old Edward John Dick's diary for July 9th reads:

> Yesterday morning when I woke up, I wash my face. Then fed my pigs and pick my rubbish [carried out the garbage]. After that, I set at our table. Then my mother called me to come and have breakfast so I went and have breakfast and we had fried eggs and boiled fish. After breakfast I had a bath, put on my school clothes, then I walked to school. After school I ran home, put on my working clothes. Then I

extracted the food for my pigs which is coconuts. After that I went to help my father to fix our bed. When we finished fixing our bed, I had my bath, got changed, then I went to my grandpa's place. When I got there my uncles were fileting fish so I went and helped them. When we finished fileting the fish we had dinner then we went to bed.

Children in rural Polynesia are given extensive responsibilities compared to their Western counterparts. The lives of their families are comparable in many respects to those of farm families on the American frontier during the 1850s. For many, food is still cooked over an open fire or in an umu, an earth oven. A six-year-old here is responsible for lighting the fires and maintaining them, for carrying buckets of water nearly as heavy as the child, and for watching over younger siblings. Akino, the lovely thirteen-year-old granddaughter of Policeman Bob, washes her family's clothes by hand, changes the diapers of her baby sister, picks and splits the family's coconuts, and keeps the house spotless. She is not praised for her work; she is slapped if she falters.

The romantic but erroneous impression persists that in Polynesia there is no violence, neither hitting nor child abuse. Unfortunately, physical abuse of women and children is common, though cases of severe beatings requiring medical attention are exceedingly rare. Still, this is a hitting society; the practice runs from one generation to another. Parents with uncontrolled tempers lash out at children at the slightest provocation. And yet love flows as quickly as castigation. Parents and relatives never praise but display physically their love and affection, and almost universally the children *know* they are loved and wanted.

Leaving the school by what would be the back door, if there were one, I walk through a grove of palms, then crash through a thicket of pandanus to find myself at the beach. The outer edge of the reef is about a quarter mile away at this point and great waves hammer it, sending sheets of spray high in the air and spilling over into the lagoon. A twenty-minute walk brings me halfway around the island. In the distance, scattered along the perimeter of the giant lagoon, other islands—some only sand spits, others of fifty or sixty acres, all of them covered with oil palms—lie low on the horizon. In the noonday glare they are slim, white horizontal bands covered with green, quietly resting on a shimmering bed of turquoise.

.

It's a Friday afternoon about three. Some big cumulus clouds hang in the sky. A light breeze blows. As I rock back in my chair on the CAO's porch facing the old church, tilting my head to the left, I look out on the glorious brilliant blue of the lagoon with a tiny white thread of breakers in the distance. The sandy main thorough-fare running between the CAO's house and the church is empty ex-cept for a few kids playing in front of the Tin House. The only sounds are the dit-dit-dit-dot-dot-dot of the radio transmitter and the incessant crowing of the roosters. The island is enjoying one of its periodic generator silences. Palms, high on their graceful stalks, swish in a momentary breeze, then droop altogether. Without the breeze a dense, wet heat settles heavily over the island.

This is the children's last day at school before a two-week win-ter holiday. The Constitution Games, celebrating the Cook Islands' independence, start soon. All the people on the island—men, wo-men, girls, and boys—form into four teams and have races, jumping contests, cricket, football, and all manner of other games. The chil-dren look forward to it eagerly. But today there's nothing much doing. A half-naked little boy roams down the road. Charming, friendly Akino is playing and picking up her little brothers and sis-ters. For a while somebody plays the ukulele in the pastel blue radio shack, incongruous with a yellow slat door and solar panels on the roof. The old Tin House, with its three-foot roof overhang that al-lows windows to be open even in the biggest storms, sits forlornly, as does the church. Occasionally a little pullet will peck across the yard. The old bell from the *Thistle* stands silent, clapper slowly moving. A little child with a piece of coconut in his hand runs by, followed by three more kids, all giggling. The littlest one is caught, squeals, and is let go again. Akino fondles her. Akino, who has no mother, is dressed always in little more than rags. Her old gingham skirt looks as though it came from a flour bag, and her stained, al-most completely filthy white top is really gray now. Often her hair is neither combed nor washed. But she's happy, and that's the essence of her. The families of the left and the right don't seem to take as much care as the families of the center. Their children are more poorly dressed and seem to have less self-pride.

Five smallish wall-eyed albacore hang upside down from the shed next to CAO John's house. He has already distributed gifts of reef fish to everyone on the island. There still is sharing here: When someone slaughters a pig or has a good day fishing, he will share with everyone. Nothing is expected in return. And anyone in need will always have enough to eat. The Palmerston people will make sure of that. Some island ways have changed; others have not.

The whole gang of kids races up the street and collapses in giggles in the middle of the road. Eventually a little one trips and starts crying. Akino picks it up and tenderly carries it home. In spite of the common practice of slapping and yelling at the children, they seem warm and happy and very loving. If it's true that the children of a society are a good indication of that society's emotional health, Palmerston, even with its problems, cannot be that bad off.

.

Giant ocean swells, having traveled thousands of miles, perhaps from the coast of Chile, roll to the northwest, stately, immutable, and relentless. They seem timeless and omnipotent. A small aluminum boat rolls over the swells, rising and falling with the soothing regularity of a carousel horse on a slow-moving merry-go-round, as each wave slides like a mountain of oil beneath it. I feel as if we are gliding, as if we and our boat are connected to the shifting surface by a giant unseen piston. My two companions pay no attention to the rollers. They maintain a sense of calm, of ease born of intimate experience with their surroundings. They couldn't tell you, but they are one with it.

Swarthy with a bushy beard, Dave looks like a Bedouin, even to his camouflage-green Arab Legion cap. Using a few deft motions he inserts a ten-gauge wire into the mouth of an iced flying fish taken from one of the buckets that line the left side of the boat. He attaches the wire to a six-ounce lead sinker, fastening it under the bait's head with a few loops of softer, finer wire. A carefully sharpened 8/0 hook, the size of a man's extended thumb and forefinger, protrudes from the bait's belly.

The third occupant of the boat is a boy in his early teens. Manea carefully takes the 250-pound test monofilament from another bucket and ties it to the other leader and bait. Dave twists the throttle on the twenty-five horsepower outboard and the boat noses over a wave, but before it can smack into the trough the throttle is eased and the bow gently nestles into the liquid crevasse and begins to rise again.

We had crossed the lagoon that morning at first light, churning over smooth water toward the eastern point of the diamond, directly opposite Home Island. From there we headed out shallow Bird Passage into the Pacific. By the time Dave and Manea had their rig set, we had been pushed about three miles northeast of the atoll. It was still cold. Dave wore an old sweatshirt and yellow foul-weather pants; the boy, just a pair of swimming trunks, a T-shirt, and a baseball cap; and I, every bit of warm clothes I possessed.

Dave normally fished alone, but today, on an inexplicable whim, he had decided to take both me and fourteen-year-old Manea, the son of Taepae, his best friend. Not that Manea was a hindrance; already he was well schooled in the routine and fairly skilled at bringing in big fish. His greatest asset, however, was also his greatest liability. He was so very eager to do his job well, so anxious to please, so desirous of becoming known as a good fisherman by the men, that often his anxiety caused him to blunder. His frenetic movements often led to missed gaffs, and the bungled attempts had let big fish off or made snarled birds' nests that weakened or broke the expensive nylon line. In a society that depends largely on fishing for its livelihood and that offers few other avenues of endeavor by which a man can be judged, such failures must have weighed heavily. At times Manea seemed on the verge of tears. His frustration and embarrassment were visible even to an outsider. But all the boy could do to atone for his errors was to try harder, to silently promise himself that next time, should there be a next time— because his father and Dave were the only fishermen who would even bother to take him—he would succeed.

When we reached the fishing grounds that morning, Dave

slipped the motor into neutral and brusquely jammed his Arab Legion hat under his arm, motioning Manea to do the same with a shake of his head. Then, barely audible, with his eyes closed, he let the words automatically form on his lips: "Thank you, God, for being kind to us through times past and bringing us this time out in these wide-open seas. We beg unto thee, Dear Father, to give us the blessing of this day to rest upon each of us. Danger, Dear Father, take it far away from us, so nothing will harm us through this day until we return home safely, in peace. We ask these things, Oh Heavenly Father, through the name of Thy son, Jesus Christ, who suffered on the cross once for our sake. Amen."

Dave guns the motor and line sizzles over the side. When forty fathoms are out, the boy snubs the line to one of the short bamboo outriggers protruding diagonally over the boat's gunnels. The bait skips once, then again over succeeding wave tops before it settles down to a constant flutter just below the surface. The boy lets out the second line, then props himself against the bow so that he can watch both baits. I am positioned by the reels attached to the cockpit combing. Dave stands at the outboard regulating our speed over the giant swells that alternately tower high above us, then push us up to the crests, making us miniature kings momentarily atop the world's most powerful horses. Semiconsciously Dave fingers one line, then the other. His rough fingers delicately sense the slightest variation in the baits' movement. "Take some turns," he tells Manea, nodding at the left side reel.

Manea rotates the big wooden spokes of the Samoan reel two revolutions, pulling in two fathoms of line. No sooner has he braked the reel again than there is an enormous hit, momentarily yawing the boat to the left before the line goes slack and wafts out to the side.

"Wahoo, big one, 'bout a hundred pounds," Dave tells us. The fish, perhaps attracted by the sudden surge of the bait as the boy shortened the line, has broken the two-hundred-pound test leader. Manea finds another leader, rigs a second bait, and attaches it to the line. Soon the second line is back in the water and the boy resumes his vigil, facing backward as he leans against the bow.

Almost immediately there is another hit. "Go easy!" Dave yells at the boy, who is already at the reel. Using his back to hold the tiller in place and leaning forward to brace himself, Dave brings the line in hand over hand, helping the struggling boy. Then Manea is at the transom with the gaff. Dave kills the engine to keep the fish from fouling the line in the propeller. Gathering the line in closer and closer to the leader, he pulls the fish's head nearer to the transom. Manea braces himself with one hand on the gunnel and tries to hook the gaff in the thrashing wahoo's gill slit. The wahoo, six feet long and sixty pounds of muscle, churns the water white in its desperate efforts to avoid the gaff. The maelstrom it creates camouflages the lightning-fast movements of the fish. It flashes in front of Manea for only split seconds before rolling away or being obscured with foam, presenting an excruciatingly difficult target. The boy plunges the gaff into the fish. It misses, only raking the fish's back. "Easy! Easy! Don't hook the body," Dave screams at him. Manea tries again, more gingerly. Either through proper placement or by sheer luck the gaff hook catches in a gill slit. Immediately, the boy pulls the fish's head out of the water. Together man and boy lift the still thrashing wahoo, carefully avoiding the snapping jaws filled with razor-sharp teeth and the powerful tail, which could knock either of them out of the boat. As soon as the wahoo hits the deck, Dave plunges his knife into the ventral aorta and immediately the floorboards are awash in blood. The fish, near death, is stuffed under the boards into the small bilge and the other bait is reeled in and checked. A new leader is attached to the line the wahoo was taken on and soon both baits are out again.

The sixty-pound wahoo, with head and tail off, will be frozen in a generator-powered freezer. When the next interisland freighter arrives, the fish will be transferred to an insulated container, actually an old freezer from which the motor and freezing unit have been removed. A half dozen or more of these stripped freezers, filled with fish, are ferried out to the waiting freighter, loaded on board with the ship's gear, and taken to Rarotonga, where the fish will feed both tourists and islanders. Since the fishing around Rarotonga is not very productive, Palmerston has become an important supplier of what used to be an imported commodity. Now Dave and the other fishermen receive sixty cents a pound for pelagic fish like tuna and wahoo and between twenty-five and forty cents a pound for reef fish. This is a princely sum to a people who previously had been so poor that they could hardly afford such basic staples as flour and rice.

.

The waves crash fiercely on the reef to the west. A mile off the reef on the other side of the lagoon Dave and Manea and I are still fishing, trying to take advantage of the shelter from the ever-increasing seas, keeping the lagoon to windward. But the waves seem to be unbroken and nearly as high as those farther away. Since the first catch we have taken only a smallish ten-pound albacore and have had no other bites. When the albacore is in the boat, the newly baited line feeds back over the side. Slight kinks have formed in the line, however, and they go unnoticed at first by both Dave and Manea. Slack in the line as it plays out allows the kinked nylon to double over itself, forming tangles. The tangles seem to feed on each other, multiplying and infecting more line until, in a few seconds, what was formerly a straight line is a birds' nest. Dave, who constantly touches the lines, feels the irregularity almost immediately. Two wahoo also are attracted by the erratically moving bait. They both attack what they perceive as a wounded flying fish. The first wahoo hits the bait. The second veers away and strikes the trailing flying fish. Suddenly there is pandemonium. "Manea," Dave yells, grabbing the first line, "you take the other one. Reel him in slow."

Dave begins pulling in the fouled line, hand over hand by himself. The nylon cuts deeply into his flesh. Only the massive callouses on his hands keep them from being torn to shreds. He also uses his body to help absorb the stress. Tangled line drops into the bottom of the boat. Manea and I slowly reel in the second fish. When he sees Dave's fish coming close to the boat, he locks his reel, hoping the fish won't take advantage of the decreased tension to get off the hook. Manea grabs the gaff and in one deft motion hooks it into the wahoo's gill slit, then with Dave's help swings the fish over the side. Immediately Manea goes back to the reel holding the second wahoo. The first one thrashes back and forth in the bottom of the boat, its rows of knifelike teeth snapping at anything within reach. Manea is barefoot and in short pants. The wahoo's nose brushes the boy's leg and with a ferocious snap the fish blindly struggles to bite him. One bite from the wahoo could mangle his entire leg, but Manea, in his desire to bring in the second fish, is oblivious to the danger. It all happens so fast that Dave can't control the fish. He lunges at it on his knees while screaming at Manea to watch out. The boy understands, looks as though he were dancing on air as he again locks his reel, jumps over the thrashing wahoo, and grabs the gaff, pulling the second fish out of the water. Dave severs the aorta of the first fish, turns, and does the same to the second one before it even hits the deck.

As soon as Dave catches his breath, he screams at Manea, "You stupid boy, why didn't you put those boots on like I told you? He gets your leg, you finished!" Dave turns away and Manea steps into a thick, decrepit pair of extra boots covered with fish blood.

Soon the lines are out again. The wind increases, driving the seas higher and higher. The little boat rolls and pitches like a cork in a hurricane. Despite Dave's masterful hand at tiller and throttle the boat is continually buried in waves. Manea is bailing full time and Dave is ready to call it quits when suddenly the outriggers heave, first on one side, then a second later on the other.

The first line has tangled again, but this time it fouls around the struggling fish attached to it. The wahoo, with dorsal entangled, shoots off on a lateral tangent and immediately fouls itself in the line holding the second fish, also a wahoo. The two struggling wahoo flash back and forth on their ever-decreasing tethers, driven into still greater frenzies. Both man and boy realize exactly what has happened. Together they pull in the first line by hand, hoping that the weakened line, holding perhaps one hundred fifty pounds of powerful, thrashing fish, does not break. The two fishermen strain mightily to pull in this huge struggling weight. With an enormous effort Dave manages to hold the line with both fish on it. Realizing that he has only a few moments before Dave will lose control of the line, Manea quickly gaffs the first fish, dumps it into the boat by himself, and kills it. Dave then immediately brings in the second fish and dispatches it, too.

It takes the better part of an hour for our boat to thread through the passage and plane across the calm lagoon. As dusk settles on Palmerston, the skiff noses into the deserted beach. In addition to the tuna, Dave and Manea have caught five wahoo averaging sixty-five pounds apiece. This is the most fish Dave has caught in a single day in years. Still, he neither thanks Manea nor offers him one word of praise for his work. When the fish are cleaned and delivered to the freezer and the gear is put away, Dave simply nods his head and walks off. Manea, too, trudges toward home, but on his face is a smile bright enough to light up the world.

3

THE THORN ON THE ROSE

The ship's bell on the CAO's porch rings insistently. It is five minutes to eight on Sunday morning, and Reverend Bill is making sure that no one in Palmerston is ignorant of the fact. The demanding peal of the bell reverberates through the morning stillness. Surprisingly, the little church, like a dusty museum exhibit with its buckled plank floors and ancient creaking pews, is nearly empty. Sule is there with Caroline, both in clean white pinafores. Akino shepherds her three-year-old cousin, Tepou. Her brother Phillip, a kind, bright-eyed twelve-year-old, sits next to her. A few other children shift restlessly in the pews, but besides Reverend Bill, his wife Martha, Policeman Bob, and me, there are no adults in attendance. Service starts with a hymn sung in Maori. Neither Policeman Bob nor the children can be heard over the booming tenor of Reverend Bill and especially Martha's falsetto screech coming from the back row. Determined to compensate for lack of numbers by sheer volume, the reverend and his wife, in fact, succeed. You can hear them, particularly Martha, throughout the entire island.

Reverend Bill is a portly yet powerful man. Grave in demeanor, he stares vacantly from the pulpit, looking somewhere out over our heads. He seems devoid of warmth or feeling, yet his sermon is powerfully spoken as if he is attempting to convince his meager congregation of its importance. Who is there to persuade? The children seem oblivious to the sermon, impatient only for the hour-long service to be over. Presumably Martha and Policeman Bob have already gotten the message. That leaves only one person. Maybe *I'm* the one Reverend Bill is trying to impress. My ears perk up. Fortunately, my tape recorder has been running since the beginning of the sermon.

Following the sermon Bill reads some Bible passages, and the service concludes with two more hymns howled as if to castigate the rest of the islanders. Anger seems to be the dominant emotion here. As we step into the bright glare of morning, I ponder the experience. Why haven't the Palmerston adults attended the island's only church? I am curious and determined to find out.

Before I came to Palmerston, I had heard rumors in Rarotonga that the three families were squabbling. Where once they had worked together for the common good, the gossipers had said they now worked against each other, although this was not entirely true. Newfound wealth from fishing prompted the men of each family to labor for themselves, but neither this nor interfamily jealousies seem responsible for the atmosphere of dissension pervading the island.

I find Uncle Tuakana sitting in front of his house painstakingly carving a bowl out of tamanu. He and his family have just finished their own religious service. Four chairs still stand in a tight circle in their front room. "Why was almost no one in church?" I ask him.

He doesn't look up from his carving. "Well, when I were running the church, there were a full church still," he answers obliquely. Tuakana had been the island pastor before his brother returned from Rarotanga.

Pondering whether there could be any crime in a place this small, I take a different tack. "Has anybody had anything stolen?" I ask.

"Yes," Tuakana answers.

"And you know who does the stealing?"

"Yes, we know who does that."

"And is it one person or a number of persons?"

"Oh, it's a few of them, a few of the youngsters, they work together during that period of time; they work together and one does his way of getting what he want from a home, and the other one does his way of getting."

"How old are they?"

"Oh they're, well, from eighteen years over. These younger ones are devils."

"It sounds very serious."

"Yeah, I could say."

"So what do you think should be done about this?"

"Well, it's something that I prefer to have a man from the justice department and a qualified police to be here so we can surely say that there will be a stop. At the moment there's no hope [of getting them to come for petty crimes]."

"Did you talk to the sergeant when he was here?"

"No, I didn't. Well, for an example, I could say this. When I were away and I learned from the next door that someone's got into my house, this house here, and taken a cylinder out, my gas cylinder. They opened the roof, one of them cames up and got it out."

"They didn't take anything else?"

"Well, I'm not sure. Everything were in my house and locked up—and nailed up, and there's no way for them to get in, but he broke in through the roof, coming in. And this man, I could say that he's been a missionary all this time. And if you want to make me tell you more than that . . . do you?"

"Tell me whatever you want to tell me," I reply, hoping that he will continue.

"Well, this man is my brother."

"Reverend Bill?"

"Reverend Bill."

"How do you know that it was he who broke through your roof?"

"Next door they were sitting and watching him."

"Did they say, 'What are you doing?'"

"They didn't say anything."

"Did he ever say, 'I went into your house, because I needed the gas cylinder'? Did he ever say anything about it?"

"Well, it's later on when I came back, when I start working with the people, then he got angry with me and he reported me that I am disturbing the life of the people here and I'm getting the water out of the cistern through the top. So they sent the police down, the chief of police, you know Goldie, the chief of police of the Cook

Islands in Rarotonga? And the justice man, man from the justice department. They sent them down to come and get me and take me to jail."

"Did they?"

"Well, this happened. I was sitting on my table here when he stand to my door, the chief of police. He pointed at me and said, 'You're the baddest man on the beach.' I said to him, 'Sir, if I'm the baddest man, you take me with you.' He said, 'I be back in a few days.' I said, 'Okay.' So he disappeared. In about three days he came back again, but during that time he went from home to home, making inquiry what I did. So they told him that I was the man that worked with the people to clean the place up and to build everything, to prop the church up, and the water catchment—to get it cleaned, the tanks, and all this and that. Well, in a few days, three days, he came back and stand to my door. He shooked his head and said, 'I'm very sorry. Just the opposite,' he says. I say, 'That's too late, sir. You pointed at me too quick. You should come and ask people first.'"

"Okay, I've heard some things about Reverend Bill—" I begin.

"Wait, I finish you up the story. Then I told him. I said 'Now you go and ask him [Reverend Bill] if he come through the roof of my house and took my gas cylinder off.' He stood up and said, 'Yes, I'll be back.' He went away, straight down. Soon he comes back and he said to me, 'You put him into my hand. He's going by this boat with me. Not less than six months in jail.'"

"For stealing a gas cylinder?" I ask.

"For breaking through the house."

Tuakana continues: "Well, I looked at him [the chief of police], and I said to him, 'Well, sir, I'm holding a Bible.' He drops his head down. I say, 'I'm holding a Bible. The Bible did not say only seven times, but seventy times seven, to forgive your own.'"

"So you forgave him."

"I forgave him. So I never said anything, kept quiet."

"Has he stolen anything since then?"

"Well, there's quite a few things I have missed from my home."

"But do you know that he took them?"

"Yes, because he . . . peoples has seen him breaking into it. He broke the locks off and came in and got what he wanted."

"And people have seen Reverend Bill do this?"

"That's right." He names the witnesses, one of whom is now deceased.

"What else has he taken?" I ask.

"Well, shortly after that I informed the police, the chief of police, that there is a barometer, a very old barometer from one of the shipwrecks during the time of my great grandfather, First William. And he [Bill] had taken that from out of my house. He got it there. So I told him [the chief], 'You come with me and we'll prove that. You ask my father.' My father was still alive. So we went there and I told my father and so my father told him, 'You go straight down and ask him [Bill] for the barometer and bring it.' So the chief took off, he went out, the chief, and tell him [Bill], 'The barometer, you must send it back. I'll be back.' So just before he leave, the chief of police came back to me and say, 'I've got the barometer back, and go and take it for your father.' So I went and brought it back."

I am saddened to hear this story. Still, in some cultures, particularly those in the South Pacific, property in a family is considered to belong to *all* family members. So perhaps, in the changing culture, Reverend Bill's actions might not be construed as theft, or at least not theft in the Western sense. Yet if these stories are true, there is much that is disturbing about the island's minister.

"Tuakana," I reply, "I understand that Reverend Bill was a minister in Rarotonga. Why did he return here, to Palmerston?"

Tuakana carves almost ferociously now. "Because he been dismissed as president of the Cook Islands Christian Church. He's taken the church money and that's why he were dismissed."

We are joined by Tuakana's son, Dave, who immediately picks up on our conversation. "When did this happen?" I ask them. They cannot recall whether it was in 1976 or 1977. They finally settle on '76. "How much did he take?" I ask.

"Well, they couldn't really tell exactly," Dave answers, "but the number we got, according to Apenera Short, he's the treasurer then, was about eight hundred dollars they found in his account."

"And this was contributions given by the parishioners? How

did they know it wasn't from his salary or something like that?"

"That's right," Dave replies. "He don't get a salary in that period. It's only every fortnight when the church puts in [pays him]."

"Did he admit taking the money?" I ask.

"When they discovered that the money not in the church account, they make inquiry," Tuakana answers, "Yeah," Dave adds, "they had this big fella from the church in New Zealand come to investigate how this money got missing, and they ask him [Reverend Bill] and he said yes, that he had taken it. And he jumped on Apenera."

"Bill did that?"

"Yeah," Dave says, "just grab him. You know, he lost his mind. Apenera has told the money didn't reach to him. When Bill received the money he put it straight in his account—and they found that money was in his account."

"So what happened? He was president of the largest church in the Cook Islands. Did it cause a huge scandal?"

"That's right," Dave replies, "They gave him so many days to clear out. A lot of peoples really talk about it, but Albert Henry [the prime minister of the Cook Islands] covered things down, because he [Bill] was the top man in [the country's main] church. So he tried to smooth things down."

Reverend Bill was never prosecuted. Instead, in disgrace, he and Martha left Rarotonga to resume life on their home island, where Bill helped to initiate a fishing business that, he said, bettered the lives of his fellow islanders. Though he apparently committed a serious crime, he had not been tried and found guilty in a court of law. So at this point, I decided not to include the story of Reverend Bill in my book. But what I was to hear during the following week changed my mind.

Later that afternoon Dawn Neale and I sit on the porch of the CAO's house watching tiny Palmerston amble through its day. We discuss Reverend Bill's ejection from the church. I ask her how Bill became the pastor on Palmerston after his disgrace on Rarotonga.

"From what Uncle Tuakana told me," Dawn replies, "the Christian Church presbytery in Rarotonga were completely surprised to find out that Uncle Bill had come here and was the pastor here because they'd apparently stripped him of whatever authority they gave him to be a pastor. When they found out that he was here, they were totally surprised and they sent a telegram to Uncle Tuakana that *he* was to be the pastor. Uncle Bob [intercepted it and] didn't show the telegram to Uncle Tuakana but went down and showed it to Bill. Bill said, 'Oh that's just a whole lot of rubbish,' and threw the telegram away, and the only reason Uncle Tuakana found out about the telegram was because Thomas [CAO John's son], who took the telegram, received the telegram, told Uncle Tuakana about it."

"And Tuakana couldn't or didn't take over the pastorship?"

"Well, didn't. But something else that Uncle Tuakana and Auntie Teinano told me: For over ten years, from 1970 to 1980, the women and some of the men, too, especially Uncle Tuakana, were carving bowls and weaving hats, mats, and baskets, and they would send their handicrafts to Uncle Bill, who was acting as their agent, to sell the things [in Rarotonga]. The funds were to take care of our church, here. And when Uncle Bill came back to Palmerston, Uncle Tuakana asked him where was the money that they made on this material, having full trust in Uncle Bill. And Bill said, 'Oh, that only come to two or three hundred dollars,' but even the two or three hundred dollars they never got. So the proceeds for ten years of handicraft work by the island people has disappeared somewhere."

"You mean that for all the handicrafts that were sent to him, they never received any money?"

"No," Dawn says, shaking her head sadly, "nothing."

"What was the value of those things? Was there a tally made of the things sent to him?"

"Well, I remember in 1976, when I came back to Rarotonga after boarding school, a lady's hat would cost between fifteen and twenty-five dollars. And the mats [often the size of small area rugs and often used by the local people as beds] take a lot more work, so were more expensive. But unfortunately, they just sent everything to him, just having complete faith and trust that the things he received would be sold and the money would be kept for them."

"So no tallies were ever made. What would you guess would be the total number of handicrafts that was sent to him?"

"I would imagine over a hundred mats, at least, because when my mother would come down to Palmerston from 1970 on, the women were making on an average about two or three mats a month, and that's a lot of hard work."

Uncle Tuakana confirms what Dawn has said. He and the others had trusted Reverend Bill. After all, Bill was family and he was revered as the most holy man in all of the Cook Islands, the president of the country's largest church, Palmerston's greatest success story. So why should they count what they sent him? That would be tantamount to betraying the mutual trust that existed among the members of this close-knit family. In addition to the mats, Tuakana guesses that fifty or sixty hats woven with tiny cowrie shells and more than one hundred finely carved bowls, as well as shell lamp shades, vases, and various other handicrafts, were shipped to Bill over the ten-year period. No one knows how much the Palmerston people should have received, but a conservative guess, based on half of the prevailing sales prices averaged over the ten years, would be three to five thousand dollars: a lot of money in view of the fact that the total income for the whole island during some of those years was only two or three thousand dollars. Besides, thousands of hours of tedious labor were sacrificed in hopes of raising enough money to repair the island's beautiful church, which was—and still is—in imminent danger of collapse. And for all their work and sacrifice, the people of Palmerston received from their most revered family member—absolutely nothing.

I asked Tuakana if Bill was ever brought to account for the missing funds. He said, "I went straight into it. I said to him [Bill], 'Where's all the result of these crafts we sent up to you and what's the amount, the sum of money you were to send to us, the balance?' He said, 'It all come to nothing at all.' He didn't give me a definite [answer]. He just said, 'Completely nothing.'"

"Did he say that *he* had received the money?"

"He admitted the money had gone to him as the agent in charge, but he can't give me a number or anything." With palms outstretched, Uncle Tuakana shrugs, as if this is the normal course of events when dealing with his brother, and what can he do?

I need to talk to someone outside the middle family. Taepae, his wife, Mary, and Martha, Taepae's grandmother, are sitting out on their stoop enjoying the quiet of the afternoon. Mary and Grandmother Martha substantiate what the others had said about the missing handicraft money. Taepae, simple and forthright, serves on the three-man island council that supposedly shares authority with the CAO, the central government's appointee, to govern Palmerston's local affairs. Tuakana and Policeman Bob are also on the council, which, however, no longer has power to enforce old regulations, or if it makes new ones, to see that they are enforced. If the islanders don't like a council ruling or ordinance, they simply ignore it. So who does have the power on Palmerston, and where is Bill's place in the scheme of things?

According to Taepae, during Bill's tenure as CAO (1980 to 1987), the island occasionally received foreign-aid donations. In 1983, for instance, New Zealand sent Palmerston a number of two-thousand-gallon galvanized water tanks. Since all the island water had to be collected during the rainy season and saved for the rest of the year, during which it was parsimoniously doled out for drinking and sponge baths, the tanks were a godsend to the islanders, who had previously depended solely on the two tanks in the catchment. Each permanent family residence expected to receive a tank, but this didn't happen. According to Taepae, Bill refused to give tanks to him, to David the dresser, and to Taepae's father and grandmother, both of whom at that time had their own domiciles.

"Why did he refuse to give your family tanks?" I ask Taepae.

"Well, I had trouble with Bill; we had little arguments. So we had our council meeting and then I asked him, you know, why he didn't give us our water tanks. He, Bill, replied that it was because I refused to cart the things from the ship. But we didn't know the things was coming on the boat. He didn't tell us. So I told him that [one of those] water tanks is my grandmother's, not mine. It's her house. And he said, 'Well, I don't care.'"

"What kind of trouble had you had with Bill?"

"Well, was a lot of troubles in years back. There was the fishing cooperative that we all were members [of], that Bill was in charge. So I asked him, 'Would you tell me how much money is in Palmerston's [fishing co-op] bankbook?' and he said to me, 'It is none of your business to know.' I said, 'I'm in that fishing company and I want to know!' And he said, 'It's none of your business to know. It's nobody's. Get out!' So I stopped [asking him] and I went away."

"There's a lot of things," Taepae continues, "that the island council supposed to own and run for the people. We got a tractor [as an aid donation]. Bill's got it now. We got a generator from fisheries. It's for the people of Palmerston, but he took it and claimed it."

"Why haven't the people taken those things back?"

"Well it's supposed to be for the chairman of island council [Uncle Tuakana] to do this. I went and asked [him] to go and get it. We can use it to benefit the island. But in that case, I don't know what's going on, really." The other members of the council apparently could not bring themselves to force the issue, he tells me.

Over the next few days other accusations pile up. CAO John accuses Bill of stealing building materials provided by the government fisheries service, the education department, and the public service department to construct public buildings on Palmerston. According to John, expensive roofing and timbers needed to replace the burned schoolteacher's house, the island generator building, and the catchment building all were appropriated by Bill and used either in the construction of his own house and bathhouse or for the building containing his personal generator, which powers the freezers used in his fishing business. According to CAO John, the government agencies never forced Bill to return the materials or pressed charges against him for their theft. Others confirm John's accusation.

·

The CAO's house consists of two tiny shed-roofed rooms, each with an adjoining porch, and a large sitting room between them. I am quartered in one of these rooms, barely large enough to accommodate two single beds at right angles to each other and a small dresser. Nearby are three freezers Bill uses for storing fish before shipping them on to Rarotonga. The shed room on the other side of the house is filled with odds and ends, including stacks of textbooks that Bill had refused to donate to the school.

The center and largest room is a parlor, by far the most ornate room in any building on the island, save the church. Wood-paneled, it is filled with old framed prints and photos. Large photographs of King George and Queen Mary occupy the place of honor, behind two high-backed, stuffed, plastic-covered chairs, circa 1950. Along one wall a matching plastic-covered sofa sits beneath pictures of Queen Elizabeth and the Duke of Edinburgh. Two dressers, a single bed, and several small coffee tables occupy the rest of the room. Flower holders filled with plastic zinnias and chrysanthemums glow incongruously on the tables. Photos of William I, Princess Elizabeth as a young girl, and Major Mane Pumare, prime minister of the Cook Islands in 1912, along with imitation velvet souvenir pennants depicting Sydney, Australia, and the Cook Islands, adorn the other walls. Ornate handicrafted shell lamp shades hang, but without bulbs; flower holders and dozens of other draped and hanging doodads, all made from hundreds of tiny pooka shells, fill every spare inch of the room.

Just to one side of the CAO house is a ten-by-twenty-foot pandanus-thatched cooking shed containing a sink, propane-powered cooker, and plastic-topped kitchen table and chairs. Between it and the CAO house sits the toilet and washhouse built of concrete. Upon my arrival Martha told me I would be staying in the CAO's house, then took me to the adjacent bathhouse. Solemnly she took a key on a string from around her neck. Handing it to me and nodding her head at a huge brass padlock on the door, she said, "Here, you lock it up when you are finished with it. Put the key on the hook on the wall." I took a quick look inside. There was only a toilet and a plastic bucket to use for giving oneself a sponge bath—certainly nothing worth locking up. I gave Martha a questioning look. She pointed to a nail on the wall next to the room where I would be sleeping. She was not about to volunteer any information, and so I asked her why she keeps it locked—particularly from her own relatives. Brusquely she answered, "We keep it locked because otherwise some other people uses it. They sneak in and uses it. So that's why you lock it." Question time was over. Martha's almost square body had already disappeared.

I soon discover that Martha and Bill have exclusive use of two of the four toilets on the island, one next to their own home and the one I use in the CAO house, which they completely control. Most of the other islanders use one of four outhouses. According to Dave, when Bill and Martha returned to Palmerston after being ousted by the church, they had no place to stay. Grandpa Ned, Bill and Tuakana's father, was the aging patriarch of the island and leader of the middle family. He allowed Bill and Martha to live in the CAO house, even though it was meant to be used by the entire middle family. Even after they built and moved into their own house they still controlled the CAO's house. Not once during my two weeks on Palmerston did any other family member step inside its doors. According to Dave, Bill also changed his father's will to appoint himself leader of the middle family instead of Tuakana, whom the old man had designated to succeed him.

While these statements further blackened Bill's character, they paled in comparison to what I heard next. According to Dave, in 1983 David Vaine, a young schoolteacher from Rarotonga assigned to teach on Palmerston, got into an argument with Reverend Bill over who was in charge of school policy. Bill insisted that he, the CAO, had the right to set policy. The schoolteacher disagreed, adamantly. The argument turned into a battle of wills and festered on the little island like a tropical sore, growing larger and uglier. One Monday night, following a nasty argument between the two men, the schoolteacher, universally popular with the rest of the islanders, joined them for an evening of entertainment at the catchment building.

Just about that time a fire broke out in the teacher's house. According to Reverend Bill, the schoolteacher had been smoking in bed and had thrown a cigarette out the window. It (somehow) bounced back into the room and started the fire. But Dave refutes this. "That's not true," he says. "Who was there watching? [No one saw the cigarette being thrown.] David came home, had a shower, and came straight here, at our place, and he was there [at the catchment building] for fifteen minutes. Then someone yelled out 'Fire!' When we arrived, the house was completely gone."

"Why do you think someone set it on fire?" I ask.

"Well, Big Bill said someone put gas on it, you know, gasoline. And the funny thing was, the stainless steel sink, the sewing machine, the pots, they all disappeared so the fire can't burn them. So somebody took those out before the fire was going."

"Did anybody see those things again?"

"No, never again."

"Do you know who started the fire?"

"Yeah, we know. The boys, Melbourne and Ray and Young Bob, were not in the catchment. Young Bob calls out, 'Fire,' in fifteen minutes' time and the house is gone, is nothing."

Melbourne, the twenty-two-year-old son of CAO John, already had served six months in Rarotonga's jail for putting out the eye of a cousin who had stolen his girl. Ray and Young Bob, the twenty-year-old sons of Joseph and Policeman Bob, had no prior arrests. But none of them will speak about the fire. In fact, the only one who will talk about it is Dave, who believes Bill paid the boys to torch the teacher's house.

The Cook Islands education department apparently did not believe the fire was accidental. After David Vaine returned to Raro, the education department refused to send Palmerston a replacement teacher. For three years there was no teacher on Palmerston. According to Dave, Tui Ngariki Short, the secretary of education, told him, "I can't promise you [another teacher]. You peoples [already] threaten the life of a teacher."

Dave continues, "A young fella, Junior Alfred, told his sister, Haua, that he was there when the house burned, but that he didn't do it. His sister told to Teipo, my missus. But he wouldn't say anything else."

Junior was unavailable for comment.

Big Bill's actions apparently have caused the whole way of life on Palmerston to change, sometimes in sad and confusing ways. Dawn says, "Traditionally, the island always held feast days for

Christmas, New Year's, a day they call Sacrament Sunday, and a couple of other holidays during the year where the whole island would come together and share their food and have festivities together, and when he became the CAO on the island, Bill virtually did away with all that, discouraged it."

"Why?"

"I don't know why. There was no reason given, but he discouraged it, said it was not going to be held and there were no plans to hold these things. When I found out this had happened, I was really quite devastated because some of these traditional things always were associated with life on Palmerston. Everyone was just devastated.

"Also for years and years the families have had their own lands that they could use for picking coconuts from, go to the taro patch, get their taro. They developed a sharing system where everybody from the middle family took from the middle part and everyone from the other sides took from their parts. When Uncle Bill came here, it got to the point where everybody, especially the middle family, had to go to see him to get permission to get coconuts from the family coconut trees for drinking, for nuts, for cooking, and that was especially bad because—now this was a firsthand account that happened to my mother when my mother came down here. She went to go get some coconuts from trees that had been planted by her father and mother on our part, on our working lands, which is part of the middle family lands, and my grandmother told my mother that she had first to go and get permission from Bill before she could climb the coconut palm."

"Was there a rationing problem, or any reason given?"

"There wasn't really any reason, but at that time they were working a lot of copra and it could be that the more coconuts you pick off the tree, the less coconuts there are to make copra. But one tree, six coconuts, doesn't make that much difference. The thing was, he wanted to control everything that happened, and when my mother went up to our family plot to work in the taro patch and my brother was up there cleaning, Bill came and told my brother to get off the land; it wasn't his land. That land was my mother's! It came from her grandmother, who was William Marsters's daughter, and it was given to her, as her family and descendants' family plot for working, which was all part of the middle family but was particularly our family plot. Each family from the children of William Marsters has land that they work on, especially when it comes to the taro patches. So Bill first wanted to be told if they were going to be going there to work on it, to get some taro out of the patch. I can only surmise that the reason why is that he felt that he was the person controlling it. To me, it was appalling, when I've always felt that I could go and pick any coconut that I wanted to."

"Basically, he was telling you what you could and could not do on your own property?"

"Right. Right."

"And with your own trees. Do you feel that he still has control now?"

"Not as much as he did before, when he was CAO. But he still controls a lot of what happens on the island."

Part of Bill's power stems from his control of the island economy. Most of the fish exported to Rarotonga, which provides the livelihood for almost everyone on Palmerston, goes through Bill's company. But his financial influence does not explain why, if he has taken advantage of his family, they do not force him to repay what he has stolen from them. How does he intimidate this little island and exploit its people for his personal gain?

The answer emerges when I meet again with Dawn. "How is Bill able to get away with all the things he has done without anyone retaliating or physically forcing him to repay the money that he has taken?" I ask her.

"Well, you know, he's got, like, henchmen, the equivalent of henchmen, so that no one would even think of physically abusing him. Tuakana has a little argument with him once in a while, but the other boys wouldn't dare come against him."

"Who are his henchmen?"

"Radio and Andrew," Dawn replies. "And besides that there's Dick, who's his staunch supporter. Dick [who has just moved back to the island] is very much in Bill's favor, so he was given *two* brand new water tanks. Also Uncle Bob [Policeman Bob, on the island council], and Joseph. People who are on his side, he treats them very well."

We are joined by Dave, who adds, "You know he wanted to do a bond, that's a liquor store, here. He's trying to change the dispensary in the catchment and use that to sell his liquor."

"How do the people feel about using their dispensary as a liquor store?" I ask.

"Most of the peoples buy liquor. Every shipment [supply boat that stops] he get about five hundred dollar worth of liquor and that is sold before the next boat arrive."

"Yes," Dawn adds, "Bill also pays his fishermen in alcohol. Cases. Because the boys like to drink. He says, 'For this amount of fish I give you this amount of a case.' Some of it is in payment and some of it is in bonus."

"Does he sell to anybody?"

"Mainly to the ones he like, his favorites," Dave answers. "Any amount they want. He sells them on Sundays, too. Quite a few times I see fellows go down to his house, you know, having a hangover from Saturday night, and on Sunday morning they goes down there and get a bottle to go to the bush to drink."

"And it is unlawful on Palmerston, and has been for years and years, for anyone to sell liquor—any alcohol? Is that right?"

"Yeah, absolute!" Dave replies vehemently.

"They also selling smokes," Dave adds, "you know, cigarettes. Martha is selling."

"Martha sells the cigarettes?" I ask incredulously.

"Yeah," Dave answers. "If they want some work to be done for them, they get the young boys to do the work and give them a packet of smokes. So you see a lot of young fellas here smoking only because of that."

"So Martha participates in all this business?" I ask, hardly believing my ears.

Dawn replies, "Apparently, from what I have heard from Tuakana, Auntie Grand, and the others, she does just as much as he does. Martha is very supportive of her husband. She defends him like a staunch defender of the truth. She does her part and will do anything he tells her to do."

[*49*]

"So Bill pays his supporters off in gifts and booze. Would they fight for him? Would they beat people up or commit a crime for him?"

"Oh yes, definite!" Dave answers.

"Do they all get drunk together?"

"Apparently, over the last couple of years," Dawn replies, while Dave nods his assent, "they've always had lots of big drinking parties and Uncle Bill has been in there with them, and it's been Joseph, Uncle Bill, Bob, the boys, the boys from the bush."

"Does Bill, Reverend Bill, get drunk with them?"

"Apparently so. He was the one that was going to convert the water catchment into a pub for the island and that was another fight that he had with Uncle Tuakana. Bill was going to take the dispensary out of the catchment and put it somewhere else and convert the catchment into a pub. The reason why the dispensary was put there was so that it would be a shelter for the people that came down for clinic days to sit there while they were being treated. Uncle Tuakana was out working in the taro patches, and Grandpa Ned sent word to him to come down and stop Uncle Bill from digging the posts around the catchment to create a pub in there. They were going to put up coconut posts to make a fence around it and so Uncle Tuakana came down and said to Grandpa Ned, 'He's your son. You go and tell him to stop it.' And so Grandpa Ned went up, and he was not well, and he tottered out there on his walking stick and said to Bill, 'You stop what you're doing; don't make this place a pub,' and Uncle Bill said to him, 'Get out of here, old man. This has got nothing to do with you.'"

"When was this?"

"It was at least six years ago, because it was when Grandpa Ned was alive. And then Uncle Tuakana told Grandpa Ned to go back in the house, and he went to Uncle Bill and he said, 'If another person puts another post down into that hole'—and there was a hole already dug—'I'm going to drop them to the sand.' And so somebody ran off to Uncle Bob, who is the policeman, and said Uncle Tuakana is threatening Uncle Bill's life and the boys that are there working with them. Bob came over and Uncle Tuakana threatened him as well. And then a telegram was sent to the police in Rarotonga."

[50]

"And I guess we've heard the rest of the story—how the police found out that Reverend Bill had stolen Tuakana's gas tank and they were going to take Reverend Bill instead of Uncle Tuakana to jail, but Tuakana said seven times seventy," I add.

Both Dawn and Dave confirm the rest of the story.

"What do people think about all this, on the island?" I ask. "It sounds like the scandal of all time. How many of the people are up in arms about this?"

"It doesn't seem like many of them are," Dawn replies. "They just shrug their shoulders and say, you know, what can we do?"

What indeed! I ponder. Still, there seems to be enough evidence to put Bill in jail for any number of crimes. While the good people of Palmerston can't overthrow Bill and his group by force, they can certainly go to the police. Do they fear reprisals by Radio, Andrew, and the other young men who seem to be under Bill's control? Probably not. By almost any standards, even South Pacific standards, these are not criminals likely to wreak vengeance on their own relatives—particularly if their leader were in jail. So what hold does Bill have over his fellow islanders? In fact, no one has a succinct answer to my question.

Perhaps Dawn's mother, Sarah, comes closest to explaining the lack of response from people who feel Bill has taken advantage of them: "I believe that people just don't like to make trouble when there's somebody's offended them or violated the laws of their forefathers," she says.

"Do you mean that your people would rather simply turn the other cheek and let him get away with the things they say he has done in order to keep their lives peaceful?" I ask her.

"You know, I would do that," she answers. "I was brought up by a woman who doesn't like any fights and she doesn't like anyone backbiting. Sometimes there was trouble and I used to say, 'You know, take it to the law, or do something about it,' and she would say, 'No, just leave it alone. *Just leave it alone!* Don't go step on another person's boots.' And that's the way I look at it." Sarah's voice trails off as she watches her granddaughter, Caroline, happily cuddling a baby chick. Dawn joins her mother and little niece.

In frustration I ask Dawn, "What do you feel Palmerston's

future is if people here continue to let Bill have his own way and if what's happening on Palmerston continues?"

Dawn considers the question for a long moment, then answers, "I don't think they're going to have much of a life on this island because the way things are going now, they're not going to be working together. There's not going to be a community. The way of life, as I remember it as a child and growing up, is not going to exist anymore unless the children can go past this feud and make something work. But I don't see these children staying on this island. I think when the old people die, a way of life is going to die, and the life and existence of this island is going to be completely changed."

Forever.

4

RETURN TO RAROTONGA

Maria Henderson looks up from behind the counter where she has been arranging pandanus handbags. She is a handsome—striking, actually—woman of about sixty, who still exhibits the fiery hauteur of a flamenco dancer. The shop she and her husband run on the main street of Rarotonga caters to both tourists and residents. On the counters, little phallic Tangaroas, miro-wood bowls, and woven mats lie interspersed with transistor radios, VCRs, and tape decks. Local teenage boys crowd the back aisle gawking at boom boxes, while an Australian mother-and-daughter team scans the front shelves with a practiced eye for status souvenirs to further stuff their already loaded Gucci tote bags.

All in all I would rather not be here, but it is necessary. I have returned to Rarotonga expressly to probe further into the dealings of this anomaly who, along with the old prime minister, Albert Henry, was once the most respected citizen of his country. It was to Maria Henderson that Reverend Bill consigned the Palmerston handicrafts, and it is with her that I must begin the process of checking the accusations that the Palmerston people have leveled against their most revered family member. When I explain the purpose of my visit, however, Maria tells me, in so many words, to mind my own business. I expected this response. I counter with a partial litany of the crimes of which Reverend Bill's own family has accused him. She is unmoved. Next, I make it clear that with or without her help the story *will* come out, and if there is no evidence that Reverend Bill had received payment from her, she will be implicated. This brings a magical response.

Maria turns to a back counter where a pile of ledgers is stacked. She selects a small book that contains her handicraft consignment transactions and begins leafing through it, trying to locate the Palmerston consignments. Finding what she has been looking for, she swings the ledger around in front of me. In June of 1985, Reverend Bill received a check, which he cashed, from the Cook Islands National Arts Council for N.Z. $724 for Palmerston handicrafts. A New Zealand dollar at that time was equivalent to approximately U.S. 65 cents. Maria goes back to leafing through the ledger. Again she places it before me and points to three 1987 payments made to Reverend Bill, in cash, for Palmerston handicrafts. The payments total more than N.Z. $800, and next to each the initials W.M. (for William Marsters) are scripted, showing that he had received the money. The initials are in a different hand from the other transaction notations. I thank Maria Henderson and spend the next hour sitting under a tree watching the waves crash on the reef.

The Cook Islands Christian Church was the largest church in the country during the time Reverend Bill was its president. Still the largest church, it has branches around Rarotonga and on the other islands and has its own theological college. The congregation of primarily influential citizens worships solemnly every Sunday in a lovely old whitewashed colonial building on a leafy lane outside town. Apenera Short was the church treasurer in 1977 when Reverend Bill was ejected for embezzling parishioners' contributions. At that time Apenera was also the chief of police of the Cook Islands.

Apenera, a small sprightly man, now enjoys retirement with his wife and family in a modest frame house on a country road halfway around the island from town. It is early evening when we meet. We sit on a screened veranda. The balmy air, perfumed with frangipani, is alive with the staccato chatter of the insect world. Apenera is a most polite gentleman of the old school, but he is not what you would call a conversationalist. "You were the treasurer of the Cook Islands Christian Church?" I begin.

There follows a long silence during which we both fidget and listen to the noises of the night, a faraway dog, a tardy rooster.

Finally, "I was the treasurer."

"When was that?" I ask.

Another interminable silence, then, "'Round about '77; '76 or '77."

"What was Bill Marsters's position then?" I prompt, hoping for a quick reply.

I am disappointed. Perhaps Apenera first needs to solve the question of the meaning of life. More probably he is wondering why he is doing this.

At last, "He was president of the church."

"And what happened?" I drawl.

More stars come out. The moon goes behind a cloud. A car passes on the island road, then silence again. Finally the story begins to unfold, one hesitant word after another.

"There was a shortage of cash, about seven hundred dollars—I can't remember the exact figure. And during that night of the argument, at the meeting, he was so furious, he pushed me out of the meeting. I had said, 'No, I can prove you took it.'"

"How could you prove he had taken the money?"

"I said, 'I know my accounting. I can find out where the money is.' I told the committee, 'Tomorrow morning I can prove to you that he got the money.' So the following day I went to the bank. I looked into the church account for the number of the check that I had issued. It was not in the church's account. It was found in Bill Marsters's private checking account."

"What happened then?"

"There was a meeting after that. A church lawyer came from New Zealand. Anyway, at this meeting it was brought before the committee and it was proven by the fact that the check was posted into Bill Marsters's account."

"Did he have any explanation for why he had put the money in his account? Did he admit it?"

"Well, he couldn't explain it, but, yes, he admits it."

"He actually admitted it—before witnesses?"

"Well, before a big meeting. I wouldn't say that he admitted it, but the lawyer said, 'You've got the money.' And he didn't say no, so that means admission."

[55]

"And then what happened?"

"So the lawyer says, 'Now, Bill Marsters, you are under a black cloud!'"

"What did Bill say?"

"Oh, he didn't say anything. But then he was voted out [of his office of president] by the assembly."

"Were there any other experiences with him that would lead you to believe there were dishonest qualities about him?"

"Ah." He refused to answer.

"It must have been a terrible shock for everyone."

"Oh yes, oh yes. At the meeting where he was going to attack me, all the others were shocked."

"And essentially he had the respect of everyone before that?"

"Oh yes. He was president before that for four or five years. He was elected to become the president and before that the secretary—and he was a good preacher, so the people respect him."

After thanking Apenera, I stroll off into the night, wondering what else will turn up about Reverend Bill Marsters. I don't have long to wait. The next day I am to meet with the chief of police and with the executive assistant to the deputy prime minister. But before I see them, I receive a note from Dave Marsters of Palmerston saying that he wants to talk to me. Dave is currently working for the Department of Fisheries in Rarotonga. He is the one who introduced me to Apenera Short, and now he wishes to tell me some previously unmentioned recollections concerning Reverend Bill and Martha.

I meet him early the next morning. "Well, I forgot to tell you about the church box," he begins.

A collection box made from an old wooden voting box and labeled "To support the rebuilding of the church—any donations will be most welcome" is placed in the church by Martha whenever Palmerston is visited by a yacht or the infrequent cruise ship.

"So what happens," I ask Dave, "after tourists come and put money in the box? Do they leave very large contributions?"

"Oh yeah," Dave replies. "They put in twenty-dollar notes—U.S. dollars, not New Zealand dollars! It depends on how much tourists come. After the tourists go back onto their boat, Martha returns back to the church, take the box home, and close the church. She takes the money straight away and check how much money she earn."

"How much does she make?"

"Well in March this year, I was there, and that time they [tourists] came on the boat, used to be *World Discoverer*, now changed to *World Expedition* or something like that. And it's about seventy tourists come. So that money—she tell her friends, 'Oh, I made six hundred dollars in one day!' So, it seems to be a big earning for her."

"Who did she tell that to?"

"To the daughter of John Dick, and she [the daughter] told me, because she's one of these talkative persons."

"And nobody has ever received any of that money for the church?"

"No, no, that money, they been doing this the past years, they just keep it. That's supposed to go into the church fund, but Big Bill is still holding it as his own personal thing. Eight hundred dollars, one time, was given [to Bill] for the island. Simon, John Dick's father, when he heard about it, he went to see Big Bill. He said, 'The money's been handed over to you for the peoples.' And Big Bill said, 'No, the money was given to me, not to you!'"

After that revelation, I decide to take Dave with me to my meeting with the chief of police. Compared to their counterparts on the Cook Islands, the policemen in New York, London, Los Angeles, and Paris look downright shabby. One never sees a soiled or slightly spotted uniform. Even in Rarotonga's heat there is hardly so much as a wrinkle on a single resplendent police tunic. The Rarotonga police's record for capturing criminals, however, does not match the perfection of their uniforms. On that small island, only three-and-a-half miles by six miles, and with a population of only about ten thousand, there have been numerous criminals that somehow the police never seem able to catch. A certain robber and would-be rapist who committed a series of crimes would run up into the hills after each strike, eluding the police time after time. Most of the Cook Islanders I talked to, though very law-abiding, thought Rarotonga would be a fine place to live and work if you were a criminal.

The national police headquarters occupies a small, 1950s modern, two-story building a few blocks from the center of town. Dave and I are led into the chief's office by a young constable.

Chief Goldie Goldie is the quintessential hail-fellow-well-met. The son of a World War II Yank soldier, known only as Goldie, and of an Aitutake maiden, Goldie Goldie shines with a wonderful Anglo-Maori friendliness. Indeed, he is so hospitable and quietly effusive that I think I am talking to the chamber of commerce spokesman. When Dave and I go over the various crimes Bill is accused of and the evidence to support the accusations, Chief Goldie Goldie narrows his eyes in an appropriate "the nerve of that guy" manner. Finally, after listening to everything we have to say, Goldie Goldie nods his head hospitably, promising that he will study the matter and bring all his resources to bear on the question, and most effusively ushers Dave and me out of his office. Smiling at what a wonderful guy the chief is, we find ourselves back out on the street.

Peter Marsters is a different story. Bright, intense, and matter-of-fact, he is one of the country's young, educated technocrats. He is assistant to Inatio Akaruru, deputy prime minister, and may be a deputy prime minister himself one day. Peter is one of hundreds of Marsterses who trace their ancestry to Palmerston's original William Marsters. So of course he is related to Reverend Bill, but only as a distant third cousin, and there is no love lost between them. In fact, according to Peter, Reverend Bill has threatened to kill him.

I ask Peter how it happened that Reverend Bill, who was Palmerston's chief administrative officer, was sacked by the central government.

"Yes, I was coordinating officer to the Outer Island Affairs at the time," Peter replies. "And I dealt very closely with the chief of Outer Island Affairs, a chap by the name of Unuia. His given name is Tou, but he's known by Man, and he controlled materials, all shipments to local governments on the outer islands. That was its main function, of course. Outer Island Affairs was to supplement their needs, to care for their affairs. Any queries on the mainland he

controlled. And at that stage there was several disagreements between Man and Bill Marsters. Things like, Bill would go direct
requesting for permission for government boats to call in at Palmerston. And if he would just go through the proper channel, request
here, tell the chief his hardship, they would weigh the situation,
and if they thought there was a need for that, then they would divert
a boat to Palmerston.

"So this carried on a couple of times and Bill was utilizing the
diversion of the [government] boat for his own benefit. You see,
when the boat arrives there, he would control how much cargo
would go. And people that he didn't want, or people that he didn't
get along with, well, you find that their fish would never make it to
Rarotonga's market. And it's about that sort of corruption that Man
spoke with me, and it's then I aired my views on what other knowledge that I have. The knowledge that I have concerns the fishing
company that was formed by Bill Marsters, and it was called The
Palmerston Fishing Company. I know for a fact that there were a lot
of people on Palmerston Island that agreed to be shareholders in his
company and that have actually paid money in to become a shareholder, and they're not a shareholder. Even today they still don't
own any part of that company. The [three] directors of that company were, and still are—I believe the company still is registered—
Bill Marsters, the skipper of the boat, and Poppy Whichman.

"This is how I see the company set up: The harbor master was
skipper on the local government schooner that called at Palmerston.
Bill Marsters, of course, he was the organizer of all of these deals,
and Poppy Whichman owned the grocery shop on Rarotonga. This
is my interpretation, that Bill Marsters robbed the people there. He
bought fish at a very low price [from the Palmerston fishermen] and
then he would put it on the boat, and they would bring that cargo
here [to Rarotonga]. And they would bring that fish across freight-
free. And Poppy, of course, had the outlet on this side to get rid of
[to sell] the fish for him. So they have a—you know—they have a
green business there.

"And there's a lot of people that paid Bill [that received neither
shares in the company nor any return on their investment]. I know
the present CAO [John James Marsters]. I'll quote him, because he

showed me, he's told me personally, that when he gave his money over—something to the tune of six hundred dollars, payment towards a thousand dollars—to become a shareholder in this business, there was no receipts given. Bill is a very crafty man. He waits. 'Oh yeah, you give me that much here, down payment, and when you've paid me a thousand dollars, I'll give you a receipt.' But the company was already registered, and to my knowledge, that company left no space for additional shareholders. Because if there was, he would have told them, but he didn't. He kept them in the dark. And that's the sort of mentality that this man has.

"During this period there were materials sent over for the teacher's house on Palmerston," he continues.

"After the first one burned, you mean?"

"After the first one burned." (Peter Marsters will not speak on the record about who he thinks set the fire, but it is obvious who he believes is responsible.) "So this material was ordered and he [Bill] came here and asked the education department, the secretary of education, if they could supply the material, the island would build [a new teacher's house] free of labor costs. So they supplied it. And once the material arrived there, he came back to renegotiate. He wanted them to pay him, and him alone. He would select the workers to build this house. You see what I'm getting at: He creates something and then he gets the full benefit.

"The changing over of the CAO," Peter continues. "That was an area that I know fully what happened, as I had to do [write] respective letters, one to Reverend Bill and one to John James Marsters. They read their respective letters; one was a termination and one was an appointment. And after those letters, things went sour. Because I was there with the chief clerk of the Outer Island Affairs, and his responsibility was to check all the government materials, the government belongings, that were in Bill's possession before handing it [the office] over to Palmerston's incoming chief administrative officer. But he refused to hand the stuff over. That's what took my trip to Palmerston. And we were there for ten days and nothing happened. He kept delaying it. And then he said he would not hand the government belongings over until the government paid him a hundred thousand dollars' compensation. That is a known fact because

he even sent a telegram, which I have. I'll find it for you. It's somewhere in my records. He even threatened bloodshed on the island."

"Who was he gonna blood?"

"You know, it's obvious, it's me. When he was terminated I
came [to Palmerston] with a delegation. I took six builders [carpen-
ters] with me on that trip. The intentions were, when he [Bill]
handed over to the incoming CAO, then he would release the materials for the schoolhouse, which my delegation would build. So
the round trip was intended that way. We were dropped off and
we would be picked up within ten days. But he wouldn't let any of
the delegation near the materials. And we have only an honorary
policeman there. (According to Dave, CAO John, Taepae, and
others, Bill didn't want an inventory made of the materials because
he had already used many of them to build his own house.)

"Well, he threatened to shoot me, anyway. I said to him, 'You
can, but you make sure that first shot connects because you only
have time for one.' This was a heated argument that happened between him and I. He sent me off Palmerston Island. He said to me,
'This is my land.' And let me tell you, I have the same rights as he
has on that land. And he knows that.

"So, therefore I left, ten days afterwards, with my delegation. I
did write a report on that and the police have that—because I filed a
complaint. My complaint was that he refused to hand over government property to the rightful appointee. As far as I know, the present CAO still hasn't received any of the government property that
he's supposed to have. And I think that's a crime."

·

I was so astounded by the behavior of the Reverend William
Marsters, a man who at the apex of his career was so popular he
could have been elected prime minister of his country, that I attempted to trace his origins to see if he had a history that would account for his present behavior. But no one I spoke with could
remember any aspect of his childhood that could account for his actions as an adult. He went to the Palmerston school, where he was
considered a bright student and very competitive. Then he attended
the Christian Church theological college in Rarotonga and the

Congregational Theological College in Auckland, New Zealand, where he graduated with a diploma in theology in 1956. There simply were no clues to why he became what he is.

After he was ejected from the church, it appears Reverend Bill felt that he had nothing left to lose. The sad fact is that most of his dishonest behavior, so harmful to those around him, might have been prevented. Two prime ministers, Sir Albert Henry, in office at the time Reverend Bill was ejected from the church, and Tom Davis, who certainly must have been aware of many of the improprieties during Bill's tenure as CAO on Palmerston, tried to sweep his dealings under the rug.

I asked Peter Marsters why successive governments have failed to prosecute Bill. He replied, "If you could comprehend the effect, as far as his status is concerned, in the church, it is quite an embarrassing situation. It's quite an embarrassing thing what he did in the church, *and* to be asked to leave the church. So naturally the public servants, the government itself, would not like to discuss such issues. Because it's quite shameful, it's a shameful act."

Inept police work, an embarrassed government, and relatives who are afraid or unwilling to give evidence against the former minister have aided and abetted his second career. According to Dave Marsters, Bill now brags about his criminal prowess. Pokura, one of Taepae's brothers, told Dave that Reverend Bill had been telling some of the fishermen working for him, "If you can get away with little things, you can just as easily get away with big things."

Reverend Bill* may not get away with either big or little things much longer. He has made some powerful enemies. As I left the office of the deputy prime minister, Peter Marsters said, "Don't get me wrong—the books have not closed between he and I. I *will* put him in jail."

---

* Prior to this book's publication, I sent William Marsters a letter suggesting that he respond to the charges made against him. At the time of publication, no answer had been received.

II

Vanuatu

THE TRADITIONAL

WORLD

5

CONVERSATIONS WITH

THE CANNIBALS

I am sitting in a thatched-roof village on the island of Malekula listening to some old ex-cannibals as they have the time of their lives laughing and reminiscing about somebody they once ate. There is no guilt here. In fact, as these old gentlemen relive feasts gone by, their animated conversation reminds me of friends at a cocktail party joyously rehashing some wild flings of youth. As their stories unfold my suspicions grow. To my astonishment, it becomes more and more apparent that with little coaxing, and if they could be sure of escaping detection, these old codgers would still love nothing better than to chew on another human once more.

My cannibal search started because I happened to pick up the March 1987 copy of *Smithsonian* magazine in which science writer Gina Kolata questions whether ritual cannibalism ever existed. She quotes anthropologist William Arens, a professor at the State University of New York: "'I don't think any anthropologist has come up with any good evidence of cannibalistic societies. And if there is no evidence, we can't say these societies existed. If I'm right, anthropologists are engaged not in a hoax and not in a lie, but in myth-making. They are retelling what is always assumed to be true.'"

There are two main types of cannibalism: survival cannibalism, in which starving people eat their dead companions to stay alive, and ritual cannibalism, in which parts of ancestors are eaten in order to pass along to kin and/or other tribal members such valued characteristics as strength, bravery, or fecundity. In what might be called superiority cannibalism—a form of ritual cannibalism—

enemies are eaten, perhaps in celebration of victory or as a final display of superiority over the deceased, or perhaps just as a time-honored practice.

Arens's book *The Man-Eating Myth,* published in 1979, labels all historical accounts of cannibalism as unreliable, however. He says there have been no eyewitness or first-hand observations of the practice. Furthermore, the author of the *Smithsonian* article states that modern anthropologists always seem to use either neighboring tribes as their informants or tribespeople who say that cannibalism is a practice that their particular tribe gave up generations ago. Apparently, there have been almost no interviews with people who themselves practiced ritual cannibalism. The exception I am aware of concerns doctors and anthropologists who interviewed members of the Fore Tribe of New Guinea and who speculated that kuru, a fatal neurological disease affecting one percent of the tribe, mostly women and children, was caused by a virus transmitted in brain matter eaten by relatives of recently deceased males. If cannibalism was practiced by the Fore—and this is not certain—it was discontinued by 1950 under pressure from Australian authorities. Professor Arens, however, discounts the evidence of Fore cannibalism.

I am not an anthropologist and will not pass judgment on Arens's scholarly arguments about whether ritual cannibalism existed. I will simply relate what was told to me and give my impressions of the informants. In three different villages in two different countries, I interviewed three people who admitted they had been cannibals and three others, two of whom were too young to partake, who all witnessed the rituals. Their testimony was completely spontaneous. According to the six men, none had ever been interviewed on the topic of cannibalism. Their stories, which agreed on most salient points, were told freely and without suggestion or coercion. There is no doubt whatever in my mind—and there was no doubt in the minds of my three translators—that the informants spoke anything but the truth. It seems that cannibalism not only existed in the western Pacific but was also practiced long after many social scientists thought it had ended.

·

The island of Malekula looks like the profile of a sixty-mile-long sitting dog as it faces the sunset. Three grass landing strips, around which small communities nestle, lie where the dog's feet, tail, and neck would be. Air transport is important on Malekula and the other rugged volcanic islands in both the Vanuatu and Solomon chains because road building is impractical and expensive. The Malekulans are fortunate, however, because they do have two roads—of sorts. One runs by starts and stops along most of the eastern coast, and another loops over the back of the dog's head to end at the village of Rautan, midway along Fido's nose. That is where my search for the old cannibals began.

The Reverend Ray Woosley, a missionary acquaintance in Port Vila, had told me that some of the oldest Big Nambas, recent converts to Christianity, were living in northern Malekula. He added, as an afterthought, that he believed some of the older men had once practiced cannibalism. Immediately the *Smithsonian* article came to mind, and I decided to seek out the old villagers to see if, in fact, they had been cannibals. Very kindly, Reverend Woosley assisted in arranging island transport and interpreters who were themselves Big Nambas and who were known and trusted by the villagers.

After a flight to Norsup, a town on Malekula's northeast coast, and a jouncing day-long truck-bed journey over an enlarged goat path, the village of Rautan seemed like a small patch of heaven. Chief Henry and I sat under an enormous fig tree framed by a crimson sun slowly falling into the sea. In front of us, muffled waves dropped softly on a deserted beach.

Henry is a powerful but aging chief, struggling to keep his village intact as it swirls into a modern world of lawsuits, property rights, concrete buildings, and gasoline engines. He told me about his people, the Big Nambas, who originated near Rautan. The traditional story is that Kinkin, the first man and the original father of the Big Nambas, came from a large black boulder; his wife, Kemken, the first mother, came from a large white boulder. Both boulders stood offshore in the surf, in the general vicinity of the village where we now sat. Together the first father and the first mother journeyed inland to Lahley, a sacred place in the mountains where they made their home. From Kinkin and Kemken came all the Big Nambas, who were to dominate northern Malekula.

Another tribe, the Small Nambas, who speak a different language and whose customs are slightly different, coexisted with the Big Nambas but were more numerous in the central and southern parts of the island. The Nambas, Big and Small, were so named for the males' only attire, a sheath woven out of pandanus leaves wrapped around the penis and fastened to the waist by a bark belt. (The names refer to the size of their sheaths, rather than for what was contained in them.) For many years, the two tribes warred incessantly, but the Big Nambas finally prevailed and drove the Small Nambas out of the northern part of the island. The perimeters of Big Namba village territories were marked with bunches of knotted grass, representing their version of skull-and-crossbones warnings. Trespassers, whether native or European, were murdered. The Big Nambas had the reputation of being one of the most ferocious tribes in the South Pacific.

Until 1940, seldom, if ever, did the few Europeans living and trading on the Malekula coast venture into the mountainous heartlands occupied by the most feared tribes, and some of those who did never returned. For the most part, white men did not frequent the highlands until World War II.

After my conversation with Chief Henry, I continued my journey until I arrived at the village of Malap, which consists of forty thatched huts clustered between the sea and the dirt road leading from Rautan, twenty miles north. The inhabitants of Malap are Big Nambas who, during the past thirty years, gradually elected to leave the traditional life of the mountain tribes to join a Christian village and the twentieth century. Malap is predominantly Seventh-Day Adventist, though some of the people belong to other denominations.

Cyrus, my translator, a village man himself, explains to the curious crowd gathered upon my arrival that I would like to talk to the old people who remember life in the mountain villages. Alam, an older man in a blue V-neck pullover, is brought out to meet me but looks away—does not seem particularly interested in talking. Another fellow, with a curly white fringe of hair and white fuzzy beard, joins Alam. Teven, whose eyes sparkle, looks like one of Santa's elves, and he seems quietly eager to converse with me. A runner is sent to the community vegetable garden to fetch the only other two old-timers who are the last Big Nambas to have left the mountain tribe. They all come from Amok, a mountain village in the center of the "dog's head" that now is connected by road to Norsup, northern Malekula's single town. Amok was one of the most important Big Namba villages, and because of the fierce reputation of its inhabitants, it was isolated from European influence and penetration. Now the descendants of Amok's Big Nambas sell photo opportunities and trinkets to the tourists.

Arriving from the vegetable garden are Joshua, a tidy little man in a neat shirt and shorts, and Norlan, a large, brooding fellow who glowers suspiciously as though he still might like to include me in his lunch. Joshua and Norlan are younger than Teven and Alam. They call Teven "uncle" and Alam, who we figure was born around 1910–1915, "grandfather," though these are not actual relationships. Since few of the older tribesmen have had any Western education, I have to gauge their ages by referring to an event familiar to all of us. By means of questions referring to their status within the tribe at the time of World War II, I can get a rough idea of when they were born: Both Joshua and Norlan were in their early teens and, by the tribe's reckoning, just on the verge of becoming men. Alam, the oldest of the four who spoke to me, already had a family of his own in 1942 and might have been about thirty. Teven was slightly younger, maybe around twenty-five.

The war affected the lives of nearly everyone in the western Pacific. Even in Malekula, which had no large military bases, there were soldiers whose presence changed the lives of the local people. Until the war there was no "white man's law" in the mountains. Tribal warfare continued not just between the Big and Small Nambas but also among different villages of the same tribes.

The traditional Big Namba tribal structure included a chief, a priest or medicine man, and also a small group of warriors known as makous. The makous led their tribe's battles and acted as assassins, killing individuals from other villages on whom a bounty had been placed. To avenge a killing of a friend or family member or to right a wrong committed by someone of another tribe, the aggrieved or a relative of the aggrieved would pay a makou to assassinate the perpetrator. The price was a ceremonial pig whose upper canines had been knocked out to allow the lower tusks to grow through the upper jaw until they made a complete spiral. The makous were not specially trained for their "work" but were accorded the title on the basis of experience. Cyrus, the translator, explained succinctly: "Just because when they shoot three or four or five men, they start calling them makou."

Below the makous in the tribal hierarchy were the village men, then the male children, and finally, as was common throughout most of Melanesia, the women.

To begin the interview I ask Teven to tell me about the wars between the tribes in the old days. How frequent were they, and why were they fought? "Sometimes there would be a war one time or two times in a year," he answers. "Sometimes a lady run away from the village [and from her husband], and she goes back to where she came from [her family's village], then that cause war. Then they must go and fight to get her back."

"Would they fight with bows and arrows or guns?" I ask.

"Musket," he replies. I ask how the people got them. "They [the men only] come down from the mountains and work for the plantations. One year work, maybe twelve pounds for a musket."[1]

"So then the men would go fight the men of the other village?"

"Yes," Teven answers.

"And would they kill very many people—kill them dead?"[2]

Cyrus, younger and more sophisticated than the older men, answers this question. "They come and hide in the bush," he says, "and when one people from this village [which is being attacked] he shot and he fell down, then they run back home. [It's] not like

---

[1] *Musket* is the pidgin or Bislama term for any kind of rifle or shotgun. Initially the traders supplies the tribes with obsolete muzzle loaders. Later, the more knowledgeable villagers demanded breech-loading rifles and shotguns. *Pounds* refers to old pounds sterling; before the war one pound might have been worth about five U.S. dollars.

[2] In Vanuatu's Pidgin English, "you kill 'em" means you beat him up or wound him. "You kill 'em dead" means you murder him.

American war, you know," Cyrus says laughing, "where you go and want to kill as much as you can."

Teven tells us that if a chief or other important man of a village dies, he is not buried. They keep his body outside the men's house until it rots. (The men's house, or nakamal, considered a sacred place, was where the men slept, next to the skulls of their male ancestors kept in a shrine in one corner.) After two weeks, he says, they put the skull in the men's house and they take a kava leaf and place it on the skull. The men drink kava,[3] maybe all night, then they worship the skull. They talk to it. They ask it for protection if they are about to go and fight with another tribe. Also if there is someone sick in the village, the family of the sick person gives a kava root to the medicine man and asks him if the sick person can be cured. The medicine man drinks the kava made from this root, and then during his narcotically induced dream tries to discover the cause of the sickness. If he and the sick person are fortunate, a spirit will tell him to go and take a certain leaf and use it as a medicine to cure the particular sickness. This was the general practice throughout most of Melanesia, though in many areas one or more pigs were sacrificed to the ancestors' spirits to aid in the cure. The pigs were not wasted, however. After pacifying the ancestors' spirits, they were eaten by the village men.

I ask what they did to people in the village who went against the laws of the tribe. For instance, if a married woman was committing adultery with some man in the village, what would they do?

The four old men discuss this question. "The punishment would be to pay a fine, they use the pig," one of them says.

"Pigs for compensation. And bride price, was that also a pig?" I ask.

"Bride price, pig too," they respond.

"How many pigs for one woman?"

"Chief's bride price is higher than ordinary."

---

[3] Kava is the seminarcotic national drink of Vanuatu and is made by crushing roots of *Piper methysticum*, a plant in the pepper family. It has a relaxing effect, numbs the tongue, and tastes like stale dishwater.

"How much is the ordinary bride price?"

"Twenty pigs for the bride of a chief," they answer.

"Twenty ordinary pigs for a chief's wife. And how many for an ordinary wife?" I ask.

The serious reply is that for an ordinary wife (presumably for an ordinary husband), it will cost ten or twelve pigs.

"Do they still have a bride price?" I ask.

"Yes, they still doing it," Teven answers. "Two cows and many yams—one hundred yams."

I ask Alam, the oldest, how long the fighting between the villages continued. He replies that it was not until the end of World War II that tribal warfare ceased. I ask him whether his people practiced cannibalism and how long it lasted. He says that, yes, it was common to eat the dead or wounded enemy warriors and that the practice lasted until the Second War, but it had been on the decline since the twenties. When the Americans came and soldiers regularly penetrated the heart of Big Namba territory, cannibalism was finished.

I ask the four old Big Nambas if they themselves have seen people eating human flesh. Yes, yes, they say, they all have seen their fellow villagers eating humans. Alam says that he has eaten people and indicates that Teven has, too. I ask Alam to tell me about his own personal experience as a warrior, and he tells me the following story, which took place a few years before World War II:

His village, Amok, was continually warring against other villages. The villagers were always living in fear of an attack. They guarded not only their village but also their vegetable garden, which even then was the source of most of their food, particularly yams, their dietary staple. On this particular day Alam, armed with a musket, was one of the warriors on guard outside the vegetable garden, which was fenced to keep the village pigs out. There had been recent attacks by the Small Nambas, and one man had already been killed. (He didn't specify whether the deceased was one of his people or the enemy.) Alam heard someone approaching and threw a stick inside the garden to alert those inside. A Small Namba appeared and Alam shot him, hitting him in the chest.

"What happened then?" I ask.

"We tied the man's wrists and ankles and put a stick between them so two people could carry him to the village. We carried him to the nakamal." The Small Namba killed by Alam was lashed to (really hung from) a tall, hollowed-out drum, usually carved in the shape of a man, called a slit drum.[4]

Then, Alam says, the women smeared a batter of crushed yams, called laplap, over the victim's entire body, after they had cut him to let out the blood.[5] "They just throw the head away," Alam says, "and then let the body lie down and just cut him up like an animal."

"Where do they cut him?" I ask.

"They throw away the intestines," Alam replies. Then with his finger he draws imaginary lines around his shoulders, elbows, wrists, knees, ankles, and hips—the joints where the pieces are cut. In response to another question, he says they don't eat the heart or liver. The entire insides are discarded. They eat just the body.

"Do they eat the buttocks?" I ask.

"Oh yes" is the enthusiastic reply. "Because that is the *big meat*. That is the best part!"

The body is split up, different parts to be cooked by three or four different families, though in all cases the method of preparation is the same. The body parts are wrapped in banana or other large leaves and are laid on top of preheated rocks in an umu, or earth oven, to steam until done, usually overnight. Then the cooked pieces are diced and mixed into laplap. Depending on the portion size, a human victim can serve, perhaps, ten warriors. Adult males are the only ones allowed to partake of human flesh.

Pierre Thevil, an older settler born in Malekula, was known to tell a story about his father, an early plantation owner there and a

---

[4] Usually the Big Nambas turned their captive, whether still alive or not, into a human appendage of the drum. That is, they beat on the captive with heavy clubs until they not only had killed him but pulverized his bones. At the time of the interview I was not aware of this Big Namba procedure and Alam said nothing about it.

[5] Laplap is still a staple for many villagers. Pounded and grated yams or taro are mixed with coconut milk, wrapped in leaves and baked in an earth oven over hot rocks to produce a dish that resembles and has the consistency of a firm custard, but tastes like wet cardboard. For special occasions small bits of pork are mixed in it.

good friend of the Big Nambas. One day his father received a laplap (about the size of a two-inch-thick waffle) as a peace offering. In front of Pierre and the rest of the family, his father bit into the laplap, remarking that it must be one made for a special occasion since it had meat in it. The father continued eating until suddenly his eyes bugged out and he spat his mouthful on the floor. From the laplap protruded pieces of human fingers.

I am told that the Big Nambas ate neither women nor girls, though male children were at times candidates for consumption. "Why did they eat people?" I ask.

"We don't have a special reason," Teven answers.

"Because he is the enemy," replies Alam. "So when we kill him, we bring him home and cut him in bits and share him among the friends around."

At the time that cannibalism was practiced by the Big Nambas, they had no cattle or chickens. Pigs and sometimes fish were their only other sources of meat, and these were not eaten regularly. But there is complete agreement among the four men that humans were not intended simply as a source of meat. They say flesh-eating is a traditional part of the victory celebration.

There is a final question that cannot go unasked. "So what did it taste like?" I ask Alam.

He shrugs. "Some of these were tasty," he answers. "Same as the meat from a cow, but the fat is yellow."

.

Gronal doesn't want to talk. The old man sits on a piece of bamboo staring into space. His tattered shirt hardly covers him, and the lenses of his cracked and broken eyeglasses are so scratched that his view of the world is gauze-filtered. He lives in the village of Esinge, a poor collection of decaying huts that sits on the side of a mountain, perhaps ten miles from the coast. Where Malap seemed if not prosperous, at least thriving, with fenced cattle, many well-tended huts, and swept environs, as well as a concrete schoolhouse and a partially finished church and meeting house, Esinge radiates desperation and bare survival. The eight huts are mostly in disrepair. There is no evidence of any livestock, not even chickens. The people are too far from the coast to have fish or other food from the sea. Thus it is likely that except for some wild nuts, they have almost no protein in their diet.

Gronal looks infirm. Still, he tends his garden daily and so far has managed to provide enough yams to feed himself. He seems to be well accepted by the younger people of the village, who assist him with his everyday needs. Gronal thought I might be from the police. Eventually Reggie Nalo, a genial minister who has consented to translate, convinces him that I am not from the police and that he can safely talk about the past. Gronal still hesitates. He has no reason to trust that he will not spend his last days in jail for admitting to an act that he may have committed fifty years ago. But finally he relents and tells about his former life.

In the early 1970s he came to Esinge from Amok, the same village where Alam and the others lived. Yes, he knew them. The main enemy in his time, says Gronal, was the village of Tenmaru, even though they were also Big Nambas. Before World War II he had been a warrior and had his own family, with an unspecified number of children. As best Reggie and I can figure, Gronal was born between 1910 and 1920; so at the time of the interview he is about seventy.

As a warrior, Gronal admits killing enemy villagers, and though he equivocates on this point, first denying, then admitting, then denying again, it seems likely that he also ate enemy warriors. His weapon was an old single-shot rifle. Of course, he had also used spears, bows and arrows, and from time to time, a war club. Sometimes the bones of the enemy killed in battle were used to make these weapons. Gronal says that arm and thigh bones were ground and sharpened to make arrows and sections for spears. Smaller bones from the hand were finely sharpened and used as spear tips. Battles were fought with these primitive weapons even as late as World War II.

The usual means of attack was the ambush. Gronal tells of hiding in the bush with his musket when a Big Namba from a neighboring village with which Amok was at war came past. Apparently Gronal fired from point-blank range, killing his adversary. Later in the interview, he becomes scared again and denies that he did this.

[75]

There is much fascination and laughter from the village boys who have gathered to listen to Gronal's stories. I ask him if he ate the particular warrior he had killed. He does not wish to answer and, of course, I do not pressure him. A young village girl is scolded and chased away by the elders for eavesdropping on this male-only topic of conversation. The people of the village seem every bit as fascinated by the stories as I am.

There were, it appears, killing cycles. Attack parties from a village would surprise or ambush men from the rival village. According to Gronal, the marksmanship of the warriors—at least with firearms—was not very accurate. Often many people were shot but usually only one was killed or immobilized sufficiently for the rival party to grab him and carry the victim back to their village. Often, it seems, the attackers would not even take aim but would just fire their weapons in the general direction of the enemy and flee back to the safety of their village.

Gronal reiterates, essentially, what the men of Malap have said. Occasionally a victim would be buried, but usually he was eaten. The victim would be cooked in the umus, then cut in small pieces and shared by the men. Only the flesh, not the intestines or the organs, was eaten. The body parts not being consumed were thrown away. Humans, according to Gronal, taste better than any other animal.

Sometimes one or two men would be eaten in a year, though if there had been a great deal of warring, four, five or six enemy warriors might be eaten in that time. This can be only a rough approximation, because while the Big Nambas kept track of seasons (wet, dry, hurricane, and so on), there was no written history or, I think, any long-term accounting of how many of the enemy were killed or eaten during a given period.

When the Nambas and other warring tribes began acquiring shotguns and other modern weapons, the mortality rate started rising. Gradually the tribal leaders realized that as they were depopulating the villages of their enemies, so were they themselves being depopulated. Fear of attack was a constant. Everyone—men, women, and children—lived in a perpetual state of anxiety. These factors, together with the encroachment of heavily armed white soldiers, led to the gradual demise of both intertribal warfare and cannibalism. But according to Gronal, it was not until shortly after the war that both practices died out.

Both the Big Nambas and Timothy, the Are'are tribesman whose people had practiced cannibalism on Malaita in the Solomons (see part IV), said they had never been interviewed by either an anthropologist or a journalist. I am not sure why. During the first part of the century and even after World War II, anthropologists covered the western Pacific like flies on sugar. Certainly they gravitated toward tribal villages whose old cultures were more or less intact. So the lack of reports or firsthand accounts of cannibalism is a little puzzling. My feeling is that anthropologists were not specifically seeking cannibals or firsthand accounts, for if they had been, they could have found them, and probably far more than I came across. Perhaps they did not have contacts to lead them in the right directions.

Native missionaries and English-speaking indigenous people who had extensive contacts or who actually were tribal members were my guides and translators. They knew the people and could usually reassure them that I represented neither the police nor any other threat. No one would have spoken openly with me about such sensitive subjects had I not been accompanied by people they trusted. Even after fifty or sixty years the old cannibals still fear retribution from the authorities. Another stumbling block is the Christian training of the Melanesians, who are now ashamed of this aspect of their old tribal life (and many other aspects as well) and who therefore usually deny that cannibalism existed except in the distant past. Even though they know they are not being truthful, they are unwilling to let outsiders become acquainted with the skeletons in their recent ancestors' closets—and certainly in their own. It's too bad that this epoch has died almost unrecorded.

6

THE LAST GREAT

SORCERER

A battered diesel launch chugs slowly up Ambrym's deserted northwest coast. The boat's bow wave is a molasses V in a cauldron of liquid heat. A quarter mile off, behind a narrow ribbon of volcanic beach, rain-forest ridges ride atop each other, undulating inland in green layers. The sun feels like a blast furnace. At any moment the sea will vaporize, eventually leaving only puddles and flopping fish. I wonder how anyone could stand to live here—and, indeed, for miles there is no one, not a single sign of life, except for the sudden flash of a red or green wing as a bird disappears through the trees. In the distance Mount Marum and Mount Benbow steam silently, angry Charons guarding this forlorn island with towering columns of ash and sulphur.

Ambrym is the magic island. Its reputation as the center of sorcery extends over the entire western Pacific. Most Ni Vanuatu[1] quiver at the mention of it. Even knowledgeable European residents of other islands are fearful of the magic practiced here. When I tell a resident European woman that I am going to Ambrym to seek out the last two great sorcerers, this lady, long familiar with local customs, says, "I would never set foot on Ambrym." Then vehemently she adds, "You are insane to go there!"

Nonetheless, I'm on my way, but already half the objective of

[1] Ni Vanuatu is the official term for one or more native inhabitants of Vanuatu, the island group which in colonial times was known as the New Hebrides.

this quest, unbeknownst to me, has been permanently placed out of reach. There were two famous sorcerers on Ambrym, but one, Gauor, an old chief feared and hated by the local people because they believed he had cast evil spells over entire villages and murdered people with his magic, died two weeks ago. Kirk Huffman, an American anthropologist and curator of Vanuatu's National Cultural Museum, was to come here and videotape Gauor demonstrating a talking head that had been severed from its body. Reportedly, the body still oozed blood while the head carried on its soliloquy. Gauor, according to local legend, lived with and was guarded by a den of vipers. Amos, my guide and translator, tells me that Gauor's specialty was to steal women's love for their husbands and transfer it to other men who had paid him. The bewitched women—no matter how much they loved their husbands—would suddenly fall in love and run off to live with the new men. Amos swears that Gauor was a master at this type of sorcery, which he calls masseng.

"How did Gaour get women to do this?" I ask him.

"He takes some kind of leaf or powder from a tree trunk," Amos replies. "He chews it or gives it to the man to chew [who paid him to procure the woman] and he spit it, like that." Amos demonstrates a hearty blow—more than a spit. "Then when the woman look at you, she would have magic attraction. It doesn't matter you sleep at night. Even a woman can do this kind of thing at you, a man, during the night. You dream [then] about that woman or man [who spit at you]. You see, can be on both sides. If a girl do it to you, you can dream and dream and dream and always, always, always—you just go [leave your spouse]."

"And you know women that this happened to? Did they play around with other men, before?"

"No, the last one I know was from my village. But it's also happened like that in some other villages, like to the north or the southeast."

It sounds to me like great cover for a husband or a wife who wishes to change partners, but I don't push this on Amos. I am surprised to hear him profess a belief in the validity of masseng, because he is not a village bumpkin. Amos Andeng, in fact, is a bright fellow who has seen much of the world. He was born in 1934 in the village of Biap on Ambrym's western tip, where he still lives. He received mission schooling and because of his ability was picked for higher education, attending Fulton Missionary College in Fiji for three years, where he specialized in teacher training. Subsequently he taught in various villages on Ambrym until 1979, when he was selected as one of ten distinguished Ni Vanuatu, representing all the islands, to debate strategies for independence. Amos and the other group members spoke before the English and Australian parliaments, as well as before the United Nations in New York and Paris. After independence Amos represented West Ambrym in Vanuatu's new parliament. He is now semiretired but is considering another run for parliament. He comes from a line of the greatest chiefs of western Ambrym, and since the great chiefs were the experts at magic, Amos is most knowledgeable on the subject.

I ask Amos to talk about tribal life. He replies, "I can tell you a bit about that because I came from one of the highest chiefs. My great, great grandfather back, and especially my grandfather, was a big chief of west Ambrym. And his name was called Maldongdong, the highest chief. And when I mention 'dong dong,' it means heaven. 'Mal' means just higher, higher than heaven. At west Ambrym are sixteen chiefs, and four of them are highest chiefs. And always from Port Vato down Ambrym's south coast and west, and from north Ambrym, they always come to my grandfather and ask for this and that. If they want to eat any person, as in cannibalism, you know, and if they want to poison anyone, they need the permission from my grandfather."

The people of West Ambrym were all Small Nambas, similar in customs to the Small Nambas of Malekula, though with slightly different languages. As in most areas of Melanesia before European rule, there were frequent wars between villages, often fought over women or land. Vanuatu has one hundred and five distinct languages for 143,000 people; this is the highest ratio of languages to population of any country in the world. Because of the rugged terrain and dense jungle, tribes even five or ten miles apart were often isolated from each other and thus developed different languages. Before the advent of plantation work or European-sponsored schools, the villagers spoke no pidgin or Bislama[2] and therefore had no unifying language. Amos describes how in his grandfather's time the chiefs of neighboring tribes used to communicate with each other during a period of intertribal warfare.

"If we want to make a peace or what, then my grandfather have to send some custom leaves to that village as a letter, because we don't know how to write a letter and you cannot [communicate] another way. But only the chief, the highest chief, have to give one leaf to one of his right-hand [men] and he have to take that leaf to another chief. Then they know that something's going to happen. And then that chief have to send another leaf back to the highest chief and the meaning of those leaves [the types of leaves sent] tell you whether we going to make peace or the fight will continue. Otherwise it [a war] will stop by killing of pigs or a woman from here have to go there and a woman from there come here [to marry a local man and to live in the village]."

Magic used to control village life. Although it is still important, it is disappearing as the old practitioners die. In Amos's opinion this disappearance is a great loss.

"Oh, I'm sorry, because I am one of the descendants of a highest chief, and we miss [forget] everything because the European come and say that we have to go to religion. Not to think of our customary way anymore because we going to be a Christian now, forget our fashion, old fashion, and something like that. So [by] 1911, 1912 and onward till today we miss everything. And we used to see, even myself, I sometime stand around and see all of the different kinds of magic."

Amos begins describing some of the powers the old sorcerer-chiefs had. In one case, if a chief wished to do away with someone he could concoct a potion or make a spell that would poison his enemy. Then while that person was dying in the bush, the chief would take on the image of the poisoned man and would actually take the man's place in his bed. So closely would the chief resemble the victim in both appearance and behavior that even the man's wife

---

[2] Bislama is Vanuatu's name for the dialect of pidgin spoken there, which varies substantially from the pidgin spoken in the Solomons and in Papua New Guinea.

would not be aware of the impersonation. Eventually the chief would leave the victim's hut and only then would the wife realize her husband had been murdered. According to Amos, this major class of treachery was called yapyap.

Often the potion used in such spells or poisonings would be powdered leaves or powdered tree bark of certain jungle species. It could be mixed into laplap, sprinkled in drinking water, or placed in the victim's bed. The result would be headache, dizziness, nausea, collapse, and death. If a man knew he had offended a local sorcerer, he might alert his wife to the potential poisoning threat and thus prevent anyone from entering his hut. The sorcerer then might change himself into a dog, a pig, or a chicken in order to steal into the man's house and, unobserved, place the poison wherever he wished. A sorcerer who had the ability to change into an animal to facilitate killing someone was known as a prosit man.

A sorcerer would often need to impress his subjects with his powers, particularly if he thought they were losing respect for him. One means of doing this was to change himself into a woman. I had been asking Amos what types of magic he had witnessed.

"Well, I've seen somebody change from a man to a lady," he answers. "You know, a boy to a girl and uh, without clothes, you know."

"He'd be standing there naked, in front of you?"

"Sometimes he just wear what we call a skirt. So we didn't see the nakedness [the loins], but the body, the breast, we call it titty.

"The titties would grow in front of you?"

"Yes."

"And would he be doing this with his muscles?"

"No."

"There would just be big titties?"

"Big titties, and, you know, if a young girl, you know, then just young titties."

"So would the whole shape of the body change?"

"Yes, the breasts all change. The breast of a man."

"Would anything else change that you could see? Hair grow?"

"Yes, the hair change and the breast change, those two parts."

"Then what would happen? Would the girl talk to you?"

"Well, I don't know, myself, but what I've seen, a boy can change and become, you know, like a girl's body. And also, he can go there in a house and change again and come up the same boy again."

"So sometimes he goes away and comes back?"

"Yes."

"But you know it's the same person and not his sister?"

"No, same person, because the face is still the same but the body is changed."

"Why would he do this?"

"He have to show that he can do magic and everybody know that. He show the village that he got a powerful magic."

"Well, I bet it did!" I reply.

Another demonstration of magic power is nearly as startling. Amos describes various klevas (the Ni Vanuatu word for sorcerers) catching fish on dry land.

"They take a fishing line, you know, and they put a hook on that fishing line with a little stick to use as a fishing pole and they just throw it [the line] in the middle of a crowd of people. And then we just watch it. Everyone say, 'Oh, come see this fella. He's going to hook a fish on the land,' you know, a dry place like this. Then everybody just watch it, watch it, watch it, won't be long you will see the fish from the sea just come out in the middle of a crowd of people."

"Even a hundred meters from the sea?"

"It doesn't matter. Away, in the bush."

"And then there'll be a fish that will appear?"

"Appear and, you know, caught that fishhook, you know, something [just] like in the sea. And then you will see the fish just moving like that and you will track it and everybody, a crowd of people, a hundred or whatever, they yell loud, 'Aye, you see the fish, see the fish.'"

"Did you ever see this?"

"Yes, I saw myself; that is why. All the things that I told you, I saw myself [when I] was a little boy and look at the magic."

"You saw this?"

"Yes, sir."

"And so there is a piece of hook and nothing on the hook?"

"Nothing on the hook."

"And then all of a sudden there is a fish on it?"

"There is a fish hung on it."

"And you can see that nobody put the fish on the hook?"

"Nobody, nobody. I myself look at the thing four times."

"You've seen this happen four different times?"

"Four different times."

"How big a fish? What kind of fish?"

"Ah, you know, like that. You see, just like that." Amos holds his hands ten or twelve inches apart. His expression conveys absolute certainty about what he saw.

"Would there be all of a sudden a little tiny fish and it got bigger, and bigger, and bigger?" I ask him. "Or would it be all of a sudden a full-size fish?"

"All of a sudden just full-size fish—either a little fish or either a big fish."

"Would the hook be on the ground or in the bushes?"

"No, no, no."

"Just on the ground where everybody could see."

"Everyboy could see. Not in the grass or any dirty thing like that. No, you know, just on the ground like this."

"Would people at that time be drinking kava or palm wine or something?"

"No, no, no. Just look like as we are now."

I shrug in disbelief and we go to other topics.

I believe Amos is truthful about what he says he witnessed, but the Ni Vanuatu people are superstitious and prone to the power of suggestion. Could group hypnosis account for large numbers of people believing they had witnessed such a phenomenon? Later I begin to question European residents, expecting that they will be able to provide a rational explanation.

.

Vanuatu's National Cultural Museum is housed in a modest, crumbling one-story building on Port Vila's main street. In front is an enormous iron kettle that tourists from the cruise ships believe was used by the locals to cook missionaries, but in fact it was left by the early whalers. The museum opened in 1961 and contains an astonishing collection of tribal icons, tools, and artifacts. It is also the agency responsible for preserving the country's culture.

Kirk Huffman, the museum's curator, is a slim, easygoing fellow in his early fifties who sports a Fu Manchu mustache. With a mischievous gleam in his eye he exhibits a childlike delight in the world and particularly the tribal cultures of the western Pacific. This likable fellow has contributed significantly to the preservation of these cultures. In fact, almost single-handedly, he established and directed a program that has saved many tribal customs of the New Hebrides from extinction.

Kirk first came to Vanuatu in 1973 to do fieldwork on Malekula's Big Namba art and culture. He had spent the previous eleven years studying anthropology and prehistoric archeology, mostly at Oxford and Cambridge. After his initial work he returned the following year with David Attenborough and a Public Broadcasting film crew to do a documentary on the Solomons. Then in 1976, in association with the Australian National Museum, Kirk returned again to collect Small Namba artifacts still being produced by that tribe. He remained to do research for his doctoral thesis on Malekula's Big and Small Namba cultures, which, when it was nearly complete after years of work, he decided never to publish. Only one who has spent years working on such a project can begin to understand the enormity of that decision. Simply put, in the course of his research he had been told in confidence so much sacred information by tribal leaders that to publish his thesis—the heart of which was information previously unknown to the outside world—would have betrayed those confidences. He refused to do that, and as a consequence denied himself his doctorate. This sort of self-sacrifice marks Kirk Huffman, and it is one reason that he has won the confidence of tribal leaders throughout the archipelago.

Kirk became curator of Vanuatu's National Cultural Museum at a time of crisis. By 1976 the country's tribal cultures were dying out at an alarming rate. Missionary zeal and disdain for the old cultures were perhaps the paramount reasons, but tourism and the attractions and influence of Western civilization were also major factors. So besides the major task of establishing the museum itself, Kirk also attempted to preserve what was left of tribal life scattered throughout Vanuatu's eighty-two islands. It was fortunate that when the country became a republic four years later, the new government strongly supported his work. Now thirty-two Ni Vanuatu employees maintain the museum and its attendant library and archives, and an additional forty-one tribal members, equipped with tape recorders and in some cases video cameras, travel throughout the country encouraging a resurgence of interest in their own particular customs, as well as making a record of what still exists. Outside of Papua New Guinea, no country in the Pacific has such an ambitious project to preserve its diverse cultures.

Magic is a very touchy subject in Vanuatu, particularly among the country's educated, ruling elite who are embarrassed by their peoples' belief in what to them amounts to witchcraft. There is also much concern that foreign journalists will sensationalize the subject, concentrating on the black or evil side of Vanuatu's sorcery. At first, Kirk would not even discuss the issue other than to say that it is a part of daily life throughout the country, and that whether you believe in magic or not, it is said to work. I ask him why he will not talk about it.

"Because, unfortunately," he answers, "what very often outsiders tend to do is emphasize the bad side of magic. But there's a good side of magic, and the klevas [who practice it] are actually traditional doctors with a very good knowledge of herbal medicine or traditional bone-setting techniques or surgery techniques or muscle-ache recovery techniques, things like that. By combining traditional medicines with a magical side—because traditionally, illnesses in many cases have a physical and a spiritual cause—the klevas here can diagnose not just the physical cause but also the spiritual cause of the physical illness. So they get rid of both. They combine the functions. While in our society, European society, the role is split into medical doctors and psychiatrists or psychologists, out here they're combined into one person."

"What kind of medicine do they practice?" I ask him. "Give me an example."

"For instance, there is a local, traditional medical cure on Efate for segotera, or fish poisoning. It is actually much more effective than anything the hospital can provide you. And there was an Australian doctor here for many years who realized that some of the medicines they have here, particularly on Efate, are better than anything that's available in European medicine today. So the Australian doctor, when he had Europeans coming to him suffering from fish poisoning, he'd say, 'Well, I mean, we can send you to the hospital, but there's an old chap down the road who's got much better medicine. I mean, we can't get the recipe from him because he won't give it out.' So I think there's an awful lot of knowledge we can benefit from."

I ask Kirk about the benign magic tricks that Amos Andeng was describing, whether feats like having a fish appear before a village full of people, miles from the sea, could be accomplished by mass hypnosis.

"No, no, not at all," he answers. "At the first National Arts Festival here in 1979, there was a particular ritual [demonstrated] whereby the spirit of a deceased person is put into a wooden stick and there's a line of five or six men who kneel down and they hold onto this wooden stick. The kleva sings a particular chant and the spirit starts to move the stick and it throws these people all around. They're holding onto this stick, and then it starts throwing them around and dragging them across the ground and stuff like that. Amazing, they actually got that on film."

"You were there and saw this—and there wasn't any kind of hypnosis associated with it?"

"Yeah, I was there—and no, no there wasn't."

Kirk has no explanation, or if he does, he is not going to divulge it. Ken Hutton, an Australian dentist and plantation owner who has lived in the country for more than thirty years, was also at the arts festival, and I ask him about this particular feat.

"I was at the show," Ken says. "In fact, I was doing the announcing. I had a European friend who did it [took part in the stick demonstration], a guy by the name of Weaks, and it was pulling him and the others [hanging onto it] all around. And so afterwards I went over to him and asked him, 'What was your reaction to that thing?' And he said, 'It had a force. It was going in its own direction, and no known force that we had could stop it.'"

"Do you think this Ambrym kleva was hypnotizing people, Ken?"

"He could have been, yes. He had this whole group of people holding the thing. And they all had the same reaction."

.

Our small boat is in the midst of a school of bottlenose dolphins. These graceful animals have come to investigate us, slicing out of the water suddenly on all sides of the boat, accelerating past our bow, then curving off to streak past us again, their underwater courses intertwining in a gregarious subsurface ballet. Soon they tire of the lack of challenge our poky tub presents and race off to the north. As the last dolphin disappears, we round a jungle-covered point and the village of Linbul appears on a bluff at the northern tip of the island.

In the hills above Linbul resides Chief Tofor, the man we have come all this distance to see. Tofor has an astounding reputation. Nowhere in the South Pacific have I heard of another man so feared. Claude Nicholls, the Efate-raised son of an old copra grower and dairyman I interviewed, happened to remark one day about a visit by the sorcerer to their farm.

"This guy, Tofor, he came to see my father," Claude says. "We were working cattle at the time. All the guys [the Ni Vanuatu employees] are sitting up on the rails of the stockyard, and all of a sudden, they went—they melt like ice cream. They are so scared of that man, you know. They really fear him. Maybe there was ten of them, and they look at Tofor like he was a god, or magic."

Ken Hutton was also aware of Tofor's reputation. "They're scared of him. They say, 'Man, Ambrym, he got strong for the magic.' He can pass through a door without opening it. There's no way you can lock him out with any sort of ordinary lock because if he wanted to go through this door, for example, and it was closed, he'd just pass through it. He has this ability and all the Ni Vanuatu know it and they fear him."

Preposterous, correct? I return to Kirk Huffman and ask him to tell me what he knows about Tofor. He says that Tofor is the son of Tyman, who was once the most powerful chief and kleva on Ambrym. It was believed by the Ni Vanuatu that at the time of Tyman's death his son assumed his powers. In fact, the local people believe Tofor has even more power than his father.

Kirk says that in 1973 Tofor caused a general panic in the north of Ambrym. He had become so incensed by some occurrence that he retreated to his nakamal and over a period of weeks cast spells so heavy that the local volcano erupted; at least that is what the people believed. The police came to take Tofor away because the whole island was being depopulated as boatload after boatload of Ambrym people fled their homeland. Tofor was shackled and, accompanied by police, was put aboard a launch to return to Port Vila. As the boat pulled away from shore all the policemen who had surrounded Tofor on the boat turned to see him standing on the beach waving at them. No one had unshackled him, nor has anyone an explanation for how he could have freed himself in the midst of all the policemen, and, untouched, returned to shore.

Tofor is also known as a flyman. The Ni Vanuatu believe that flymen can transport their bodies through the air to any place they wish without benefit of an airplane or other mechanical means. Although Europeans won't admit that Tofor has such power, they can't explain his movements. Kirk says that, once, after visiting Tofor at Craig Cove on Ambrym, he flew to the village of Lamap on Malekula; and that when his plane landed, there was Tofor waiting for him. When Tofor was asked how he got there, the sorcerer said he had used his flyman power. Kirk did not have an explanation, but he said that Tofor did not arrive by plane and that even the fastest speedboat could not have covered the sixteen miles quickly enough to have arrived there ahead of him. Other Europeans report witnessing similar occurrences, and no one can explain them.

Tofor has had a history of severe emotional problems. One explanation given me is that he has not been able to abide the encroachments of European culture on the lives of his people. Reportedly he felt, with just cause, that the entire "custom area" of northern Ambrym was disappearing, that his people were adopting

Christianity and European ways—changes with which he simply could not cope. Another probable source of his emotional behavior was his training as a sorcerer. I was told, for instance, that during one of the ceremonies initiating him as a kleva, stakes were "attached" to his scalp, but apparently not driven into his head. The extent to which this or other ceremonies had physiological or psychological ramifications is impossible to gauge, of course. Then, too, he has had a major problem with alcohol over the years.

Tofor has continuously run afoul of the authorities. Some years ago he told Kirk that he had been on the beach at Ambrym and suddenly the Christian God came out of a cloud. God identified himself to the surprised chief and told Tofor that the custom man's time was coming again and that he, Tofor, would have the power the Christians then had to collect money. Tofor told Kirk that the Christian God looked a little bit like him and also like Jesus. Anyway, Tofor said that God said that Tofor would be in charge of all the money that He had allotted but not yet doled out to all the Ni Vanuatu villages.

Upon receiving this revelation Tofor went to Port Vila, where the French and British colonial governors were meeting. Tofor broke into the meeting room and angrily demanded all the money God had told him he should be in charge of. The appearance of the feared kleva wreaked chaos, and the Ni Vanuatu fled the meeting hall in panic, prematurely ending the assembly, to say the least. Subsequently, Tofor was judged insane and committed to the local mental asylum.

The "house-blong-cranky," the Ni Vanuatu mental asylum, looks like a small fortress on the outskirts of Port Vila. From the time the building was constructed during the "snake pit" days when mental illness was considered to be virtually a crime, it was believed to be escape-proof. Tofor, having been declared "cranky," was confined in a steel-walled room with inch-thick bars on both door and window. Yet the authorities could not prevent him from escaping.

One morning shortly after Tofor's incarceration, Kirk walked into the cultural center to find Tofor sitting on the floor in his office. They started talking, and after a while, two Ni Vanuatu policemen came in, because they had figured Tofor would go there. Tofor said to them, "You are Christians. This is a custom area. You have no right to be here." Tofor then raised his hands in front of him in the symbol of the hawk, and before the soldiers could run out told them: "I can come and go from house-blong-cranky anytime, walking through walls. And when I want to come back, I will come back without you."

His escapes notwithstanding, Tofor spent years in the house-blong-cranky. It was closed at independence and now houses the cultural museum's archives.

Tofor has also been prosecuted for a more serious offense. In 1976 someone insulted or put a curse on him. The insult was so severe that according to tribal custom, Tofor was justified in killing the individual who had cursed him. Apparently he did just that. The colonial authorities did not agree, however, that the murder was justified by the curse. This time Tofor was put in prison, which proved no more able to hold him than had the house-blong-cranky. Making their morning rounds, the authorities would find his cell empty, the lock still secured on the cell door, and in his place would be a type of laplap with ingredients that could only be found on Ambrym. Eventually he was allowed to return to his home island with the authorities' fervent wish that he would stay there.

Those responsible for Tofor's incarceration no longer live in the South Pacific, and no one could provide more information on his prison sentence. What was clear, however, was that while few Europeans still living in Vanuatu were willing to say they believed in his magic, or magic in general, nearly all had a profound regard for it—and for him.

While talking to Reece Discomb, a retired salvage expert who has been a resident of Vanuatu since shortly after World War II, I come to realize how much the Melanesian magic affects even Europeans. I ask Reece if he knows any Europeans affected by the klevas' sorcery.

"I know people who were sick for a long time and were cured by them," he says. "And I can speak from experience on this. One of our daughters went to all the European doctors over a period of six months. And finally the house girls got to her. They said, 'You better go see this man.' At first she wouldn't do it, wouldn't go. Finally it had gotten so bad that she did."

Reece's oldest daughter, Paulette, is a lively young woman in her middle twenties, with a husband and a small child. She speaks unhesitatingly about her illness, which occurred when she was twenty. "What happened to you, Paulette?" I ask.

"I began having really bad migraines," she recalls. "Maybe I'd have seven of those killers in a week. I lost about twenty pounds, and I had no energy. I couldn't lift my head up—couldn't lift it off the pillows—could hardly move."

"So what did you do?"

"I didn't do anything. Mom and Dad tried to get me the best treatment they could here. The doctors took blood tests, X-rays, and things like that. And they couldn't find anything. So eventually it was my husband who got me to go."

"And what did the kleva do?"

"He took a sort of liquid, made from leaves, and I had to put that in my nose. That cured it. Within three days I was walking around."

"When this happened, did you believe in any kind of magic— that Ni Vanuatu magic could affect you? Did you do anything to bring any kind of a curse on you?"

"No, no, I didn't. Absolutely not."

"And do you believe in it now?"

"Well, not too long ago my sister, Denise, got something like it—well, not quite the same, but I took her to the kleva where my husband took me, and it worked for her, too."

Folk medicine, or a placebo coupled with the power of suggestion, might have been responsible for the cure of the Discomb girls. Folk medicine, however, had no part in the cure described by Claudia Huffman, Kirk's French-born wife, who told me about an illness that almost killed her husband.

In 1984 someone brought some nasmas—rounded magic stones—into the cultural center. The Ni Vanuatu individual seemed in a hurry to get rid of them, giving them to Kirk. The stones, considered by the Ni Vanuatu to be among the most powerful carriers of magic, did not appear extraordinary in any way except that they were covered with some type of cobweb that no one could identify. Shortly after receiving the nasmas Kirk began experiencing a tremendous loss of energy. It was almost impossible for him to do anything or even to get out of bed. Like the Discomb girls, he also began rapidly losing weight. Kirk spent a week in the hospital in Port Vila undergoing tests and was then flown to the Sydney University School of Tropical Medicine. The Australian doctors were mystified by the illness. Their extensive testing could pinpoint no organic causes of his deteriorating condition. The illness continued to worsen.

Back in Port Vila, Kirk and Claudia both thought he was going to die, having given up on Western medicine after four months of testing and unproductive treatment. One day Kirk decided he would contact an old kleva called Apif, who had come from the island of Epi and was then living in Efate. Kirk set out for the old man's house. Perhaps coincidentally, this old kleva was on his way to visit Kirk at the same time. When Kirk dragged himself out of his truck in front of the old man's house, the man's wife said, "Well, Apif has been looking and waiting for you. He knew that you were in trouble and has gone to the cultural center to help you."

Claudia Huffman says that before that day Kirk had not talked to the old man in years. She does not believe it was coincidental that on that particular day Apif knew Kirk was looking for him and needed his help.

At the cultural center Apif identified the magic stones as the cause of his sickness, did some incantations and spells to discharge their power over him, and told Huffman that within four or five days he would be well. This was exactly the case; within four days Kirk was back to normal. "It was just a miraculous recovery," Claudia says.

A few days later Huffman saw Apif in the street. The old man's right arm, below the elbow, was swollen double its normal size. Kirk asked, "What happened to you?"

Apif replied, "The magic bounced off as I was taking the spell out of you and hit me in the right arm, and that's the cause of this."

Eventually the old kleva was able to heal his swollen limb. Kirk

Huffman won't talk about whether he believes or not, but it's quite obvious that both he and Claudia believe in the powers of the klevas, or at least in their healing powers.

·

Linbul is a Christian village of about five hundred people perched on two hills overlooking the sea. Our small boat anchors in a protected cove and I am led up winding hillside trails to the only concrete house, the schoolmaster's office and guest house, in the otherwise thatched village. Then Amos and I climb a series of hills beyond the village. We traipse through groves of banana palms, past tethered goats and slow-munching cattle, toward Chief Tofor's nakamal.

Tofor's men's house sits in a clearing surrounded by gigantic old ficus trees. Their thick canopies provide shade and an aura of solemnity. Intricately carved slit drums—some fifteen or twenty feet high, others smaller, all with human, wide-eyed expressions above hollowed-out bellies—stand as mute guardians of the clearing and of the single bamboo-and-thatch hut set back from it. Interspersed with the slit drums, which double as shrine sentinels, are carved fertility figures, all eight to ten feet high.

Tofor's nakamal itself is not much different from simple huts in villages throughout Vanuatu. It has a steeply pitched roof supported by bamboo beams and posts. A heavy-set, long-nosed, gawking door-guard carved from coconut palm warns intruders away. Next to it a battered old metal teapot rests on a flat stone beside the door. Both the clearing and the hut are unoccupied. Presently some young boys, Tofor's sons and nephews, join us in the clearing. They tell us that the chief is away but is expected to return by nightfall.

I would like to see inside Tofor's nakamal, but it is strictly prohibited. The penalty for unauthorized entry into a nakamal used to be death. I don't know what it is now, but I don't plan to find out. In fact, no one, not even Tofor's brothers, is allowed in his nakamal. Only chiefs of the very highest grade are allowed in a high chief's men's house, and since no one approximating Tofor's rank is left, nobody else may enter.

I ask Amos how Tofor arrived at the highest rank and where he learned his magic.

"He train from the highest chief [in this case, his father, Tyman]," Amos replies. "But only chiefs can do this magic, and you cannot become chief until you do the [steps]; so you go grade one, two, three, four, five, and so on, learning little by little. If the chief says, 'Don't eat this,' then you have not to eat this for ten days, or if he says, 'Don't go in bath for ten days,' then you have to do that. And the highest chief and boy, they pick leaves and come together and they worship them in the customary way and make powerful magic. So the boy learns this."

Amos goes on to say that the student kleva pays his professor in pigs. The fee is one small one for class one, a little older pig for class two, and the higher the class, the more and larger the pigs, until at the top level of apprenticeship the levy is about fifty pigs, including some bomado, or pigs of seven or eight years whose tusks form a complete circle. If you can't afford so many pigs, you might give the chief twenty-five pigs plus your sister. I ask Amos what happens if your sister doesn't want to go live with the chief.

His reply is succinct, "Too bad—she must."

"How old are the boys when they start training to be a kleva?" I ask him.

"Past time of circumcision," he says.

"Do they also circumcise girls?"

"Yes, but different," Amos answers. "For girls, they knock out front teeth."

I am shocked that this practice continues. Nevertheless, a girl losing her front teeth is more fortunate than girls who are forced to undergo the horrible clitoridectomies practiced in parts of Moslem Africa. Still, this is a tough price to pay for reaching puberty.

During all our discussions of magic, Amos answers my questions matter-of-factly, even about the most gruesome or what we would call "unethical" practices. As a devout Christian, however, he makes it very clear to me that he does not condone the type of sorcery involving murder or wife stealing. Nonetheless, he is sad to see his old culture disappearing. We start back down the hill, stopping at Tofor's village of six large thatched huts to tell Tofor's wives that we will wait for the chief at Linbul.

The following morning at a little after eight o'clock, Christian hymns float out over the sea. Most of Linbul's adults are in attendance at a small thatched church resting on a bluff at the outskirts of the village. I am enjoying a bit of solitude with my coffee as I savor the relatively cool early morning air. Privacy in a country village is an unknown commodity. Since the local people's curiosity about foreigners is almost overwhelming, there is nearly always someone—particularly children—sitting quietly looking at you. And all at once, that is the feeling I have. I turn suddenly to look into the eyes of a slight man of about sixty years who has been sitting on a rail fence fifteen feet away, silently watching me. It is not one of the villagers. It is Tofor.

I expect a piercing stare as befits if not *the* greatest sorcerer in this part of the world, then at least one of the world's great hypnotists. Instead, I find his gaze friendly and disarming, though quietly appraising. Tofor does not seem in the least imposing or threatening. He is small-boned, of medium height, with a wiry body unencumbered by an ounce of extra flesh. His narrow face is framed by a full head of close-cropped hair and a well-trimmed Vandyke beard. He is dressed in a spotless blue T-shirt and denim shorts. Though he is shoeless and obviously accustomed to being without shoes, his feet are narrow, without the calluses and knobby protrusions usually seen on islanders who have walked barefoot all their lives. In fact, the Tofor I am gazing at seems entirely out of character as a sorcerer or chief. He looks as though he would be more at home in a United Nations office than in a village nakamal. His eyes, in particular, reflect an extraordinarily alert, active, and intelligent mind, and his whole demeanor is sophisticated and worldly.

Tofor tells me, in Bislama, that his friend Amos is in church with the others. He seems content to sit on the fence rail to wait for the service to end. I try to engage him in conversation, but he does not wish to talk, and in any case he speaks only Bislama and Small Namba, or so he would like me to think. A tall woman perhaps in her middle thirties, bucket in hand, on her way to the village well, pauses to wish me a polite good morning. Then she notices Tofor sitting on the fence, and an involuntary shudder runs through her whole body. The greeting freezes in her mouth, her head snaps forward, and she hurries on. Tofor seems unaware of the effect he has had on her.

Eventually the church service is over and Amos joins us. We walk out of the village up the hill and sit on the stoop of an unoccupied house under construction, where we will have privacy. Amos explains who I am and why I wish to speak to the chief. Tofor listens impassively. He seems very much at peace with himself and totally in control. Jacques Nicholls, Claude's father, the dairyman who had talked to him several times, described him as very smart and different from most Ni Vanuatu, with a sharper, very cunning look in his eye. To me, he does not have a cunning or sly look at all.

Tofor is speaking Bislama in a low, moderated tone. Slowly, calmly, he tells me that he does not know any magic, that he has never practiced magic, and that he had made the decision to join the church, to become a Christian. Amos is as shocked as I am. At first he tries to persuade Tofor at least to tell me something of his past. The chief refuses. Only upon departing does Tofor say to me, "Many people think that Tofor is cranky. Not so. Someday it will be like Noah with his ark. They think he cranky and too late they find he not cranky. Someday they will know about Tofor."

Not until later does Amos tell me that a young man in a nearby village has recently been accused of killing someone by witchcraft. The accused has been chased out of the village and, pursued by the police, is hiding in the mountains. The remaining Ambrym klevas—Tofor included, apparently—are extremely worried for their own safety: If the police think you are doing magic, they will arrest you, whether you are doing it or not. There is much bad feeling here toward the klevas just now, and of course Tofor is considered to be *the* most powerful of the living sorcerers.

Disappointed that our long-awaited conversation has been so fruitless, I spend much time pondering the meaning of his words during the slow return voyage from Ambrym.

7

RAMROD

Rosalie is out of control and so is her rider. Trailing along on a tropical cattle roundup, my well-behaved nag suddenly has gone berserk and I find myself in a most precarious position—one stirrup lost, chasms separating me and the saddle, and one bounce away from going head over heels into a thorn bush. I have been looking for a modern-day expatriate living and working in the jungle, but this is not how I expected to interview him.

I am in the company of Marcus Thompson, a bright-faced Western hell-raiser who dropped into the wilds of Vanuatu to manage the six-thousand-acre Tuku Tuku Ranch belonging to the Trammel Crow family of Dallas.

Robert T. Crow, the son of Trammel Crow and Marcus's partner, also owns Vanuatu's largest hotel, the Intercontinental, as well as movie production companies in California and substantial U.S. real estate holdings.

Marcus has just charged after three errant steers that decided to go left when they were supposed to go right. The animals are crashing through heavy brush, heading toward an even denser thicket filled with long-needled thorn bushes. Marcus and his mare, Doolittle, a high-spirited strawberry roan, have galloped over a small ridge to head off the steers, and suddenly Rosalie has decided to throw good behavior to the winds. Apparently she is not going to miss out on whatever Doolittle is doing and jolts off with her reluctant rider at a manic pace in single-minded pursuit. Horse and I engage in a terrible trot-canter, my camera bag flying into the air at every second step. A dense cloud of red dust rises above us, shrouding the sun in a hazy glow. Bushes and trees emerge as if projected from fog, and only my death-grip on the saddle horn prevents a head-first swan dive over Rosalie's ears. I yank on the reins to turn her head and finally bring her to a halt. Rosalie is totally nonchalant. I, on the other hand, am panting and my hands are shaking. Just as I begin to relax, the three steers suddenly crash past in the opposite direction with Marcus hot on their tails, driving them back to the herd. I swear at them and Rosalie as we all clatter back the way we came.

Marcus and two Ni Vanuatu drovers are pushing four hundred thirsty cattle to a new pasture where there is more water. We are in the dry season of a drought year, and the grass is short and withered; the tall, elmlike white gums hang morosely, and even the ubiquitous mynah birds are too dry and hot to twitter.

Slim, young, and with the grin of a devil, Marcus is the picture of a clean-cut American cowboy. Eventually, when we have rejoined the herd and I have digested a mouthful of red dust, I ask him about his background.

"Well, I was born in Storm Lake, Iowa," he says. "I'm thirty-three. I've lived in fifteen different states. Went to four different high schools and then to Texas Christian University, Colorado State, and Northwestern. Studied psychology, animal husbandry, and education. I sort of went around the horn. And the last thirteen years I worked mostly on cattle operations. The first one I broke out in, I was just beginning my senior year at Colorado State. A guy by the name of J. Evan Roberts out of Livermore, Colorado, offered me a full-time job on his ranch. I was a real greenhorn at the time. I'd never done any ranching, but my dad always talked about doin' it, and he was a bushman, but he never got into cattle. Anyway, the guy had about twenty-six thousand acres north of Fort Collins. I worked for him two and a half years. After that I moved around a little bit just on a few small places. Then I ended up going down to Texas on a dairy farm for six months, and I worked the oil fields in between jobs. I also worked a couple small farms in Wisconsin, but in 1981 I was down duck huntin' in Louisiana and I broke my neck in a motorcycle wreck and was in a halo brace for about fourteen months.

"At that time I went back to school because I didn't know for sure if I was gonna be able to physically get back into the cattle business. After about, oh, close up to fourteen months, I still had some trouble, but I was ready to go back and started puttin' my applications back out again. I ended up gettin' back in the dairy business in east Texas, and after that I worked in the oil fields again. Since I'd had over a year of clinical psychology, I got a job at Brentwood Hospital in Shreveport, and I worked at Timberland Psychiatric Hospital in Dallas for about seven months dealing with from adolescents to adults, ranging from drug and alcohol abuse to schizophrenia and bipolar personality disorders. It was good experience."

"But how did that get you here?" I ask.

"Well, I always have my applications out everywhere, talkin' to people about ranchin' and just lookin' for the right place where there's an opportunity. In the United States it's so hard for a man my age to get involved in something that doesn't take a big stake, something where you can have part interest.

"Anyway, I was home in Dallas, and my mother saw it, an ad someplace, and she said, 'There's an opportunity.' She doesn't think too much of me bein' down here, but she was told by several people that it was on the up and up. She said, 'Well, there's a job down in the South Pacific that's open, and they've been takin' interviews for a month or so. Why don'tcha call this guy up?' And so I called him. Mr. [Robert] Crow's not a cattleman per se, so I was interviewed by a couple other cattlemen. We talked here and there, and I think they were lookin' for a guy that had . . . what's the word for doing a lot—versatility or something?"

"Yeah, sounds like you filled the bill," I say.

"Well, that's what that guy said," Marcus answers. "He said, 'Here's your guy.' I said, 'Well, wait a minute, I need to go down there and take a look at this place and see what I'm in for. I'm not gonna sign a contract and head down there without lookin' at it.' So he said, 'Fair enough.' I came down just to look at it, they gave me a month's wages, and after Bob came down, we negotiated a contract on a handshake deal—nothin' was signed for a year—and with promises of shares in the company. And after he'd come down, after the cyclone, there was a big drastic change here, and he liked what he saw and offered me a full partnership.

"Now I'm a fifty-fifty partner in all the assets and transfer of leases which are under way. The letters of intent are all signed, and it looks like it's just gonna be another month and things will be wrapped up. The only thing," Marcus adds with a smile, "is I've never had a financial burden of debt, and now I'm in debt up to my butt. This is gonna be three or four years down the road before any of us get any payback out of this deal because it was so rundown, there wasn't anything to sell when I came. It's gonna take three years to build up that herd to get the stocks up to even make ends meet. Mr. Crow is financing this mostly; I've put some money into it."

I interrupt to ask Marcus what assets he had to put into the deal. "Well, a deluxe '59 Chevrolet pickup, lots of hunting and fishing gear, and a few horses," he says, laughing. "I can't compare moneys with those folks, but we're doing everything on a minimum. Like I said, there was no machinery here when I got here. There was the very minimum. There were four tractors, but they were all broke down. We put one together. We did most of it by hand, and finally after one year I said, 'Bob, we need to get some equipment.' And so we decided on this partnership. I assumed fifty percent of all debts and he put up the initial capital. I put in the little bit that I had, and, you know, donated a pretty big commitment. And as long as this ranch and, politically, the nation is sound, I'll probably be here for a long time."

Along with the herd we head east at a slow walk. Steers, heifers, and cows trailing bright-eyed calves are being pushed by Marcus and his men through a ghostly looking valley past the bleached skeletons of leafless milkwood trees under the bright tropical haze. The previous winter, a terrible hurricane denuded much of the island's foliage and destroyed hundreds of thousands of palm trees. Where once they provided shade for the cattle, the downed palms now lie helter-skelter in the narrow valley. Marcus and Frederick, the young foreman, along with wizened Willie Batiste, an experienced Ni Vanuatu stockman, ride one behind the cattle and one at each flank, slowly turning the herd as if they were a rudder steering a boat. The cattle, calm now, move ahead steadily. They are packed close enough so that they cannot stop to graze without getting pushed by the animals behind them. Even considering the dust and the heat, it is an agreeably lazy way to spend the day.

A large, square-headed, reddish-brown cow carelessly flaps her long ears against the voracious insects buzzing around her head. She levels a malevolent gaze at me. Marcus says she is a "Braford," a Brahman-Hereford cross that combines the beefiness and manageability of the Hereford with the tick resistance of the tropical Brahman. The herd also includes some of the smaller Herefords, as well as enormous white and buff-colored Charolais and Limousin-Brahman crosses. Some lighter brown cows—wilder, with spread horns—mingle nervously with the others. These, Marcus says, are the progeny of wild bush cattle and will soon be sold to the local abattoir.

·

In 1980, when Vanuatu achieved independence from Britain and France, the new republic's fledgling government decided that the local tribes had been cheated out of much of their ancestral lands by the colonial Europeans. The two countries had claimed the New Hebrides and established joint rule in 1906 by means of an agreement called the Anglo-French Joint Condominium, which specified that each nation would establish its own legal and educational systems. Britain and France also promoted the islands to their own people, each hoping to attract a plurality of investors and settlers, thereby gaining a population advantage that could eventually translate into greater control of the islands. They needed no coaxing. Many French and British businesspeople saw potential fortunes waiting to be made. One such speculator was Sir William Lever, founding partner of Lever Brothers, the huge English soap conglomerate, which owned vast tracts of land in the South Pacific. In 1912 he wrote:

There are millions of acres of waste land in tropical countries waiting
to be developed and all that is wanted is a little help from the
authorities to convert waste tropical possessions into veritable gold
mines, producing wealth beyond the dreams of avarice.[1]

The Levers and other large land buyers received plenty of government assistance, nearly always to the detriment of the local
people. To facilitate investment and to fulfill the Foreign Office's
request that the islands produce greater revenues, the British government had, in 1907, declared all "unoccupied" lands—those not
owned by native tribes—to be the property of the Crown. A panel
made up of district officers, European plantation owners, and missionaries decided which lands the tribes were not "occupying." This
"alienated" land was subsequently leased or sold for development.
Land was also purchased directly from the tribes. Since the native
people had no concept of land ownership, they had little understanding of the ramifications of selling land they had used for centuries. Tribes were duped or coerced into selling their land for almost
nothing by European (French as well as English) government representatives and developers working hand in hand to swindle them.

The prevailing attitude among the colonials with regard to the
native Melanesians was one of stark racism. In 1933, J. C. Barley,
an old planter in the Solomons, wrote:

Speaking with over 21 years' experience of conditions in the British
Solomon Islands, I regret to state that my considered opinion [is]
that—with the notable exception of the Missionaries—scarcely 10%
of the European settlers in the Protectorate regard the native
otherwise than a "necessary evil" in the economic life of the
community or as being entitled to any sort of sympathetic attention or
interest outside his sphere of utility as a customer or labourer. He is
almost universally looked down upon as belonging to a somewhat
unclean and definitely inferior order of creation, as one who does not
know the meaning of gratitude, loyalty or affection, and who will
invariably mistake kindness for weakness and immediately take

[1] *Wealth of the Solomons*, Judith A. Bennett. University of Hawaii Press, 1987, p. 125.

advantage of any person rash enough to trust him and treat him as a fellow human being. My personal experience of the native of the Solomon Islands has always been diametrically opposite to this.[2]

Within fifty years the native people had lost possession of nearly all their tribal lands. This situation was not redressed until independence, when most land titles reverted to the tribes, who in turn subsequently leased the lands to whoever wanted them, compensating the old European owners from part of the proceeds.

Independence also influenced race relations. Prior to 1980, the majority of white planters in Vanuatu held racial views that probably were not far removed from what their predecessors had held a hundred years earlier. Racial supremacists generally cannot tolerate living in a country that their race does not control, however, and most left prior to or soon after independence. Many other European landowners left in disgust after losing title to land for which they felt they paid an honest price (usually to another European).

"After independence," Marcus says, "Colonel [Trammel] Crow was kinda tired with it [the ranch]. He had paid for it once. They, the custom owners, took it all back, and he said, 'All right, let's sell and get out.' So when I first came here, they were starting to liquidate this place. They had just kinda gave up on it, and they were trying to sell everything off. They hadn't put any new cattle into it. When I got here the youngest breeding cow in the place was at least six years old." Nodding toward the healthy-looking cows we are pushing in front of us, he continues. "The bad thing about this herd here, when I got here they hadn't been wormed and they looked skin and bones. Every one of these you could see their ribs as plain as day. Besides, the whole cleared part of the place, over two thousand acres, had been let overgrown and it was covered in lantana, pico, and thistach—those are the major weeds in this country. It took us about. . . well, the first seven months I was here we did nothing but clear land and rebuild fences.

"After I'd had time to look the place over, I called Bob Crow to give him an assessment of what was here. He's an absentee owner.

[2] *Wealth of the Solomons*, Judith A. Bennett. University of Hawaii Press, 1987, p. 179.

He was under the impression that it was in immaculate shape, and when I got here it was a disaster. I immediately called him and said, 'You need to come down here and look at this. If I'm gonna take this job, you've gotta know the status of this, eyesight, not just take verbal word on it.' He flew out here and he was astonished. It was . . . well, you see up here on the hill, just up there next to the bush where you get that maybe six-foot-high stuff? The whole place was masked like that." Marcus points to an area of brush that is so high and thick that a cow could not get through it, much less feed on it. "All that you're lookin' at, everywhere was masked. What it does is, it shades the grass and kills your nutrients and your legumes so you don't have any feed. The first thing I did was I pulled a bar, like an eight-inch by ten-foot steel, one-inch-thick bar, over the whole property, just to knock down stuff.

"Then, all the cattle were mixed. They had calves, yearlings, two-year-olds and bulls all together. None of the calves had been cut [castrated]. There was a hundred bulls on the place, you know, and they were all scrawny. Nothin' had been done with the herd. We sold off a lot of the bad ones. They hadn't knocked off any of the horns. When I got here I knocked off about eight hundred head, you know, cut the horns off of 'em, and you need to. It settles down your cattle. You couldn't get close to the cattle when I came. We do a lot of horseback riding, a lot of moving, and you got to be able to work 'em. As soon as the grass gets to a certain length, you've gotta get the cows off. Otherwise, you know, you wear the grass down so much it won't grow back. And the cows were just kinda not very workable. Now, after fifteen months and putting 'em through the corral several times, you can see that they're very cooperative. And you need to talk to 'em, you need to work your cows about. These cows hadn't been touched for three or four years.

"But everything's been castrated in this bunch," he adds, "so it's okay to run them together, and I'll run 'em together until December when the grass starts comin' on and I've got my separate heifer and steer paddocks. Also when I came down here in June of last year it didn't rain once till December. It's real difficult. I'm real concerned about my cattle counts. I don't wanta overstock. People have overstocked here before, and when it got September, October,

November with no rain, they lost a lotta cows; they just dropped dead. They just didn't have enough feed for 'em. All the cows just sit by the water and drink and they don't go out and graze. Hopefully, time willing, if I go slow and be conservative, I'll increase my herd between ninety and a hundred thirty head each year. And I'm putting in about four hundred acres of new, improved pasture this year. So in two years' time it will feed around nine hundred cows, which will be full capacity the way the ranch sits now."

We have come to the head of a slight rise. Below us is a fence line and another pasture. "The reason we're moving these cows," Marcus says, "I've got seventeen paddocks ranging from a hundred to three hundred acres that the cows stay in year-round. I keep rotating 'em and they stay there. I breed three months out of the year. I got a three-month breeding program, and for those three months all my bulls are turned in with the breed cows. Then I take the bulls out and the cows are by themselves again until the next breeding season. I wait approximately six months and I pregnancy-check the whole herd, and the ones that aren't pregnant get sold. That's about the only way that you can bring your fertility rate up is to cull your cows that aren't cycling properly and aren't comin' in. So then I've got five or six hundred calves on the ground every year, which I might take ten bulls from the whole lot. I work all my calves at six to eight weeks. I can throw 'em on the ground, we dehorn 'em, we brand 'em, do all the necessities basically, and then at nine months, at weaning time, you get a second shot, you can see everything you've missed and you go back over 'em."

We are interrupted by cattle backing up in front of us. Some are balking at going through the gate into the adjacent pasture. Marcus snaps a twelve-foot bullwhip over the heads of the cattle at the rear of the herd. There is a crack like a rifle shot and the cattle thrust forward, pushing those in front of them through the gate. I ask Marcus about the whip, where it comes from, and how you use it.

"I've seen whips used mostly in Australian films," he says. "I've seen a few old-timers in the States use 'em, and I practiced around with 'em there. Then, about the last couple years in the States, I got ahold of one and started usin' one. When I got down here, there was one here that nobody had used for years. They come in handy because you're so vocal otherwise. You yell a lot and if you can crack the whip, it saves your voice."

"But nobody actually hits the animals with them?" I ask, "I mean they're just used for sound-making, aren't they?"

"Sound-making, and if a cow's bein' hard to move or she won't move, I usually take my horse and just push her along. But if she's out of my reach a little bit, I'll reach over and peck her on the butt with one. Doesn't hurt 'em but it sure gets 'em movin'."

Willie Batiste, the sixty-seven-year-old stockman, sits relaxed, flipping his quirt idly while he listens to us. In his old tennis shoes and tractor cap, he seems as worn as time itself. Marcus says that he is the best stockman on Efate and that he has super savvy about cattle. He knows what's wrong with a cow by the way she's walking or bawling. In the forty years that Willie has been tending stock he has developed good cow sense, an invaluable quality for a drover. I ask Marcus if Willie can reach in a pregnant cow that is having problems in delivery and check to see if the calf is turned around.

Marcus says no, that Willie has never been inside of a cow. "How can you have a stockman who's never been inside a cow?" I ask.

"Because in this country they never did any pregnancy checkin' or pullin' of calves," Marcus replies. "If they saw a cow lying down over there, in trouble, they wouldn't go see what's wrong with her. Like one day we were pullin' a calf, where the calf was half out and it was stuck and the stockman that was here said, 'Oh, master, we must shootem bullet, she dead finish anyway.' I said, 'Shootem! One of mine?' Then I used the example, 'You got one pikinini[3] he come out, he stuck, just shootem?' They shook their heads. 'No, you wouldn't.' Then I said, 'You get 'em in the stockyard and we'll pull the calf and she'll be all right.' 'Oh, no, no, she's too wild,' the boys told me. 'You can't work with her,' you know? So I went up there and I lariated her. I told the boys to grab hold of

---

[3] The terms *master*, which means "mister," and *pikinini* (baby or small child) are vestiges of the colonial era that have been retained in the Pidgin English, or Bislama, that is the official language of Vanuatu. The government would, understandably, like to see the word *master* forgotten, though it no longer conveys its original meaning. Still, it is an indication of the recent state of servitude that existed throughout Melanesia.

her tail, and we jerked her down and had the calf out in about ten minutes, and the cow was on its way. Now I have two calf-pullers, and I'm working with the guys. I'm showing them how to use them so if I'm not here they can just go ahead. One guy can pull a calf with a calf-puller easy. And that's a long way from where we started. I remember when two of my boys were with me when I stuck my hand inside the rectum of a cow to do a pregnancy check—that's the only way you can tell if there's a fetus inside—they just all thought I was crazier'n a hoot owl and they took off and ran. And then when I stuck a chaw of tobacca in my mouth—the word for eating here is 'kai kai,' and they said, 'My God, this guy's gonna kai kai tobacco.' So their first impression of me was kind of a skeptical one."

I ask Marcus about the differences between the Western and Vanuatu cultures and whether it is difficult to bridge the gaps that exist. "It's real hard," he replies. "When I first came, you ask 'em if they understand, if they're savvy, and they'd say 'yeah,' and then you ask 'em, 'Okay, repeat back to me what I just said.' And they didn't understand. That's the biggest problem amongst ex-pats, I think, with Ni Vanuatu. They're shy, but they'll say, 'Yeah, I understand,' and then they'll walk away. But they don't understand a word you said. And the first six months I was here, I made every one of 'em . . . any kind of a request of mine to do some kind of work, I had 'em repeat back what I wanted 'em to do and how I wanted 'em to do it. So then if they screwed up, it was because they voluntarily screwed up. At least they understood the job, and they understood how I wanted to do it.

"For the first eight months I was here, I would say 'I need it done this way,' and as soon as I would leave, they'd go back to their old ways and do it their own way. And everything that I've asked them to do I've jumped in and showed 'em and worked with 'em, and not just told 'em to do it, and showed 'em why it would work. And now in the last, oh, I suppose six months, I've got four or five guys that are startin' to become self-starting, takin' some pride in their work, getting' to work on time—well, everybody gets to work on time now or they don't work here. But at first I thought that they never would, because it was just like at 4:30 they dropped their tools, no matter where they're at, and it seemed they had no pride in their work at all, *at all*. And just through showin' 'em that it can be done, after a couple months here everybody started working pretty hard. And when they came to an obstacle, they just usually gave up on it, and I said, 'No, no, we're gonna fix this.' During the year they've gotten to trust my judgment, and when I say we can do something, they believe it and do it. But it's really frustrating, too," he adds, "because ya work with 'em and a lotta times as soon as you turn your back, they'll go back to their old ways, or you've trained a guy and he's come along really, really good, and on the spur of the moment he'll say, 'I'm going back to my [home] island,' and he leaves ya.

"I have four married men working here and the rest are single, but I went through about thirty guys to find the ten that I have now. About six of 'em were here originally and they stayed; they're good men. I went through quite a few to get these other guys, and they're startin' to come 'round. All of 'em are startin' to become a family. I made them clean up all their kids. They all had head lice, they were dirty, real dirty, and I . . . almost mandatory, if you're gonna live and work here, you're gonna keep clean, keep your kids clean. When I got here I bought thirty toothbrushes and toothpaste. Then one day we got everybody together and had toothbrushing lessons. I make good living conditions for 'em, but I expect them to take care of themselves and their families." He explains that each family has a small apartment, and the single men occupy a bunkhouse.

"What I've tried to do is get younger men that have a little bit of savvy about carpentry or whatever and try to teach 'em something, make a situation here, a likable situation and some kind of incentive program. I think I've got probably the only incentive program in the country. If the boys are workin' good, I let 'em have my eighteen-foot runabout with the seventy-five-horse Mariner on it, and I trust 'em with that. Anytime they've shown me they're trustworthy, they can use my equipment. Every Saturday night I buy 'em kava. We sit and story—almost every Saturday night the boys and myself sit down for two or three hours, drink kava by the fire, and talk about work. We talk about the future and I try to get 'em enthused. I told 'em all that they could each have a horse if they take care of it. So they can have their own horse. And they're liking it more and more. They're just now in the last month forming a family unit, which a good working community's gotta be. Everybody backs each other. If somebody needs some help, you see 'em help each other. It's a good change."

Labor conditions on Tuku Tuku are a far cry from what they were in colonial days. Blackbirding—the name given to foreign labor recruiting—began in the 1870s to supply labor for plantations in Fiji, Australia, and Samoa. Recruiters, arriving by sailing ship, would barter trade goods with coastal chiefs, or big men, in return for providing laborers, either local tribesmen or captives from other tribes. The indentured laborers were paid upon completion of their three- or four-year contract, but often they never lived to see their homes again. Many died of sickness brought about by poor conditions on the plantations. Some, instead of being returned to their tribal lands, were simply dumped on the most convenient passing shore, often to be murdered by tribes on whose territory they landed.

Though the majority of laborers were eager to enlist, blackbirders sometimes shanghaied unwilling Melanesians, often enticing them onto a ship with the promise of gifts of trade goods, then forcing them below deck at gunpoint and sailing away. After stories of blackbirding outrages spread to Britain, the practice was finally banned, but labor conditions in the New Hebrides and the Solomons remained despicable. Plantation living was difficult and dangerous, often in isolated malaria-infested areas, and European companies usually had to accept whomever they could find to manage their properties. Lonely, despondent overseers took their personal problems and frustrations out on the laborers. Many plantation managers shot or whipped Melanesians with impunity. In cases of outright murder—not uncommon up to the 1930s—the European would usually be expatriated rather than stand trial. Gradually, labor laws promoted more humane working conditions but there were never enough government regulators to enforce them properly. Major labor abuses diminished, but unfair practices continued except in areas where there were shortages of workers. Only after independence, however, did any labor–management power balance come into existence.

The cattle have settled in and are grazing peacefully. Marcus and Frederick, the twenty-six-year-old foreman, talk together about the next job to be done. Frederick answers thoughtfully. He has a friendly, eager look about him. When he rides off, Marcus says, "I myself work twelve to sixteen, eighteen hours a day, and Frederick has got tons of energy and he's right with me all the time. I got all the respect for him, and I believe he's got all the respect for me. Him and I work a lot together. He's about the only one that's got the initiative to do a full day's ranching job. Most of the other help are not used to workin' that eight hours' time. And we had a little trouble one time about Frederick 'cause he is such a hard worker. I don't favor him but I work with him a lot because I gotta go do this and, bam! He jumps in the pickup, 'Let's go,' and everybody else just kinda doesn't work, and I say 'Come on, you guys, let's go, you're gonna learn something' here,' and so *then* everybody comes. Anyway, Frederick got in a little trouble one time, and they brought him in front of a custom court, and the boys wanted him out. His wife was back in his village for three months and one of the other women approached him here on Tuku Tuku, and he was tempted but didn't do anything. But the boys turned on him. I think it was premeditated to get rid of him."

"Because they were jealous, because they thought he was your favorite?" I ask.

"Yeah, they're jealous because he's a tough, hard worker and probably, yeah, him and I spend a lot of time together. But like if I go fishing and everything, I try to bring a different guy with me all the time and not get that favoritism. Anyway, in front of all Mele village, all the chiefs and everything else, I told them, I said, 'Part of this problem is that Frederick is a hard worker and these boys can't keep up with him. They want his job, but there's not a man in this room that belongs at Tuku Tuku that can replace Frederick.' And I said, 'If you, Mele village, ask me to have Frederick leave, I would have to go elsewhere to find another foreman. There's nobody on my place that can fill his boots,' and I said that in front of about five hundred people.

"Then the chief asked me, 'Marcus, what do you want to do about this?' And I said, 'Well,' I said, 'I don't believe that one mis-

take should ruin a man.' I said, 'Frederick, yes, should be punished.' I said, 'I believe in a good Christian attitude, and talkin' to
somebody's wife about this and that isn't really kosher, and he
should be punished. But I don't believe that one mistake should
ruin his life. He's got a helluva future at Tuku Tuku and we oughta
give him another chance, and that's how I stand on it,' and the chief
looked at me and he says, 'That's the way I feel about it too, Marcus.' And that was the end of that.

"And then he asked this woman [with whom Frederick was
seen] about what the dealings was, and he says [to her and the man
she was living with], 'Are you two married?' And they both hung
their heads and said, 'No.' And he said to this other fella, 'If you
wanta keep your woman, marry her.' They were just livin' together
for years and years and not custom married or not church married,
and this chief said, 'Hey, you want to keep your woman at home,
looks to me like she's out temptin' guys, and you know, marry her
and keep her under control.' It's pretty chauvinistic here."

"Frederick didn't actually take the woman to bed or anything.
So what were they all upset for?" I ask.

"It was just because he approached her," Marcus replies, "and
asked her to come down by the saltwater and talk and maybe something woulda happened, I don't know. But anyway, it didn't, and it
got resolved. We went and said our piece, and he ended up payin' a
head of kava, one pig, and a thousand vatu[4] to David for the insult
that he had done to his woman."

We pause on a knoll eighty or ninety feet above the beach. Below us waves crash on the reef, a few hundred yards offshore. Our
horses snort as we all unwind. Standing on the most westerly point
of Efate Island, we face out over the Coral Sea. Twenty miles to the
southeast lies the picturesque little French-flavored capital of Port
Vila. Due east is the jungle-covered center of the island. And in
front of us there is only ocean for one thousand four hundred
miles—until it strikes Australia. Small wooden ranch buildings sit

---

[4] One thousand vatu, at the time of writing, was about U.S. $10; a small pig was worth
$20, and a head of kava about U.S. $8. So Frederick's illicit conversation cost him about $40
or nearly a week's pay.

nestled in groves of milkwood and whitewood a half mile off to our left. Marcus seems pensive, a mood I had not observed earlier.

"You seem as if you were a free spirit, Marcus," I say, "and probably you still are in some ways, but now all of a sudden you've got more responsibilities than most men ever see in their lifetimes— and more potential rewards than most men ever see in their lifetimes. What's the difference between the before and after Marcuses?"

He is silent for a moment. "I'm a recovering alcoholic," he says finally. "I'm on my year four of sobriety. My dad died of alcoholism at the age of fifty-three, and I saw myself going in the same direction. I sobered up, and the last three years I've gotten my finances in line again and got my physical senses all back. I mean, not that I was a guttered alcoholic, 'cause I was holdin' a good job and everything else, but it was just really holdin' me down. Now I see a promising future. I quit! It's hard, real hard, but in a few years' time . . . " His voice trails off.

"It's to your credit that you could accomplish something as difficult as that," I say.

"Well, I tell ya, I was luckier than hell. I was gifted, I can do any kinda athletics. I've been gifted with hand-eye coordination. I got the best in the world. In college I got good grades, but I . . . it was easy enough for me, but I never learned how to read very well. I can read, but I listened to lectures and would go to review sessions and get through. It is a real detriment to me now, I'll tell ya, because I do have to do all the business. I do all my own bookkeeping now, and I wish I'da, you know, done a little bit more in school. My dad was a real super, I mean super, outdoorsman. He was a helluva intelligent fella, and my senior year I was on full scholarship and I quit to work for three hundred dollars a month in Colorado, and he about disowned me.

"So I didn't get the education I coulda, but I've done a lot of things," he continues. "I've worked with a lot of youth programs. In Shreveport I worked with the Off the Street Program in the heart of . . . I mean I was the only white guy for miles around and working with a bunch of kids that nobody else, you know, could do anything with. I went down there to the YMCA and started a basketball program, and Christ, I had more kids comin' in there than you could shake a stick at. And, uh, I don't know, sometimes I wonder if I'da just stayed in one field I'da accomplished something, you know?"

"What about friends?" I ask. "Is it difficult to find people you have much in common with?"

"The few white people that I do have friends with here are in the cattle business," he answers. "Most of the expatriates, the white people here, are into the social life and such as that; I'm not too much into that. I spend most of my free time on the ranch. But I've come to be friends with my boys, which a lot of the expatriates say you cannot do. Don't be friends with your workers. Well, I believe that if you can't be friends and work together, then you don't have a family unit very well, and now we are friends, and we work hard together and play hard together, and they're gettin' the attitude there's nothin' that we can't do—which is great."

"Are there very many single women around?"

"Not too many. I was datin' a gal that was an air hostess from New Caledonia, but her contract was up and she went back to France. There's a lotta young local French half-caste women here, but you have to speak French, and my French is just now gettin' to the point where I can greet people and listen a little bit and catch a little bit of what they're sayin', but I'm so involved with the priorities out here that in the first year I've been here I just haven't had a chance to get involved. And I do like to play sports and stuff, and so the free time that I do have I'm tryin' to organize softball teams and such as that or play basketball with a bunch of Ni Vanuatu guys. I'm the only white guy on the team. Hopefully, somethin' down the road'll happen. A woman would make my life a whole lot easier, and I've always wanted a family. It sure would be nice."

"It'll happen sooner or later," I tell him.

"Sometime, God willing," Marcus replies.

As we ride past hundreds of fallen palm trees, strewn like dead soldiers across a battleground, Marcus tells me about the effect of the recent cyclone—the Pacific term for hurricane—that hit Efate with winds of more than one hundred and forty miles an hour. It destroyed almost half of Port Vila, taking over forty lives and leaving tens of thousands homeless.

"It completely took every building we had," he says. "About six o'clock. . . we knew it was comin', we had some notice, but I don't think anybody had any idea at all that it was gonna be as strong as it was. The boys. . . we were kinda gettin' prepared for it, and I was talkin' about goin' up in some cliffs and stuff, but the boys said, 'No, no, cyclones aren't that bad,' and they kinda twisted my arm a little bit, said it was all right. Well, it waddn't all right, and about six o'clock all hell broke loose, and the first thing I noticed, the heads of coconut palms, big heads, you know, like four, five, six feet across, full of coconuts, were flyin' horizontally, not falling to the ground but gaining height. My eighteen-foot boat with two 25 Mariners on it went about a hundred meters up in the air and didn't hit the ground until it was six or seven hundred meters out to sea. And it just increased by the minute. I got all the kids, everybody into the shop where there are some steel beams. We got in there and gave everybody huddled together, almost like a snake line. I moved a little bit, everybody moved a little bit. And you know, 'Massa, massa, what we do?' 'Shit!' I say, 'Hey, stop the wind, guys,' you know, and parts of my house were just disintegrating and crashing into the shop, and whenever something would crash into the shop, it would just take a big chunk of it away. And for seven hours it blew unbearably and just seemed to get worse and worse and worse. I had been through tornadoes, and, you know, slept on ice at thirty-five degrees below zero, and lotsa other things, and I'm tellin' ya, I had a holda my butt pretty hard. It was a life-threatening situation. It takes a lot to scare me. I mean I'm cautious and I'm respectful, but it takes a lot to scare me, and I was real, real frightened for my life."

"And nobody was seriously hurt. How many head of cattle did you lose?"

"Remarkably, I lost only six head of cattle and one horse. A tree fell on it."

"A tree fell on it?"

"Yeah, flyin' debris. There were four or five with broken legs that we had to shoot, but everybody ate 'em. I got ten men, four of 'em are married, and there's fifteen children on the place, so you got thirty people here, and we ate lots of beef.

"But that's not all," Marcus continues. "Friday a barge from Santo was comin' down to the abattoir with a load of cattle, and the ballast was leaking or something. They got tipsy-turvy and they crashed into the west side of Tuku Tuku. We gathered up cattle all day Saturday, and all these cows were bush cows—they were all wild, they all had big horns. Thirty-two animals came ashore, and they hadn't been to water in two days. Every one of 'em were fightin' us. Instead of pushin' 'em, they'd turn around and they'd wanta gore ya and everything else, and 'bout halfway through the day—I push cows pretty hard, I get up on 'em and literally push 'em with my horse—this one turned around, and he gored Doolittle right here in the front. I don't know if you can see it or not." He point to Doolittle's chest where there still is a puncture. "It swelled up, but she's all right. Went in about two inches, a puncture wound, and the rest of the day we had to rope cows and drag 'em to the corral. We pulled ten up off the bank that were dead and burned 'em, and I dove on the wreck yesterday morning and there are thirty-five head up underneath the barge, dead. Tuku Tuku is a disease-free ranch. We've been tested for tuberculosis, which they did have on Santo, and brucellosis. We don't have any, and what I'm upset about is these seventy-seven cows comin' from an area of the country that hasn't been heavily tested could create a problem for me."

"You moved them out of here or are they still around?" I ask.

"No, I moved 'em out immediately, and I segregated 'em away from my herd, but they still drank out of the troughs and were in contact with a couple of my cows, which I now have quarantined. As soon as those live animals are tested and prove to be okay, I'll say my prayers. Only trouble is, those eighteen head of mine they were in contact with were eighteen really nice three-year-old heifers, and I hate to butcher 'em, you know?"

"So you kept the eighteen segregated?"

"Yup, I still have 'em segregated."

"Well, chances are you'll be okay."

"Nine hundred ninety-nine out of a thousand you're fine, but when you got close up to one thousand head of animals on your place and your future in front of ya, you hate to screw it up with one deal like that."

Above: A quiet morning on Palmerston; the beach, facing the lagoon, with the reef and breakers in the background. *Below, top right:* Dawn and the children at recess. *Below, left:* Sarah Marsters is a wise and kind woman. *Below, bottom right:* Palmerston's church, built entirely with wood from old sailing ships that crashed on the reef, must now be propped up.

Above, left: Dave Marsters with a freshly caught wahoo. *Above, top right:* Island girls are delighted to pose for an infrequent visitor. *Above, bottom right:* Uncle Tuakana feeds his pigs. *Below:* William and Martha in the CAO's house. Above them are photos of England's King George V and Queen Mary.

Above: The four old Big Nambas. From left: Teven; Alam; Joshua; and Norlan. *Below, left:* Marcus on Doolittle. The Bislama slogan on his T-shirt translates: "My Cattle." *Below, right:* Tofor, the last great sorcerer's sacred nakamal, is guarded by a carved slit drum.

Above: Inspector Taafaki and his men on patrol in Funafuti. *Below, left:* Men on Nukufetau build a dugout sailing canoe. The work will take them about two days to complete. *Below, top right:* Four generations of Tuvaluan women. From left: Frieda, her grandmother Laki, Frieda's daughter, and Frieda's mother Mafua. *Below, bottom right:* A traditional fale in the center of Nukufetau.

Above, left: Timothy, the old Are'are warrior. *Above, right:* Lysander, the Are'are guide, who related the story of his grandfather's murder. *Below:* Looking east toward Mount Nggatokae over Morovo Lagoon from the mission station.

Above: Children play in the shallows of the bay next to the Batuna Mission Station at Vangunu. *Below, top left:* Ken and Jill Hiscox, the missionaries of Vangunu. *Below, bottom left:* Ken prays with men from the mill before starting the day's work. *Below, right:* A nursing sister examines a small patient at the mission's clinic.

Above: A group of Kwaio women and children inspect us as if we are from another planet. They smoke wild tobacco in homemade cigarettes and pipes. *Below, left:* Women, children, and dogs eat their meal of yams in the cooking hut. *Below, right:* Two old men. The one on the right is ill and pigs have been sacrificed to the ancestors in hopes they will cure him.

Above, left: Adobo, headman and feastgiver, wears his wealth in chains of shell money. *Above, top right:* A man scrutinizes us as he chews his betel in the men's hut. He dips lime out of hollow bamboo. *Above, bottom right:* Lumale, Lameuka's and Mamani's daughter, is of marrying age and highly prized as a future wife. *Below:* Lameuka teaches his son to play the bamboos. The pipes the people smoke are made from the remains of a World War II fighter plane that crashed in the mountains.

The quality of Marcus's herd seems excellent, and I tell him so.

"You're right," he replies. "My beef here, I've eaten a lot of beef, corn-fed beef in Iowa and everything else, and my beef is as good as I've eaten anywhere, and that's what's gonna help us, I think, on the export market. Most people realize that we do have good beef. The export market is gonna go, and we need it, because there's gonna be too much beef here for the local consumption."

"So how does your future look to you?"

"I feel like I'm managing a piece of property that hopefully in ten years' time will be worth something, and I'll get somethin' out of it. But it's not a sure-bank thing. You don't know what's gonna happen in the future politically. And dealing with the custom owners is a real touchy situation. On any given moment if you rub the wrong person the wrong way, you could probably be asked to leave. So, I try to have good relations with my custom owners. I bring 'em shark meat. I bring 'em a bullock every year for Christmas. I try to involve them if I can with some Tuku Tuku operations, and I just try to be diplomatic."

"Do they have a lot of political pull?" I ask.

"That's funny," Marcus answers, "because you might have somebody that's workin' for ya that is a cousin of a cousin that's in parliament, and if you sack him, he runs to somebody and says somethin' bad about ya, and pretty quick you're in trouble. But I don't think I'll ever have a problem because I'm straight as an arrow. I'm honest with people, and I don't care how bad it hurts, I tell the truth. If it's the president of this country of if it's the president of the U.S.A., if I don't like his attitude, I'll say something."

"Well, that might be a quick way to get thrown out of here," I reply.

"Yeah," Marcus replies with a laugh, "that's right, but you can't surrender all your integrity. You have to keep some of your pride, and if my straight honesty and position isn't good enough for 'em, then I don't wanta be here."

8

JOHN FRUM'S

NOT DEAD YET

Standing on a volcano's rim watching it erupt beneath your feet is your basic nightmare, like being thrust into the center of the earth. Clouds of smoke and sulphur fill the air, and periodic explosions blast torrents of molten lava skyward before they fall back into the inferno at the base of the cone. The crater bottom, a cauldron of fire, seethes under clouds of smoke.

Each explosion causes the mountain to shudder. Not to worry, says Terrence, my lanky Tannese guide; there hasn't been a major eruption here in many hundreds of years. I am not convinced: Another guide has told me that the last major eruption was only about thirty years earlier. Now, as I look around at the giant hunks of lava covered only with a light coating of ash, the reassuring words definitely seem suspect. They become more so a few minutes later when an atom-bomb-size explosion blots out the sky. Pieces of lava the size of Volkswagens come hurtling through the air hundreds of feet above the rim on which we are standing. I am caught flatfooted, awaiting my fiery demise. Not so Terrence. He is galloping back down the trail, jet-propelled, as fast as his long legs can carry him. Later, he shrugs and gives me a sheepish grin, as if to say, 'So, that's why I am still a volcano guide.'

Mount Yasur, on Tanna Island, is one of the few viewable volcanoes in the world. Just to the northeast lies the village of Sulphur Bay, the center of the John Frum cargo cult. Some of the John Frum people believe their savior lives in the local volcano with his five-thousand-man private army. The John Frum is not a small band of renegades. According to local authorities, they command more than a quarter of the villages on Tanna and the same proportion of the island's twenty-five thousand people—and much to the consternation of Vanuatu's Christian government, the movement continues to grow and gain adherents.

The John Frum is the only large cargo cult remaining in the South Pacific. From the beginning of the colonial era to the end of World War II, many such movements sprang up, primarily in Melanesia but also in some Polynesian island groups, as naive islanders attempted to practice the magic by which they believed Europeans obtained vast cornucopias of material wealth. Because the islanders never saw the Europeans work or make the automobiles, lanterns, tools, clothes, and other items they coveted, it was natural for them to ascribe the accumulation of possessions to magic. This coincided with Melanesian tribal beliefs that those who were successful and wealthy carried magic with them and, conversely, those who carried magic were bound to gain fine possessions.

The Frum movement did not start as a cargo cult, however; nor has it been cargo-centric, strictly speaking. During the 1930s, lush, mountainous Tanna was still isolated from the outside world. Only the sporadic arrival of a trading boat broke the seclusion. It would load copra or supply the twelve to fifteen Europeans—mostly British planters, traders, or missionaries—who resided there. The Scottish Presbyterian Mission (a successor to the London Missionary Society) and Church of Scotland missions established on Tanna in the 1840s and 1850s dominated religious life on the island. The Scottish mission's strictures were severe. It banned many tribal practices, particularly custom dancing, polygamy, and the ritual uses of kava. Unbeknownst to the missionaries, the drinking of kava was a ceremony the Tannese believed vital to their tribal welfare. They thought it brought them protection from their dead ancestors. The mission's ban unhinged the tribesmen emotionally, and many Presbyterian Tannese left the church in defiance.

At first the rebels simply manifested their displeasure by non-stop kava drinking. Gradually they began to practice other banned rituals, but they still had no focus. Perhaps they had learned too much from the missionaries to revert to their old tribal life, but a major turning point occurred in 1937 or 1938—no one is sure of the date. Villagers at Green Point, on the southwest tip of the island, saw a vision of a man walking across their dancing ground. He was a slight figure, dusky but not black, wearing a handsome jacket with shiny buttons. At first the apparition did not speak. But on subsequent visits he told the astonished people in a squeaky high-pitched voice that the Ten Commandments were real, but so was their "custom" life real. He said that while the Bible was true and that Jesus would come to fulfill the law, their custom beliefs, to which they should return, were true as well. Word flashed around the island, and soon people came from dozens of villages to hear this spirit, whom they called John Frum or John Broom. (The John Broom variation may have symbolized the movement's desire to "sweep the whites out" of their lives, or off Tanna.)

Many accounts of the movement incorrectly ascribe the name's origin to an American soldier who came to Tanna during the war. According to early histories, however, the Tannese were already using the John Frum name by then. The source of the "John from America" variation was the early belief that the Messiah was king of America or the son of the king of America. This would seem at odds with another belief, still held, that Frum is also the Son of God—not Jesus, but a man whom humans must follow to find Jesus. The Frumers consider themselves children of John, who promised that one day he would return to lead them.

At first the Frum devotees kept the appearance of their savior a secret from the church and civil authorities, but word soon leaked out that banned kava drinking and licentious dancing were regularly taking place. Tannese church attendance dropped to almost nothing and all the Frum children left the mission schools. James Nicol, then British district agent on Tanna, who apparently served as magistrate, prosecutor, and policeman, sent two of his trusted native assistants to investigate. They joined the Frums, as did three subsequent assistants. The Frumers then descended on the island's trading posts, spending all their money. John had told them to buy out the stores and thereby eliminate the white man's money, which was thrown into the sea for the same reason. They also believed that when their messiah returned, he would provide them with every-thing the white man had, including, according to some reports, white women.

The Europeans feared that even though the Frumers showed no signs of violence, they would take over the island. Nicol began arresting the leaders and sending them to jail in Port Vila. One of those arrested, Tom Meles, is now a chief of the Frum. Meles, now slight and wrinkled, with a perpetual squint, was twenty-eight years old when he was arrested by Nicol's policemen in 1940. I met him at his Sulphur Bay home, where he told me about his arrest: "They [the British] told me to stop the order. The judge said that it will take two hundred dollars and they will let me free, but in 1940 it was a hard time; there was no money. Still, I work hard and find the money. So I give them the two hundred dollars. But they still put me in prison. I went to prison for four years [his first of many incar-cerations]. They never tell me why."

In 1940 Nicol sent thirty-three Tannese men to prison even though there had been no laws broken, other than church dictates. Over the next two years fifty more Frum men were sent to jail in Port Vila for such crimes as "adultery" and "incest." No evidence of these crimes exists. Apparently, any charge sufficed. There was no right of appeal and no due process. The British hope—to end the Frum movement by jailing all its leaders—nevertheless failed. In-carceration seldom is able to suppress dreams and ideals; indeed, it seems to be a hothouse for their propagation.

Poita Peter and other activists served sentences of one to eight years, but Tom Meles spent a total of eighteen years either in prison or in exile for having committed no offense other than being a Frum leader. If Meles was bitter over his unjust incarceration, he seems to have resolved the issue; at least he appears to bear no grudge against his British malefactors. James Nicol did not live to see the failure of his attempts to quash the Frum movement. He died after his jeep overturned on the outskirts of Port Vila in 1944.

The national prison, in a valley adjacent to urban Port Vila, is a rather homey, countrified affair, as prisons go. Still, it could not have been pleasant, especially during the eleven years Meles served there. I asked him how he survived his imprisonment. "John Frum with me," he replied. "He comes like a spirit. The government and the police, they cannot see John Frum."

"And did you talk to him?" I asked.

"Yes. He tells me I must keep doing the John Frum order."

Meles said he often saw John Frum in prison, that Frum slept with him, and that he still sees the spirit and has visits from him, as do some of the other older Frum believers.

Even with the mass imprisonment of Frum leaders, the movement continued to expand, especially after the arrival in 1942 of thousands of American troops, who came to Efate and Espiritu Santo to build airfields, harbors, and military bases. The American forces needed enormous numbers of laborers. A Caucasian Seabee bosun from Mississippi, Thomas Beatty, was put in charge of Melanesian laborers building the Efate bomber field, then became the labor recruiter as well. Whereas many colonials and military officers mistreated or took advantage of the native people, Beatty was fair and kind to them. Under his supervision, the eleven hundred men recruited from Tanna received tasty new foods, shiny military uniforms, and chances to ride in ships, trucks, and jeeps. They saw the best that Hollywood had to offer at the movie theater, and their twenty-five-cents-a-day earnings, although meager, were twenty-five times that which the miserly British and French paid them on Tanna. (In fact, the military wanted to pay them a dollar a day, but the French plantation owners complained so strenuously that their pay was cut *back* to twenty-five cents.) A new world had opened to them. Beatty led labor-recruiting trips to Tanna and soon he, without realizing it, became integrated into the Frum mythology as Tom Navy, benevolent American friend of John Frum.

With their new riches, the Frum devotees bought clothes, calico, tobacco, and chocolate bars. They gaped at black American soldiers who had even greater wealth. Their new impressions fused with their prewar beliefs in the certainty that John Frum—American for sure now—would one day return, bringing them all the wealth that the whites, but most especially the Americans (of both colors), seemed to possess.

Attempts were made to convince the Tannese that their American messiah was a false god. An American army colonel was invited to Tanna to talk to the Frumers. He brought his submachine gun and blasted a picture of John Frum nailed to a tree, scaring the Tannese out of their wits but not changing their ideas. Some years later another American by the name of Johnson, captain of the National Geographic barque *Yankee,* arrived to tell the Frum people that, contrary to their beliefs, John Frum was not the son of the American president and that the American government would not be bringing them the luxuries for which they had been waiting. The Frum, who lavishly entertained Johnson and gave him gifts, had believed he was a man of power in the United States, perhaps the president. After his lecture they felt he had deceived them and was an impostor.

Meanwhile, the war ended and the American soldiers and all the luxuries associated with them suddenly disappeared, leaving the Melanesians dumbfounded. Into the void stepped numerous Frum disciples. One by the name of Neloig told villages he was Frum, king of Tanna and king of the U.S.A. He had his people build "airstrips" in hopes that the American planes would return with more possessions for the faithful. Many of these model-size airstrips bordered with whitewashed stones once adorned Frum villages, though now they are disappearing. Another disciple, Captain World, appeared repeatedly dressed in red at the village of Green Point until the British jailed him for "subversive activities."

The center of Frum activities was (and still is) the village of Sulphur Bay on the east side of the island. In 1956 a John Frum army began drilling there with realistic-looking bamboo rifles. When the army marched across the island toward the Presbyterian mission, the British panicked. Three boatloads of real soldiers armed with machine guns and tear gas were brought in. They prepared to attack the Frum army at Sulphur Bay, but the Frumers had disbanded, leaving no one for the British to fight. Eventually, the invaders piled back into their boats and returned to the capital without having saved Christianity from the wrath of the John Frum. Never had there been any violence on the part of the Frum, and as time passed the Europeans realized they were not threatened by what they referred to as the "mad coons."

Time and further contact with the outside world have changed the people of Tanna, including the Frum devotees. They certainly are more sophisticated and knowledgeable about the ways of the world. No longer do jungle innocents crawl wonderingly under an airplane to determine its gender. Every day now three or four twin-engine planes land on Tanna, each bringing a handful of tourists who travel by minibus along the island's winding jungle roads to the volcano or the Frum villages. Schools abound, and even the Frum children attend. Missionaries abound, too—they probably outnumber planters four to one—and they are united in their desire to bring the Frumers to their bosoms. The government of newly independent Vanuatu no longer jails Frum leaders, but it doesn't care for them either. The government has devised its own tactics for dealing with what it considers at the very least a potential political threat.

So how do the Frum practice their religion and withstand the constant pressures to abolish their faith or to convert to a mainline Western church? These questions are much on my mind as my battered pickup-cum-taxi bounces along the dirt tracks leading to Sulphur Bay.

The capital of John Frum, the biggest village on Tanna with 559 people, looks as if it had been laid out by a town planner. Thatched homes shaded by giant banyans surround a broad meadow, the focal point of the village, behind which is the bay itself. To the south, low hills separate the village from the volcano, only a mile away. Three flags fly from tall bamboo poles at the entrance to Sulphur Bay. On the left is a tattered remnant of an American marine ensign, the kind flown from yachts. In the center is the John Frum flag, a blue block of large white stars set in a field of broad red and green stripes, a design clearly inspired by its American counterpart, which flies on the right.

A committee of Frum leaders forms in two rows to meet me. The senior chiefs, Tom Meles and Poita Peter, are flanked by younger devotees, all neatly dressed in jeans or shorts and T-shirts. I had half expected a wildly costumed and coiffed contingent—South Pacific Rastafarians with dreadlocks, perhaps spaced out on kava. But these guys, with the exception of Poita Peter, who could pass for an old hippie, look straighter than straight. You could mistake them for a group of Protestant missionaries. Because I had been introduced by intermediaries they trusted, and because they clearly knew the value of publicity, the Frum hierarchy give me the three-dollar tour, including photo opportunities and a special prayer session in their church. No question but that the Frums had learned the white man's ways since World War II. I strongly doubted that I would see them still throwing money into the sea.

We begin talking about what the Frum believe, the crux of their religion. Only about half of the dozen men gathered around me speak English, and so my questions are translated into Bislama. After some consultation, one or another answers and his response is translated back into English. John Frum, I am told, has prophesied that certain events will take place: Jesus will return and he, Frum, will prepare the world for Christ's coming. "John Frum will clean you," one young man tells me. "You will confess with John Frum and then you will go to Jesus." Another man says that many Frum devotees believe Frum *is* Jesus. It becomes evident that there is still no single body of Frum belief or doctrine. Some devotees, for instance, believe Frum is Noah and that his coming will coincide with the sea rising up to overwhelm all but Frum believers, who will, of course, be saved by Noah/Frum. This does not seem an unreasonable belief if you have lived your entire life on an island in the middle of the sea. All the Frumers do believe that Frum is alive, and his spirit is felt by them all. But he talks to only a few of the old-timers, whom he tells to keep the faith and await his return. He also advises them of his present whereabouts—he is currently on his way to America, according to Meles.

Much Frum doctrine has been adopted from other religions. The Frumers seem to put great emphasis on millennium concepts, which probably were inspired by their experience with the Seventh Day Adventists. The belief that they are too sinful to go directly to God or Jesus without first being absolved—cleansed by John— certainly appears to have been derived from Catholicism, with which they also had contact prior to the 1930s. Frum's spirit among them may or may not be from one of their other religions. Perhaps not even the Frum devotees could say for sure. Not that borrowing from other religions lessens theirs; they are doing only what every major religion in the world has already done.

I ask if many Christian missionaries come to Sulphur Bay and the other Frum villages to convert them. "Yes," a Frum spokesman answers, "they always come here and we cheer and ask [them] to join our religion."

"So what do they say?" I ask with a smile.

"They say that we are doing the evil spirit."

"So you still believe that John Frum will come from America or will send Americans to bring you wonderful gifts?"

"We believe the first promise when John came. He told us that the only man [who is] your friend and [who is] with him is American people. So we keep the American flag."

"And was that flag given to you by John?"

"Given by the American people." (Apparently both the American flag and marine ensign were given to the Frum by a passing American yachtsman, I later find out.)

Elizabeth, a graying older woman who is the children's religious teacher, comes to tell us that the religious service is about to begin and asks if I would like to attend. Significantly, only a few of the men I have been talking to decide to go. The thatched chapel is large enough to hold about a hundred and fifty people standing, but only about forty Frumers of both sexes, ranging from children to elders, are in attendance. There are no seats or benches in the chapel. Where the altar would usually be is a large, somewhat crudely constructed cross painted red. Tacked on the front wall are numerous pictures of Jesus, but none of John Frum that I can see. No explanation is given of why this is so.

The service starts with what I imagine are prayers in Bislama. Everyone is standing with hands clasped piously in front of them. Some of the women hold small bouquets of flowers. There is no minister or other leader. After prayers the worshipers sing the following hymn, in which *Kalbapen*, the Tannese word for God, is invoked:

> We are in a boat and our boat leaves shore in a storm.
> God tells Noah, place your sights on the rainbow until you find land.
> *(Chorus)*
> I am the spirit,
> I am Kalbapen and my spirit spreads everywhere, all over the world.

Noah steers the boat toward one end of the rainbow.
On the end is Malekula or Santo.
The boat has landed and they meet the unseen spirit.
Kalbapen is with us all the time.
The eye of the sea snake comes out and in it is Jesus.
(Chorus)

The committee gathers again after the service, and they tell me more about their religion, as well as their relations with the churches and the government. The Frum sabbath is on Friday, when no one works or gardens. Services are held in each of the twenty-six Frum villages, after which the men drink kava. In the evening men and women alternate ritual dancing. On the special Frum holiday, February 15th, clans get together from all over the island to celebrate the day in 1957 when the Frum flag was first flown. Ceremonies begin with hymns and a flag raising. Then there is a military-style parade led by flag carriers and the chiefs representing each Frum village. A battalion of Frum men—whose bare chests and backs are painted with the initials USA—march and carry bamboo replicas of rifles. Following the parade is a great feast, kava ceremonies, and finally an all-night concert of songs and dances performed by members of the various villages. Christmas and Easter are also observed, but not with the fervor and enthusiasm exhibited on "Frum Day."

While no longer jailing the Frum people, the government, still fearful of their growing numbers and mortified by the fact that the movement has a greater affinity for the United States than for its own country, tries to isolate them as much as possible without entirely killing a golden goose of Tanna tourism. The former Prime Minister Walter Lini is himself a Presbyterian minister, and he defended the Frum's right to exist. Yet his government had, at one time or another, confiscated the Frum's American flags and censored their mail. On an ad hoc basis, it also banned foreign journalists from visiting them. Policies under the present government do not seem to have changed.

Where both colonial and independent governments failed to affect the Frum movement, the missionaries and tourism have been more successful. At Port Resolution, just to the southeast of Sulphur Bay, a Seventh Day Adventist congregation shares the village with a sizable contingent of Frum believers. The two peoples seem to live side by side in harmony. Pastor Rini Bong, the garrulous Tannese SDA minister, says that many Frumers attend his services and they get along fine. In fact, he adds, many Frum devotees attend their own services on Friday, worship with the SDAs on Saturday, and pray with the Anglicans on Sunday. The Frum people seem to accept the other two religions as being complementary to their own and as playing a major part in their lives. Perhaps the accusation that Frum is the devil in disguise is having an effect and the Frumers want to cover all bases. Or maybe, in this most fluid of all religions, sentiment is simply bending toward conventional Christianity as the Tannese become more worldly.

Certainly the Frumers have become more sophisticated. They are in daily contact with Western tourists, and many devotees have lived in the capital. Some have even visited foreign countries. As the days of belief in aircraft as magical birds are long gone, so for many of the younger Frumers is the notion that John will one day return with his everlasting largess or that the king of America will deliver them from poverty. Though the old people may cling to traditional Frum beliefs in the face of reality, there seems to be growing skepticism among the young. During my interviews with the Frum hierarchy, questions about John's being king of America or returning with automobiles for everyone brought amused glances, even attempts to hide giggles, from the younger men. It is likely they were embarrassed by their elders' naiveté.

It is hard to say whether the doubters still stay in the Frum villages because of the family ties, the filter-down benefits of tourist donations, or simply because of a residual belief in the Frum doctrine. What is certain is that the Frum religion is undergoing a rapid metamorphosis. Not even the John Frumers know where their religion is taking them.

III

Tuvalu

A POLYNESIAN

SOCIETY

9

A MOST PEACEFUL

COUNTRY

Inspector Taafaki and I head north on the main road one morning, past the Vaiaku Lagi Hotel and the broadcasting station. For a big man, probably about two hundred and thirty pounds, the inspector handles his bicycle with the grace of an athlete. He pedals easily ahead of me with no wasted motion or effort. Uaelesi (pronounced Y-less-ee) Taafaki is the number-two man in the Tuvalu National Police Force. He answers only to the chief and is responsible for the day-to-day operation of the twenty-four-man department.

It's still early, but the temperature already approaches ninety degrees; the air is dead with moisture. Sweat stains bloom under the arms of my shirt and at the neck of Uaelesi's khaki uniform. Fortunately, the inspector doesn't seem in a hurry to reach wherever it is we're going. Narrow lanes meander a few hundred feet off the main road to each side of us before they abruptly end at the lagoon, the airstrip, or the ocean. And as Uaelesi passes each lane, he slows and peers down it before moving on. Palms and breadfruit trees line this road and the other runs parallel to it. Small concrete cottages bordered by frangipani and hibiscus hedges nestle next to plantings of beans, taro, and arrowroot, some of the few vegetables capable of surviving in this bleak, coral-laden soil. Mynah birds chirp and cane toads hop in the puddles from last night's downpour. Two ladies wearing sarongs pedal demurely by on their way home from shopping at the Fusi, their food-filled woven baskets dangling from the handlebars. As they pass they give us a prim greeting. Uaelesi says good morning to them, and I smile and nod politely.

The inspector and I are riding two of the police department's seven bicycles. The department also has a Land Rover, but it is sitting on blocks in the headquarters courtyard, awaiting repairs that may never take place. Anyway, bicycles are an appropriate means of getting around. Almost everyone here in the capital rides them, or walks. There are only twenty-seven cars and trucks and about a hundred scooters and motorbikes on the entire island. A battered van serves as the island bus, and for about twenty cents you can ride the mile and a half of coral roads. To the north and south the roads turn into bicycle tracks that peter out among pandanus, family tombs, and mounds of coral stones worn round by the sea.

Little Funafuti is the capital of equally small Tuvalu, one of the most diminutive nations in the world. Its nine coral atolls stretch in a rough line nearly three hundred and fifty miles from southeast to northwest, yet their total land area is only fifteen square miles. A thousand kilometers north of Suva, Fiji, the islands used to be the Ellice part of the Gilbert and Ellice Islands Colony. After a countrywide referendum in 1978, the Ellice people were granted independence from Great Britain and given autonomy from the Micronesian Gilbertese to the north, who formed the Republic of Kiribati (pronounced Keer-a-bass). Now Tuvalu basks independently and, for sure, quietly—since almost no one ever comes here. The country averages fewer than a hundred tourists a year, and most of those arrive on private sailboats cruising through the Pacific.

After pedaling about half a mile we reach the Fusi and pull up to the bicycle racks at the south end of the building. The Fusi is the country's Sears and Safeway rolled into one. It supplies basic commodities to this island's twenty-seven hundred residents and to the fifty-eight hundred inhabitants of the other islands. Though there are a handful of private shops on Funafuti, they are no larger than closets and do relatively little business. The Fusi itself is not much bigger than a large convenience store, with about the same selection of food and a miserly assortment of clothes, household items, and hardware.

Uaelesi isn't shopping, however. He appears to be checking bicycle registrations, though he doesn't actually tell me what he's up to. For the last week I have been bugging the inspector to let me accompany him on a criminal investigation. It seemed like a distinct possibility except that the island turned out to be short on crimes. On the department's "crimes reported" sheet, the only notation for the preceding two weeks showed that a small pig had escaped its enclosure and was caught freewheeling on the airstrip. The owner paid a fine and got his pig back. Not exactly Sodom and Gomorrah.

As Uaelesi checks to see that registration numbers are painted on all of the bicycles' rear fenders, he begins telling me about a recent criminal case. It seems that two months ago a man by the name of Daniel reported his bicycle stolen. A week later he returned to the police station saying that he had seen the thief riding the bicycle. Inspector Taafaki and a sergeant confronted the accused, one Pani, who denied taking it, saying that the bicycle Daniel had seen him riding actually belonged to one of Pani's relatives. Since the painted identification would quickly settle the matter, Uaelesi asked to see the bicycle. It would be impossible to show it to him, Pani told the inspector, because it had broken down continually and in disgust he had thrown it over the sea wall into the ocean.

Uaelesi had a diver meet them at the sea wall, whereupon Pani confessed that the bicycle was not there but in the banana plantation at the north end of the island. The group repaired to the banana grove, where they found the stolen bicycle hidden under a pile of rubbish.

Twenty-five-year-old Pani, who had two previous arrests for drunkenness and one for fighting, was charged and convicted of taking a bicycle without the owner's consent. In court he was fined $30 (the Tuvalu dollar, tied to the Australian dollar, equals U.S. 80 cents at the time of writing), ordered to repair the damage he had done to the bicycle, and warned that his next conviction for any offense would bring at least six months in jail.

Pani's case, a true one, illustrates "major crime" in Tuvalu. During the month I spent in the capital the errant pig was the only crime reported. Could there be any capital or any country in the world with less crime? In 1987 there were no murders in Tuvalu. Indeed, there have been only two murders in its history, one in 1967 in Funafuti and the other on an outer island in 1980, and both were committed by foreigners. In 1987, the last year for which records were available, only eleven thefts were reported nationwide. In those cases, three thieves were convicted and three were shown to have committed the crimes but not judged to be guilty (one of the latter involved a mentally retarded individual). Five thefts were unsolved. There had been one rape during the previous ten years, although when I was there an individual on another island was being investigated for attempted rape. The only other major crime occurred in 1986 when an employee of the national copra board embezzled $21,000 by forging signatures on checks. This woman, a foreign national married to a Tuvaluan, was required to repay the amount stolen, jailed for three years, then deported.

How does Tuvalu's incidence of crime compare with that of other countries? Fiji, with a population of 717,000, is the only nearby nation that submits statistics to Interpol's report on international crime. Fiji's 1988 rate per 100,000 population for homicides was 2.25; for rape, 6.1; for aggravated theft (theft involving violence or threat thereof), 22.5; and for all types of theft, 4,336. In Japan, the country with the lowest crime rate of all large nations, the rate per 100,000 population for homicides was 1.2; for rape, 1.4; for aggravated theft, 212; and for all thefts 1,160. Tuvalu's rates for these same crimes in 1988, per 100,000 population, would be 0.0 for homicides, 10 for rape—though if averaged over a ten-year period the rate would be 2—and 110 for thefts of all types. Compare this to the rate per 100,000 population in England, a fairly peaceful European country (homicide, 1.92; rape, 5.7; aggravated theft, 1,690), and Tuvalu's extraordinary record becomes more clearly focused. There is virtually no serious crime.

Of course, minor infractions do occur, mostly drunkenness and fighting, but even these are not as violent as one might expect. Inspector Taafaki was quick to point out why an attack with a knife or gun is almost unheard of. "If you use a weapon in a fight here," he said, "people will call you a bloody coward, and that goes with you all your life. That is the custom of this country—anybody who use a weapon is a weak man. He is *not* a man. If people see you with a weapon in a fight, they will attack you to take it away so the fight will be fair, and then you are always known as a coward."

Somehow Tuvalu's national attitude toward the use of weapons seems correct and normal, but of course it is not the norm in the rest of the world, especially in the United States where the homicide rate in 1991 was 10 per 100,000 population. Male Americans learn from childhood that weapons symbolize manhood and virility and are the primary option in a conflict. In Tuvalu children are taught that weapons are not an option, nor is their use readily expressed in the vocabulary of islanders, though this may change as more violence-filled videos make their way into the country. Presently there are no theaters and few VCRs, though movies are shown three times a week in one or another of Funafuti's *maneapas*, or community halls. Weapons are not readily available in the country, either. Only twelve shotguns exist outside the police department, and pistols and rifles are illegal. Even if there were a market for weapons Tuvalu's diminutive size, together with its few visitors and high population density, precludes successful weapons smuggling.

Tuvalu's freedom from major crime and violence is not a product of a wealthy society. Many Westerners would consider Funafuti a tropical slum. The population density—294 persons per square kilometer—is the greatest in the Pacific and one of the highest in the world. Houses are tiny, usually only one or two rooms, and are jammed together with little privacy and few comforts. Extended families of three generations usually live together, and there is an extremely high occupancy rate: 6.8 persons per house in Funafuti and 6.2 on the other islands. In the capital more than 20 percent of families have no toilet or outhouse, 28 percent have no electricity, and nearly 15 percent must still obtain their water from public cisterns.

Tuvalu ranks among the poorest of Third World nations. Unemployment is a staggering 89 percent, though most adults are involved in subsistence agriculture or fishing. Per capita income is about U.S. $400 per year and the average wage, for those lucky enough to have jobs, is less than a dollar an hour. There is no industry, with the exceptions of tuna fishing and crafts, and little likelihood of developing any. Copra is the only crop, and now, because of health studies damning palm oil as a saturated fat that contributes to heart disease, copra prices are at an all-time low. The government is also poverty-stricken. It must depend for most of its $4 million-per-year income on the interest from a $27 million trust fund established for Tuvalu by England, Australia, and New Zealand. The government's only other major sources of income are import duties and sales of postage stamps to collectors.

United Nations and World Bank studies indicate that this tiny country, whose only natural resource is fish, and which is far from any sizable world markets, will never be self-supporting. Tourism initially was considered to be the economic savior, but owing to Tuvalu's distance from tourist markets, the lack of land on which to build hotels, and the need to import virtually everything foreigners would want, it was eliminated as a viable proposition. The social disruption and resentment fostered by luxurious enclaves of wealthy tourists were also factors in the government's wise decision not to opt for major tourist development. The country has one old, seven-room hotel, which is scheduled to be rebuilt or replaced, but so far nothing has been done.

Perhaps the absence of foreigners and their unsettling influence allows the islands' social fabric to remain intact. Aside from some Micronesians living on the island of Nui—whose forefathers arrived centuries ago from islands to the north—Tuvalu's population is almost totally Polynesian and always has been. The first Polynesians, who most likely arrived about 300 to 400 A.D., probably from the east, had the islands much to themselves for the next fifteen hundred years. The first Caucasians to visit the Ellice Islands (named by an American captain for an English benefactor) were American whalers in the early 1800s, but for most of that century little Western influence sullied traditional values.

Two beachcombers, Jack O'Brien, an Australian, and an American by the name of Tom Rose, settled in the islands around 1850, but like the few European traders who had taken up residence, usually one on each island, they observed local customs. Rose was later implicated in an outrage that still shrieks in Tuvalu history. In 1863 Peruvian blackbirders sailed first to Nukalaelae, then to Funafuti, and with Rose's assistance they assured the local people, who had heard of Christianity and were joyously eager to learn more about it, that they could go to a Christian country to learn about the new religion and then return home. Naively, 421 of them agreed and were kidnapped to slave in the Peruvian guano mines. None ever returned. If O'Brien hadn't warned many Funafutians not to board the ship, even more would have been lost. Proud O'Brien descendants still live in the islands. There are no Roses.

Britain, whose sphere of influence included the Ellice Islands, declared them a protectorate in 1892—not to safeguard the islands but rather Britain's trading rights to them. In 1916 the archipelago was upgraded to colonial status. American forces built air bases on three islands during World War II, but because of the islands' remoteness, other foreign influences remained at a minimum. Today only about fifty expatriates live in the whole country, mostly on Funafuti, working on aid projects or as consultants to the government. In general, they are considerate of the islanders' culture and careful to blend in as much as possible. They would not dress immodestly, for instance. A foreigner, or *palagi*, wandering around in, say, a bikini or even a conservative bathing suit, would shock and disgust the local people and might be approached by the police and politely requested to cover up.

Culturally, the islanders still control their own destiny, though that control is beginning to slip. Many Tuvaluans are frightened by cultural changes under way and they are adamant about protecting their heritage. Talakatoa O'Brien is one of those most concerned. A great grandson of Jack O'Brien, Talakatoa, with his curly black hair, olive skin, and flashing brown eyes, looks all Polynesian. He is the closest thing the government has to a cultural officer. While his title is Youth and Welfare Officer, a major part of his job is trying to preserve his people's culture. He plans festivals and programs and is helping to develop the nation's first cultural center and museum.

When asked how his people have managed to preserve so many of their old values—including those associated with peaceful coexistence—Talakatoa replied, "We still have extended families where the old ones teach the younger ones the correct values and we have a very strong sense of community here. It's like we—especially on the outer islands—are committed to each other. We are like one family. Everyone knows everyone else."

Inspector Taafaki had said the same thing, that unity and harmony were important considerations in day-to-day living. For people to live peacefully, so close together in such a small place, they have to get along well. Also, everyone still shares. The Western concept of "what's mine is mine" hasn't yet fully permeated the culture.

The Tuvaluan character itself makes for peaceful living. The prevailing attitude is one of gentleness, of polite interaction, of what a Westerner might call "old world courtesy," extending even to debate in the twelve-member parliament. Of course, people here do get angry, but then they have it out, usually verbally, let the other person know what they feel, and the next day, perhaps, have a reconciliation and go on with their lives. Not only are they tolerant of others but they also do not seem to carry grudges. Expats say that if you bring up past wrongs committed by another person you, the accuser, are looked down upon. "Forgive and forget" seems to be the motto.

The local outlook is radically different from that of other island peoples nearby. The Micronesian Gilbertese, to the north, have a custom the Tuvaluans call *ita fakamoemoe*, which means "to hold a grudge and to hope that you will be able to retaliate, to settle the score." The Polynesian Samoans, to the southeast, have similar customs, and in both those countries the level of violence is much higher than in Tuvalu. Prior to European intervention, intertribal or intervillage warfare was the rule rather than the exception in nearly all the neighboring island groups. Thus, the absence of internecine warfare in Tuvalu is unique in the history of the area.

No social security exists here, and as I accompanied Taafaki on his rounds I asked him how the old are cared for. "Well, in all Tuvalu families, you get married and you must have children," he replied. "You *must* have a house and you *must* have children. Then they or the grandchildren will look after you. And if your wife, she can't have children, then you must adopt some of your sister's or brother's children. If you don't adopt, then there will be no one to care for you when you are old." The house is then bequeathed to those children, he explained.

"What happens if the children don't take care of the old one or if they die before him?" I asked.

"There was a case like that on Funafuti," Taafaki answered.

"An old man with a wife and children remarried when she [his first wife] died. And she [the second wife] looked after him very well [as did the second wife's children—the man's own children did not care for him]. When he passed away the land [his house] was given to those who looked after him during his last time in life. The children of the first wife bring up their case before the lands court, for the land to be returned to them, because they are blood, but the lands court gave the land to the people who looked after him. The first children are very sad," the inspector added, "because now they don't have any chance to get the land back."

The major source of welfare assistance to Tuvalu families comes from family members working abroad and remitting part of their earnings to support their brethren at home. A member of almost every family is employed either by the government (the only domestic employer of size), overseas as a seaman on foreign vessels, or at the Naru phosphate mines. Usually a share of the wage earner's salary goes to his parents, who then divvy up the income among other dependent family members. When the breadwinner retires, or if he should become sick, he is cared for by those he has supported. In this way, in a land where there is almost no employment, everyone survives.

My poll of Tuvaluans as to the reason their country is so peaceful produces one prevailing reply: the Church of Tuvalu. Its Christian dictates permeate nearly every islander's consciousness almost from birth, and no influence is as strong as *the* Church. While not the official state religion like the Church of England, and while other faiths are permitted (Catholic, Seventh Day Adventist, Jehovah's Witness, Baha'i, and Moslem at present), the Church of Tuvalu caters to nearly all the churchgoers in the country. Or rather they cater to it.

Perhaps in no other country does a church so dominate the finances of its parishioners. Enormous pressure is imposed by the church on each family to tithe much more than the traditional tenth—often twenty-five or thirty percent of the family's total income. Isa Paeniu, brother to the prime minister and Tuvalu's former minister of commerce and natural resources, as well as a former editor of the government newspaper and for most of his life a

Church member, estimated that the average *extended* family, with an income of only $6,000 a year, might contribute $900 to $1,000 in cash, divided between their pastor and the national church fund. In addition, there are weekly cash donations, and every family is expected to make daily contributions of food to their pastor—not just rice but fish, pork, chickens, cakes, and imported foods. The pastor's yearly take in cash might be $12,000 and his food supply so large that, besides sharing it with the needy and with his friends, he will also feed it to his pigs. The fattest pigs on each island usually belong to the pastor.

How do the pastors convince their poverty-stricken congregations to part with such largess? They wield extraordinary influence.

One genial European who has been a resident of Funafuti for many years, speaks fluent Tuvaluan, and is on intimate terms with the country's customs told me: "The pastor has political power. He has taken over most of the power the chiefs used to have. And he has spiritual power because he is God's representative [in the minds of his congregation]. Even today, many people believe that a pastor can curse someone. If he gets up in church and says, 'Look, someone stole from my food safe [a screened nonelectric cooler used to store food]; that person will be eaten by sharks or will fall out of a tree and break his leg,' many people still believe that will happen. He has that power because he is God's representative."

Isa Paeniu concurred. "The belief, normally," he said, "is that if you don't give away [to the Church], you won't get any place in heaven. The pastors don't say it directly—it's a shameful thing to them now to say it directly—but they always do it indirectly. And another thing," he added, "is that they always stand up behind the pulpit and announce the names of the contributors and how much they have contributed. And if you don't [contribute] you don't get any blessings."

"The people believe they won't get a blessing from the pastor, Isa, but what about God?" I asked.

"From both," he replied. "Neither from the pastor nor from God."

Isa also accused the Church of Tuvalu of pressuring the government to abolish the competition, to deregister the other churches in the country, and by ousting them to give it a religious monopoly. Isa's accusation is corroborated by others, including the leader of the small Moslem group in Funafuti and the Jehovah's Witness minister whom the Church of Tuvalu hierarchy tried unsuccessfully to have ejected from the country. But perhaps the strongest case of persecution was against the Seventh Day Adventists.

In 1985, when Pastor Valokolone was preaching on Nanumea, the most northerly of the islands, the Church of Tuvalu pastor, who was also chairman of the island council, told him that if he didn't leave the island immediately something, presumably violent, would happen to him. On other islands, Church of Tuvalu pastors threatened from the pulpit that any of their congregations' members who went to hear the visiting SDA minister would be expelled from the Church. Persecution in the past was even more forceful. In 1949, a group of young Church men, called the Volunteers, burned two houses and a boat belonging to prominent SDAs on Funafuti. They then proceeded to destroy the vegetable gardens of most of the twelve or fifteen SDA families living on the island.

For more than one hundred years the Church has dominated island affairs. It all began in 1861 when a Cook Islands pastor of the London Missionary Society established the first mission in the islands. By 1880 LMS pastors were on each island and were so successful in their proselytizing that they reported there was not one heathen in the archipelago. The Ellice LMS was supervised from regional headquarters in Western Samoa until 1956, when it began to operate on its own, calling itself the Ellice Islands Congregational Church. In 1975 the church changed its name to the Church of Tuvalu. Today the Church, now partially funded by the World Council of Churches in spite of its bigotry—or perhaps because of it—tells visitors that its congregations comprise ninety-seven percent of Tuvalu's population. Whatever the figure, the Church is a major force within the country.

Pastor Laumua Kofee is a well-educated Funafutian who is secretary of the national Church of Tuvalu. He would not discuss church finances but was frank about the Church's desire to rid the country of other religious groups. He stated that other religions were divisive and should be banished from Tuvalu. The Church's many attempts to persuade the government to accomplish this have so far not succeeded, but its lobbying efforts go on unabated. The Church views alcohol as the other major threat to the stability of the people.

The Friday night scene at the Vaiaku Lagi provides some evidence that, indeed, alcohol plays a major role in destabilizing the society. The hotel's seven decrepit, unairconditioned rooms[1] are usually filled with foreign-aid people, technicians, or perhaps a traveling salesman on his yearly sweep of this remote island group. But the hotel is also the center of Funafuti social life. Every Friday night comes "the twist." This is not the old Chubby Checker twist. Instead it signifies a chaste shuffle reminiscent of a chaperoned sixth-grade dance at Saint Theresa's—with one major difference: Most of the males at this dance are happily, staggeringly, drunk. In contrast, the females are all drinking Coke. Tuvalu women, more than men, feel the Church's disapprobation regarding alcohol and their society's condemnation not just of an inebriated woman, but of one drinking at all. They seem resigned to the men's drinking, often having to prop up their leaning dance partners or simply dancing with other women, the only companions still able to move their feet. Many of the men sit in the corners, putting down can after can of Foster's Lager until they run out of money, pass out, or are forced to stop drinking by the genial giant of a bouncer. Arguments and fights do break out, but generally they produce no more damage than a bloody nose. Still, many families' meager incomes are diverted from food or other necessities to alcohol, and most of the "crimes" in Tuvalu are committed by males under its influence.

•

The Tuvalu National Prison sits at the end of a row of government buildings across the airstrip from the island center. Surrounded by an eight-foot fence of barbed wire over chain link, the prison's old concrete blockhouses look like World War II fortifications. The compound contains a tiny, unoccupied women's enclo-

[1] As this book goes to press, I hear that the new hotel has opened.

sure and a six-cell men's block attached to a kitchen with dining area and a rec room. Today the main gate is closed but swings wide at a touch. All the doors are open. No one is home.

I eventually find the seven male prisoners picking coconuts and clearing downed palm fronds on the grounds of a government guest house. Inspector Uaelesi quietly supervises their labor. The prisoners are innocent-looking young men, mostly in their early twenties. They are dressed only in blue prison-issue *lavalavas*. One expatriate said he recently saw the seven all standing in the back of the slow-moving government rubbish truck in their underpants, with their lavalavas fastened around their shoulders and flowing out behind them, playing Superman.

The prisoners are not looked upon as outcasts, but rather as naughty boys paying for their mistakes. Inspector Uaelesi says that most of them are in jail for drunk and disorderly conduct or for fighting. The penalties for these minor crimes are not insubstantial. The first conviction for either offense brings only a $20 fine, but the second conviction entails a prison sentence of three or four months. Conviction for theft (other than of a bicycle), even a first offense, will bring a six- to twelve-month sentence.

I ask a tousled young prisoner if being in prison is difficult. He smiles and shakes his head, no. In fact the prison is known in Funafuti as "the university." "Where is so-and-so?" someone might ask. "Oh, he's doing his degree at the university." Their life at the university does not seem bad at all, especially when compared to what they would face in outer-world jails. The prisoners cook their own meals and work in the prison vegetable garden or elsewhere on the island with a minimum of supervision. It is not uncommon for a prisoner to stop off for a few minutes during the day to say hello to his family. And the work is not onerous. One story tells of a prisoner proudly using the government's first power lawn mower in front of an admiring crowd of onlookers. The next day the prisoner was sitting in the shade while a civilian mowed the lawn and a line of islanders waited to take their turns.

Although the prison building itself is rundown, most of the young prisoners, having never been acquainted with luxury, are content with their surroundings. Then, too, with the lax security the prisoners could escape easily, but there really is no place for them to go and they are not considered risks to society. A few years ago, a slightly deranged man stole the keys to the prison and in the middle of the night unlocked all the doors, yelling to the prisoners, "You're free, you're free, you're free!" The prisoners immediately went to the warden and complained about the noise.

Geoff and Jenny Jackson, two island missionaries from Australia, pointed out that the barbed-wire fence surrounding the prison is angled out, making it more difficult, they said, for someone to break *into* than *out of* the university. They told the following story to explain this unique fencing design. "One time we had a slide show here on the island," Geoff said. "So we decided that we'd go over and show it at the prison. We went across one evening and got to where the gate is. Here's a prisoner on guard listening to the radio. So we asked him, 'Can we come in?' And he said, 'Sure, come in.' So here's a prisoner looking after things. We went in and set up everything. The prisoners came in and sat down and we started showing slides. The next thing we knew, people were hopping in the windows, people from the village who wanted to come and watch the slides. And even an off-duty policeman came in through the window. This formed our theory that the fence is to keep people from going in, rather than to keep prisoners from going out."

While little major crime exists, one crime—almost unique in the world—is perpetrated here regularly. Called sleep crawl, it is the national adolescent pastime of Tuvalu. At night a boy will sneak into a house where a girl is sleeping and lie next to her. The boy and girl may whisper together, or if she is asleep he may just lie alongside her for a while, then crawl away and disappear in the darkness. The couple may have furtive sex, but this is most unusual—and extremely daring, since in the traditional Tuvalu *fale*, and even in the more modern one- or two-room bungalow, the unmarried girl generally sleeps in the same room as her parents and brothers and sisters. So while getting in and out may be easy for a young sleep crawler, particularly through a wall-less fale, the major challenge is not to wake anyone except the object of his affection.

Sleep crawl has been going on here for at least a hundred years, but adult Tuvaluans are usually embarrassed to talk about the prac-

tice with outsiders. They feel that sleep crawl reflects poorly upon
their culture. One elderly couple, Alicia and Richard, were the exceptions. I found them in their fale. Seventy-nine-year-old Richard
(he looked to be in his late sixties) was reading; Alicia, his wife,
slightly younger and with hardly a furrow on her brow, was weaving
a mat. They had been told why I wanted to talk with them, and between giggles they recounted their *moe tolo*, or sleep-crawl liaisons,
which had taken place when they were adolescents, some sixty years
earlier.

In the puritanical Tuvaluan society of their youth, which has
not changed dramatically since then, boys and girls were not allowed to meet, secretly or otherwise, for any reason. "This is against
our custom," Richard said, "but we would meet anyway. I would
see her somewhere and tell her 'I want to come tonight.'" Alicia
blushed. "She would tell me, 'Be careful. Be careful. The boys, my
brothers, will smack you if they catch us.'" Alicia confirmed that
her very large brothers would have thrashed Richard heartily if they
had caught him. Richard said that it wouldn't have mattered. Lying
next to Alicia, whispering in her ear, kissing her—and, Richard in-
dicated, possibly more—would have been worth the thrashing had
they been caught. But they never were. "Nobody ever saw me," he
said with a wistful grin.

Besides male drinking, moe tolo appears to be the primary
symbol of teenage rebellion in this conforming society. Perhaps it
takes the place of bungee jumping in a land with no bridges, or drag
racing for a country with almost no cars or roads. Aside from the
goal of lying next to each other despite social prohibitions against
even speaking, the bravado of the act is motivation enough. A moe
tolo, whether or not successful, provides proud retellings to peers by
both boy and girl. No doubt it enhances the reputation of the perpetrators—though perhaps boosting *his* status more than hers. Yet, a
girl is proven desirable by a moe tolo attempt, which enhances her
image as well. To show their daring, boys will even try occasionally
to moe tolo a visiting European woman, though they will run like
scared rabbits if the woman should happen to awaken.

The penalties for apprehended sleep crawlers vary, from a
shake of the head by a sympathetic parent who still remembers his

or her own moe tolos, to a beating at the hands of an angry father or brother, to an infrequent four- to six-month jail sentence if the girl's relatives take the boy to court. Perhaps the most unusual punishment was recently meted out to a repeat offender caught in the act by a disgusted father and brother. After being captured, the young man was stripped and bound naked to the center pole of the house, there to spend the rest of the night while the girl's entire family laughed and went back to sleep.

10

DOWNTOWN FUNAFUTI

In the world's quiet hamlets, those endangered municipalities where engine, siren, television, and radio racket is still largely absent, you are able to pluck an individual sound from the air, to sift it, to caress it in your mind, and to savor it.

At six o'clock in the morning I am doing that. The roosters have been carrying on for an hour, but now, in the otherwise silent outer world an open bedroom window away, a muted, rhythmic scratch-scratch-scratch takes over. The women of Funafuti are raking the dirt in front of their houses. This daily ritual, as punctual as an alarm clock, is completed in an hour. Next comes the sound of soft, soothing voices, the foreign melodies of Funafutians walking sporadically down the road, not fifteen feet away. They are on their way to work, or more likely to a public bathing spot; there's one in the backyard of the small guesthouse where I am staying. A few trucks pass by carrying workers to the dock or the warehouse, but generally these motorized intrusions are over quickly. Across the road someone picks up a crying baby and cuddles it. A new day has begun.

On the lagoon side of the house the early bathers have already come and gone, but now a young man in a yellow lavalava comes down the path toward the water. He tenderly cradles a naked baby, cooing to it and kissing it. He sets it down and watches it wobble unsteadily, then take three or four drunken little steps toward him. The proud father whoops with joy, snatches his son to his chest and walks off. As they leave they greet a young woman carrying a yellow potty chair. Leaving the chair on the beach, she wades out in the shallows and washes under her sarong. Returning to shore, she deftly cleans a pair of mullet she has brought, during which time two ample-bodied women arrive. They greet her, then wander out in the shallows, spacing themselves apart, and sink down in the lagoon and wash under their lavalavas. They also rinse out small bundles of clothes. The young woman finishes her fish cleaning, washes out the potty chair, and leaves. An older man wanders up. He, too, wades out to his own spot in the shallows, equidistant from the two women, and with a bar of soap reaches up under his sarong and proceeds to lather himself.

The bathers all face away from shore. In this lifelong ritual of public bathing, they observe utmost modesty and decorum. No one watches anyone else and no extra skin is ever on display. Everyone seems composed and serene, unperturbed by the presence of the opposite sex, even though separation of the sexes is a prime cultural tenet here. Probably I am more abashed at observing the bathers than they are at being observed. Yet the changing scene outside my window is so fascinating and tells me so much about the people that even though I try not to stare, I all but ignore the pile of notes in front of me awaiting attention.

Along with a constant dribble of people, the yard holds a dozen scruffy hens and chicks, plus two imperious little roosters, all of which spend their day picking through the grass for insects. Squat palms provide some shade, though not for my sweltering little house, which is set back a hundred feet from a concrete boat ramp. A nine-foot-high steel lamppost guards the top of the ramp, and on each side low stone walls run parallel to the coral-covered beach. Homemade two- and three-man outrigger canoes lie stored in the grass. At low tide two old stone fish traps emerge from the lagoon, though I never see a fish caught in them. Farther out in the placid water, the rusted remains of a World War II pontoon float rest on a shallow coral reef.

Because big waves ceaselessly pound the weather side of the island, the sheltered lagoon here is the incubator, the central focus of Funafuti life. A long outrigger canoe with a side-mounted outboard has just gone by and now, heading in the opposite direction, comes the maritime academy's launch, smartly manned by two cadets in sailor suits with short pants and white middie caps. The academy, which is situated on a small island in the lagoon to the north, graduates forty able-bodied seamen from its year-long course. They subsequently work on foreign vessels to help support their families at home and bring badly needed foreign exchange to Tuvalu.

As I watch the boats pass, a stocky young man with curly black hair wearing a green lavalava deftly climbs one of the palms directly in front of me. Two small bottles tinkle from a cord looped around his wrist. Upon reaching the head of the tree, he empties sap-filled coconut shells that have been fastened beneath cuts made in the trunk. The empty shells go to new locations. With his bottles half filled he descends the tree, probably to tend one or two others on the island. Each family has two or three trees from which they may obtain both coconuts and sap, for later consumption as is or for fermentation into toddy, a beverage with the alcohol content of wine that is much favored by the men and that sells for a fraction of the price of imported beer.

Two little girls about five and six arrive, led by their slightly older brother and with their baby sister in tow. The children, skinny, healthy, and bronzed, are chatting and laughing, oblivious to the adult world. They are clad only in cotton underpants. Totally unself-conscious, the two older girls strip off their drawers and squat, still chatting, before scampering down the boat ramp into the shallows. Their brother strips and runs to join them. Soon they are all splashing together. Then they run naked along the wall leading to the hotel next door. Baby sister has been dawdling, not sure whether she wants to join the others. Finally, she grabs her own underpants and those of one older sister and, still naked, marches off toward home. Moments later, an angry older sister rushes off after her.

By midmorning the day has become hot and sultry. Activity slows. Two young men carrying a monofilament fishnet take the small outrigger and, with gentle, practiced movements of their spade paddles, head out into the lagoon. This may be the only capital city in the world where outrigger canoes outnumber automobiles. Midday lassitude settles over the island. The quiet is broken by a sudden *thunk* as a heavy coconut traveling about thirty miles an hour hits the ground. (The tropical warning "Don't sunbathe under a coconut palm" often goes unheeded by tourists until they see the first coconut fall.) A pretty matronly woman with graying upswept hair wearing a faded cotton dress comes to sit under the lamppole on the seawall. She stares out over the lagoon lost in her thoughts, probably in her dreams, maybe in her fantasies. After a while she leaves.

Two small boys stroll down to the beach, chatting. They space themselves a few yards apart and, with their backs to the water, drop their drawers and proceed to do their business. With twenty percent of the population using either the beach or the lagoon for their latrine, this is not an uncommon sight, though most adults squat in the shallow water. In general, a beach defecator will kick sand over his feces. Still, walking the beaches here takes on a little of the adventure of strolling through a minefield. It seems amazing that there is not more cholera and typhoid fever, especially with people bathing and cleaning fish in the same lagoon. Tourism is also affected. When tourists travel the distance required to reach Tuvalu, they usually like to be able to swim, but there is really no safe place to do it here.

The heat suffocates now, draining energy from the body like blood from a severed vein. Nearly everything has come to a stop. Only a few chickens poke listlessly in the weeds. Far out in the lagoon a man slowly paddles his canoe with rhythmic strokes. A very large woman comes to bathe. She shuffles toward the water, her hips shifting from one side to the other in unconcerned, graceful slouches as languid as the paddler's strokes. Her mind seems somewhere far away. Time has little importance here. It seems to melt, one minute into the next, one hour into another, one day into other days. Whole lifetimes could slip away. With so little to do, no one is ever in a hurry. No one even seems to know there is such a thing as time. Yawn.

A cool breeze abruptly springs from the east, a sure precursor of a downpour. Where only minutes ago the sky was blue, it is now dark. A moment passes, expectantly. Then the deluge hits. Rain pours down in drenching torrents. Rivers of water form instantly where there is any nonabsorbent surface. The little islands in the lagoon are obliterated from view. Just when I think that everyone has taken shelter, I see three little boys in swimming trunks laughing and jumping rope in the downpour. They are only sixty feet away, yet are nearly obscured by the rain. A man who has been out fishing gathers up his net. As he passes the boys he gives them each a small fish. Gleefully the boys devour the raw fish. As quickly as the rain came it is gone, leaving only the rich smell of wet soil and dripping trees.

A stocky man of about forty with a bushy mustache, wearing a soccer jersey and a bandage on one foot, inspects his canoe, then sits on the grass staring out to sea. He fishes, and one day, as he was returning with his hand net, he showed me his catch—mostly small reef fish—but there was a nice mullet which I admired. Generously, he offered it to me. With regret I declined, for I have no cooking facilities.

In the afternoon glare the islands in the lagoon look like tiny smudged pencil lines on the horizon. Far offshore an artillery barrage of water suddenly erupts. It is a school of spinner dolphins twirling like tops as they rocket five and six feet into the air. These Pacific dolphins, *stenella roseiventris,* swim in large schools, often in the hundreds, and feed on bonito and squid. No one knows for sure why the spinner engages in its airborne acrobatics, but the prevailing theory is that the behavior is simply an outlet for the animal's exuberance and high spirits, though it could also be a mating ritual. In any case, to see hundreds of spinners exploding together from the water is a remarkable sight.

Later that day I run into Tim Gentle. This kindly, bespeckled Cook Islander is the chief fisheries officer of Tuvalu. He describes a unique encounter with the school I have been watching: "We were in the center of the lagoon," he says, "in a little monohull [sailboat] and they surrounded us and followed us for hours. They were taking turns bow riding. They would pass from the stern up to the front of the boat and coast on our bow wave for a few seconds before heading off. There was one big male, I presume it was a male. It had his dorsal fin all chewed up, so I guess he'd been fighting, and he was hogging most of the time in the front. Apart from that they just seemed to take turns.

"I was interested in seeing them up close to determine how they would react to us, and we thought, what about jumping into the water and hanging from the back of the boat? It took a while for us to get up the nerve to do it. Basically, I wasn't scared of the dolphins, though they're mammals and if they're breeding the males might be antagonistic. I was worried that there might be some big sharks feeding with them or hunting them. If you want to see big sharks, the best way is to swim around a seal colony; there's always big sharks hanging around waiting for a seal that's a bit doggy. A lot of people who get attacked by great whites or tigers are doing that. So finally two of us got our nerve up, jumped off, and hung from ropes attached to the boat with our snorkels on so we could stay underwater.

"The boat was going pretty slowly, maybe a knot or so. And the most immediate impression was the tremendous noise in the water. It's just incredible. It's an amazing noise. It's like all the birds singing in an early morning rain forest, just overwhelming. And when we got in the water we saw them all around us right away. And they didn't take a lot of notice. Some of us had them approach very closely, within two or three feet, and then they took off again. But the thing I noticed most was that the ones we could see on the surface were only a small part of the whole school of dolphins below us. About sixty feet below there was almost a continuous floor of dolphins. You could see clearly in the water. We were in sort of indigo blue water, and you have a sort of searchlight effect when it's deep like that. I think it's from reflected plankton; it looks just like searchlights. It was very attractive.

"Anyway we were in the water about two and a half hours and the dolphins were coming and going. There was a lot of interaction between them. They would be jumping and so forth, and then when they saw the boat coming, they would join the boat instead. Then they would dive and join the ones below and some of those would come up, a constant interchange back and forth, just dolphins everywhere. It was fantastic," Gentle concludes.

The dolphins have disappeared. The turquoise lagoon seems

empty without them. The fisherman with the bushy mustache who offered me the mullet is back. He wears only a checkered lavalava and carries a towel over his shoulder. He wades into the lagoon, swims and bathes, then sits on the seawall staring wistfully out to sea. It seems as if he wishes he were somewhere else. I go over and talk to him.

Elia is a seaman and he looks the part. Tattoos cover his barrel chest and thick arms. He walks with the rolling shuffle of one long at sea, and his friendly brown eyes narrow in a perpetual squint. For twenty years Elia has worked for a German shipping line, sailing, he says, from Europe to the Caribbean and South America and then through the Pacific. A voyage usually takes four months, after which he has time off. He is on holiday now. He lives in a small house across the road with his girlfriend, a thin, attractive raven-haired woman in her early thirties. They have one of the better collections of popular music on the island. On his next holiday, Elia says, he and his girlfriend plan to get married. No doubt she is feeling pressure to marry; their living-together status still is rare and shocking to most of the island people.

But Elia says Tuvalu is not enough for him now. When he is on holiday he lazes in his house, talks with friends, or fishes with his hand net. Within a few days, however, he is bored and looks forward to going back to sea. Since he has seen the world, he says he can no longer tolerate the smallness of his country. He would like to move to someplace larger, but he has no great hopes of being accepted anywhere as an immigrant. He shrugs, his quiet smile personifying for me the peaceful demeanor of the Tuvaluans that I like so much.

The bells of the church, a large, rather modernistic affair near the Fusi, peal their 6:00 P.M. call to worship. Trucks pass, bringing workers home from the dock and warehouse at the other end of the island, then some motorbikes and a few motorcycles, but this traffic soon dwindles. A news broadcast drones background to nearby conversations and the occasional crying baby. Rock music thumps from Elia's house across the road. Fortunately, he and his girlfriend are considerate and soon turn it down. Then quiet again falls on the island.

I have been half expecting to hear a violent argument from one of the surrounding houses, as is so common in most other cities, but there is nothing of the sort. Considering that twenty-seven hundred people are squashed together on this small island, there is remarkably little bickering or fighting. My impression is that this is a nation of extroverts. Not only do the people survive together, but like plants in a hothouse they seem to thrive in each other's company. Talakatoa O'Brien, the cultural officer, told me that even if his people lived on an enormous island where everyone could have large pieces of land so they could live apart, they wouldn't. They still would build their houses right next to each other and congregate.

Not only do these people have the desire to be together, but they also have the ability to do so. One Tuvaluan trait is the capacity to be easy—easy with themselves and easy with others. They also love to laugh. Small moments of joy are important and the now is important. Not much time is spent worrying about the future. God will provide—or at least something will—and in the meantime, why not have a good time?

Long into the night the murmur of talking and the tinkle of gentle laughter float through the balmy air as these gentle people enjoy themselves and each other.

11

NUKUFETAU, A BLISSFULLY

ISOLATED ATOLL

When bicycles first came to Nukufetau in 1977, no other mechanized transport existed except for the government tractor. At first the small boys were the only ones who could ride. There was great resistance to the bicycle introduction, as the older people in particular predicted dire consequences and lamented that Nukufetau would never be the same again. Nonetheless, an adventuresome minority of adults soon began cycling nervously around the island.

At first it seemed that the old ones had been right. Disasters were only a pedal away. Sulus became caught in chain guards. Stately Polynesian ladies found themselves upside down in ditches with their sarongs up around their necks. Cataclysmic smashups vibrated across the island when novice cyclists traveling in opposite directions simultaneously lost control of their machines. And the local chickens, once peaceful and serene, now lived in near-constant clucking hysteria. Gradually, though, the islanders mastered this newest of Western challenges, and today the tinkle of bicycle bells is common throughout the island. Hardly anyone speeds. Riders are cautious and courteous. But most important, Nukufetau really hasn't been devastated as the old people had feared. Nor has it changed much from what it probably was like at the turn of the century. Separated from the capital, Funafuti, by fifty miles of ocean, the atoll has no airfield and the government supply ship comes only once a month. Occasionally, a foreign sailboat stops on its way across the Pacific. The rest of the time Nukufetau is by itself.

·

Today seems like a meandering sort of day and this little island, only a half-mile long, is certainly conducive to meandering. The government supply ship dropped me off the previous day, along with a small mountain of supplies and about thirty islanders return-ing from the capital. Now, to get the feel of the place, I begin wan-dering down its sandy lanes shaded by giant breadfruit and fetau, then stroll past neatly thatched fales, some with elaborately painted designs on the two-foot-high boards that form the only walls. People working or sitting outside their houses pause to offer quiet greetings, usually accompanied by a shy smile, before resuming their chores or conversations. One man is building a modern house of concrete blocks. Already he has the sheet-metal roof erected and the window spaces framed. His house will be one of only about thirty-five of the island's one hundred sixty structures that are not traditional, thatched fales.

The fale is but a simple room with a packed dirt or concrete floor. Tree-trunk cornerposts support peripheral beams, which brace pole rafters and the pandanus thatching of the roof. Aside from the knee-high wall around the outside, that's all there is—no doors and no windows. Thatched screens can be dropped at night for privacy, then rolled up during the day. Sometimes a small screened alcove is built into one corner, usually not larger than a closet, for added privacy. Outdoors, behind the fale, a fire pit, an enclosed privy, and often a tiny vegetable garden are jammed to-gether on the tiny plot allocated for each home.

Houses, packed neatly together in orderly rows, fill the large end of this key-shaped island. It's called Savave and contains the only village and most of the people living on Nukufetau atoll's fifty-odd islands. So everyone in the outside world refers to it by the atoll's name. As I wander through its tidy collection of fales, a square of sand fronting two large buildings opens before me. One building is a Spanish colonial-style church with whitewashed ce-ment, buttresses, and domed windows. The other, also of cement but newer, is a large covered meeting hall, the island maneapa. It has a sharply peaked tin roof but is otherwise open to the elements.

The maneapa's broad expanse of floor is empty, except for a group of old men sitting in one corner playing cards and a circle of women in another corner taking basket-weaving lessons from a gray-haired, wrinkled matriarch.

The lane that runs from the maneapa to the narrow end of the island is bordered by more fales. I pass a woman hanging wet clothes on a line beside her house. Another woman scrubs clothes in a plastic wash pan, and two houses down a small baby is being bathed in a similar pan. Although rainwater collection provides the only fresh water—as on most atolls—houses, clothes, and people are sparkling clean.

No washing machines or motorbikes, almost no motorized anything here—only the village's portable cement mixer and its tractor, which is used for all major hauling. The fishermen own a few outboards, and the Fusi has a generator-powered fridge and freezer. Otherwise, this is as premechanized a village as you are likely to find in an educated society anywhere in the world. And this *is* an educated society. There are a handful of college graduates and one Rhodes scholar here. The government mandates at least a tenth-grade education for all the island children. After seven years of primary school, children receive either a three-year secondary education or equivalent vocational training, though almost thirty percent of Tuvalu's young people attend privately funded church schools, usually in Fiji, Samoa, Tonga, Australia, or New Zealand.

Without thinking about destination, I have been walking toward the school, a one-story concrete building divided into five or six classrooms. It's a little past noon, and the children, nearly all barefoot, are outside for their lunch break. The boys wear short-sleeved white shirts and blue shorts, the girls, white blouses with blue cotton jumpers. They are surrounded by mothers and grandmothers bearing teakettles and covered plates or woven baskets. As I pass, the children and their sarong-clad elders are beginning to sit on the low wall opposite the school to eat lunch together. This noontime ritual is a good indicator of the closeness of families in this culture.

A few minutes later I reach the end of the island where at low tide you can wade across a coral shelf to a smaller, uninhabited island planted in coconut palms. To my right, where the teeth on the key shape of the island would start, are areas consigned to pigpens, chicken coops, and garbage disposal. Garbage is becoming a nightmare for residents of the tiny atolls as both their numbers and their reliance on foreign packaged foods and goods increase. There seems to be no practical solution but sea dumping, and the long-term ramifications of that could certainly be undesirable. Even more undesirable are the waste-strewn beaches. As on Funafuti, they and the lagoon shallows are the toilets for about a quarter of the population. It does nothing for a beautiful morning to step on a fresh turd.

I stop for a few minutes and gaze at the other islands scattered around the periphery of the lagoon. They look to be four or five miles off, but distances are deceiving on the lagoon. The tide is out and a man in black swimming trunks wades across the exposed coral, a mass of reef fish at the end of a pole resting on his shoulder. He has neither rod nor net and I wonder how he caught the fish. There is not a boat in sight. Two black reef herons fish in the shallows of the small adjacent island. No one else is about. While enjoying the feeling of solitude I suddenly sense someone behind me. Vanguna Satupa has pedaled up on his bicycle, but seeing me lost in reverie he has approached quietly, respecting my privacy, and stands a few yards away leaning on his handlebars.

Vanguna is a bright twenty-seven-year-old, tall for a Polynesian, athletic, with a full crop of hair and a bushy mustache. He is joyful and personable, yet conscientious in carrying out his various duties. Vanguna is the government clerk, responsible for recording the judgments of the island council and judiciary. He is also the island's executive officer, representing the central government on Nukufetau, seeing that its edicts are carried out. This post is an honor, for he was elected by the islanders, and Vanguna hails not from Nukufetau but from the island of Niutao, a hundred and twenty miles to the northwest.

I wish to find out about Nukufetau's political and economic structures, and Vanguna freely describes the island hierarchies. We start with the six-person island council, whose elected members are paid about two hundred dollars a year to meet one or two days a month. It supervises the maintenance of the island and its infrastructure. What power the council has comes mostly from its hiring authority: It rents out its cement mixer, its tools, and its two home-made cargo catamarans, which are used to carry coconuts and copra from the outer islands in the lagoon. It employs two coxswains to operate the catamarans, a tractor driver, treasurer, typist, carpenter, and fee collector, all of whom are paid about thirty cents an hour. In spite of the tiny wages the jobs are much in demand. Six hundred dollars a year goes a long way on Nukufetau toward feeding a family—and there aren't many other jobs.

The council establishes regulations concerning littering, rubbish dumping, evening twist hours and the like, but it has no authority over more important matters, which are decided by the central government and enforced by the court in Funafuti. A local justice settles small disputes and levies one- and two-dollar fines for minor offenses.

The central government provides eleven other paid positions, including six teachers, two dressers (medical assistants who may set broken bones and treat minor illnesses), and a constable. These people earn about the same as Vanguna, two hundred dollars a month. Six Fusi employees make seventy-five cents an hour, or one hundred twenty dollars a month. In addition to these people there may be thirty or forty locals working for the government and living in Funafuti. Perhaps another forty or fifty work overseas, either as seamen, as laborers in the Naru phosphate mines, or in New Zealand. Nearly all these people provide the greatest part of their Nukufetau families' incomes, perhaps remitting fifty or a hundred dollars a month. The only other employment is the national seawall project, a government-financed program to build a wall to protect the weather side of the island from high seas. Each adult male may work a maximum of one month per year on this project for which he is paid ninety dollars.

Vanguna tells me that about half the island's two hundred families are supported by relatives working or living in Funafuti or overseas. Another twenty-five have an employed family member on the island. This leaves seventy-five families with no major source of income. "What do these people do?" I ask Vanguna. "How do they live?"

"The only way they can make money," Vanguna replies, "is to go out fishing, or some will collect shells and make those into neck-laces that they will sell to the market. Some will weave mats. I think that's all the ways they can get money."

"It must be very difficult for these people then. They must live very poorly."

Vanguna nods, "They do. They can only buy some rice, some soap for washing, and maybe a little kerosene for their lantern."

While no one looks underfed, no one seems rich either. I don't see houses that look grand or much bigger than their neighbors', nor do I come across any individual who is flush with possessions. Most people appear to be just getting by. Vanguna, who earns more than almost anyone working on the island, tells me that his salary is not quite so good—his polite way of saying that he, his wife, and their child can barely get along on what he earns. As a government em-ployee he receives a bicycle and a fale for a nominal rent. Vanguna's family also has fifteen chickens. Most other families have five or ten pigs and a few dozen chickens, as well as a vegetable garden usually surrounded by a banana, pandanus, and breadfruit tree. Because Vanguna has no land on Nukufetau, his family must purchase their vegetables.

Two people on the island do have greater wealth than the rest, the minister and the *eleaki*, or chief. The eleaki is a jovial, heavy-set man in his late fifties. We sat with him over a cup of tea in his mod-est Western-style house while he talked about his role in the com-munity, past and present.

"I've been told that you are very wealthy. How many islands and how many pigs do you own?" I asked him.

The eleaki nodded happily. "Two islets over there," he replied, pointing in a vague northerly direction, "and one islet over there," he added, pointing toward the east. "And for pigs—round about three hundred."

"And they are on those islands along with your copra planta-tions?" Another big affirmative smile. "So who feeds these pigs? Do you do it?"

The eleaki seemed a little shocked that I would suggest he feed his own pigs. He told me that he assigns four families at a time to handle this chore. Their piggery duties last two weeks, at which time another four families take over. "What if a family refuses to do it?" I asked him. "Then what happens?"

"Then that family is not considered so good," Vanguna put in. "In the past if the eleaki tells such and such family, 'Do this,' and if they don't, then that family was totally excluded from the island."

"You mean no one would talk to them or they would be put off the island?"

"No," Vanguna answered, "they would not be allowed to any functions, any ceremonies."

I was still fascinated with all this pig wealth. "So with all these pigs the eleaki must have plenty of money." Yes, he does, Vanguna assured me. "Well does the eleaki get to spend some of this money for himself?"

"No, he doesn't." Both Vanguna and the eleaki shook their heads, the chief a little wistfully. "It's all for the good of the community," Vanguna told me. "If some old people are poor [and presumably without family], he can give some money for food to help them, or he can use some of the money, but only for the good of the entire island."

"Does the eleaki have any special powers anymore?" I asked. I was told that he does not, except as an advisor. Together with the older men of the island the eleaki meets at the maneapa. His group advises the island council and also the pastor on community matters. I thanked the eleaki and told him that I appreciated his talking with me and found it a great pleasure to be on Nukufetau. He warmly welcomed me and said he hoped I would continue to enjoy my visit.

The following day was Sunday, and along with the majority of the adults I attended morning service in the lovely old church. The pastor was already standing behind the pulpit with a stern look on his face when I came in. The church was almost full, and after dropping my shoes on the pile beside the door I quickly found a space in one of the orderly rows of parishioners, all sitting—men on one side of the aisle, women on the other—on clean woven mats covering the floor. A few moments later the pastor began speaking in Tuvaluan. The gist of the message was quite clear, however.

Quickly the pastor's voice rose in both tone and volume until he was shouting at his congregation. He didn't pound his Bible, but he might as well have. His flock seemed to have shrunk before him, turned into four hundred cowering mice. He continued to shriek at them. I was stunned. I felt browbeaten along with everyone else. People's eyes were closed or turned to the floor. Some seemed to be cringing, near tears.

Mercifully, the next items on the agenda were hymns, and everyone sang reverently together. These were followed by another blast from the pastor, some more hymns, and a final benediction. Then, quietly, everyone left. I asked some of the people I had already met what the pastor was saying. They were embarrassed to answer, but they told me he had been saying they are not good Christians and they must do better. I couldn't believe these people weren't good Christians. If the meek shall inherit the earth, the people of Nukufetau will certainly be first in line. It seemed incomprehensible that screaming at these gentle islanders would make them better than they already are.

The next day I went to see the pastor. Seve Iotama greeted me in a newly pressed sport shirt and sulu. He was a young-looking man for his sixty-six years, and with his black pompadour and aviator's sunglasses, he looked more like a playboy than a minister. Nervously he puffed on an unfiltered cigarette as he ushered me into his ranch house, the largest and most luxurious on Nukufetau. Minister Iotama led me through one room after another, each with hardwood floors and well-worn, good-quality furniture. He told me he was married and had four grown children, now on their own. When we were seated in his parlor, I asked him about yesterday's sermon.

"This Is the Way—Follow It, was what I called my sermon," he said. "There is *only* one way, Jesus Christ, and you *must* follow it," he added.

I said that his congregation seemed so devout, so pious, why did he feel he must shout at them and threaten them?

Pastor Seve apparently was not used to anyone questioning his preaching tactics. He sputtered and only repeated the message of his sermon. We went on to discuss other subjects. He said that the original church, still standing but remodeled and now used as a Sunday school, was built in 1865 and was the first building on Nukufetau. The present church was built in the 1920s. After describing the history of the Church of Tuvalu, he began to rail again, this time against the destabilizing influences on Nukufetau. First, he lambasted the dances, or twists, which, he said, "turned the minds of the young boys and girls upside down"—this in spite of the rule that males and females must dance apart and may not attend dances at all until they're eighteen. Then he attacked the other Christian religions, which "only half-believed in Christ," and finally, pointedly, he denounced *outside meddlers*. Though he never specified what area was being meddled with or who the meddler was, the object of his anger was never hidden. I could feel Pastor Seve's eyes glaring at me behind his aviator glasses.

Well, touché. I asked him how many pigs he had. Then, in my most polite, lighthearted tone, I continued, "Do you use some of the food donated by your congregation to feed your pigs? And when the pigs are sold or slaughtered, does any of the money or food go to help the poor of Nukufetau?" Silence. It was as if the pastor had suddenly gone deaf. It was also the end of the interview.

From other sources I found out that Pastor Seve didn't have as many pigs as the eleaki, but he had more than a hundred, fed partly with food contributed by the parishioners, and most, if not all, of the pig profits stayed in the minister's pockets.

While the Church is an important thread in the Tuvalu fabric, so is the family. Here "togetherness" has an old-fashioned meaning: Many Tuvaluans live three generations in the same small house, apparently in harmony, without the divisive influences common in the West. Once I became friendly with nearby families, they began to share feelings about their lives. The Botongo family, who lived down the road in a tiny Western house, was particularly open; married daughter, mother, and grandmother all consented to be interviewed together.

Frieda, the bright, independent, twenty-four-year-old daughter who had been married only about a year and had a two-month-old daughter, did most of the translating, since neither her mother nor grandmother spoke much English. Mafua, Frieda's mother, was fifty-five. She had been born on the island as had her mother, Laki, who was twenty years older. Laki's marriage had been arranged when she was thirteen and consummated when she was sixteen. Her husband, now dead, had been a minor chief who, before the war, had been responsible for carrying out the edicts of the most powerful eleakis. Most of their ten children died early, usually from childhood diseases. Mafua's marriage had also been arranged by her parents, when she was sixteen. Since her husband had worked for the colonial and then the Tuvalu government, the family had spent some years living in the Marshall Islands. Mafua had nine children of whom Frieda was the youngest and the only one still at home.

The three generations viewed their culture very differently. Mafua and Laki lamented the weakening of their old customs and especially the traditional values, though they all agreed that the two main influences changing the culture were foreign videos, which had an especially negative effect on the children, and education—particularly when older children went abroad, as had Frieda. After having attended the national secondary school on Vaitupu, Frieda went to college for three years in Fiji, then returned to work for the Red Cross, assisting handicapped people on the island.

Frieda's grandmother had perhaps the strongest views. "I don't like our culture to be fading away," she said. "It's really hard to bring it back. We are taking on other people's customs."

Mafua was nearly as adamant. "I prefer that *all* the old customs still existed. In the olden days the young people are respectful and they are not, you know, cheeky like her generation," she said with a dismissive nod toward Frieda. "It's what I learned," Mafua continued. "When your parents talk to you, you just keep quiet and listen. Or when you see an old person carrying something, you help that person. A young person doesn't shout when old people are around. Nowadays they just swear or do anything when older people are around."

Frieda herself remembered growing up in a traditional household. "When I was young, before secondary school, I feared my mother 'cause she used to beat me up when I talked back to her. But after going away to school I felt I had a right, you know, to talk back to her—well, not talk back, but to give my opinion if it's different from hers. And when I argued with her she would say, 'You know, you are very different today. You learn those new things from school and you think that you are cleverer than me.' She would say, 'I don't like you talking like that,' but just lately, in the last three years, she accepts when I talk back. She understands."

Defiantly, Frieda shook her head. "I'm for the Western way," she said, "so women can run their own family and live by them-selves and be independent. Because in our culture even though you're married, you're still under your husband and your husband's parents, or your parents. And to me, as a woman, I don't want any-one to boss me around."

Laki and Mafua disagree. They both feel that the traditional way is better, even if the man is the boss. Laki said that the old life was a happy one. She prefers the traditional food, like fish and pulaka, which they can get easily (and inexpensively). That's the way she wants to live. Frieda added that it is a sociable life, that all the family is together, not like Western societies where the husband and wife live apart from the rest of the family.

Having made this point, however, Frieda returned to the ad-vantages of Western culture, not only for herself but especially for her daughter. "I want my daughter to be educated well and to travel around the world to different kinds of places and to work for the people, like helping people, dedicating her life to serving others," she said. "And I want her to be able to have any kind of job she wants, like maybe a pilot, and to go to church where she would like to go and not be forced to go to *this* church. So that's why I see some good in foreign cultures."

But even Frieda appreciates many of the values instilled by her culture and passed on by the older generations. "At times the older people will advise us how to behave," she said. "When I got married I was really stubborn, you know. I don't want my husband to tell me what to do. Whenever I want to go out, I just go without asking him or informing him that I'm going somewhere. And I just come home anytime I want to. So my grandmother told me not to behave like that because our marriage will end up [badly], you know, won't be a good marriage if I continue to be like that. And she said, to be a good wife I have to listen to my husband and share, and try to forget my own life, just share with my husband, everything, and discuss [things with him]. If I don't agree with him, I have to talk to him instead of just yelling at him, you know."

Apparently Frieda feels that her grandmother's advice was valuable and helped her marriage. Although not as common as in the West, marital strife and divorce do exist, and single-parent families are often the result.

Two other women I talked to mentioned male drinking as the reason for their divorces. When I questioned them a little more, it appeared that wife beating was also part of the picture. While I didn't see anyone drinking beer here, I was told that men do drink, often to excess, though women don't. One of the two young divorcées was about twenty-eight and had a ten-year-old child. I asked her if there were many divorces, and she said, "Oh yes, many." There were many women living without husbands. She said that Nukufetau was a good place for her to live, that she could go safely to dances and that there were many men who either had never married or who also had gone through a divorce; so she had a counterpart group. Both these young women seemed a little sad, however—left out of a society in which the great majority of women are married and where the strength of a complete family unit is almost always in evidence.

Lack of a mate is viewed here as a greater problem than in Western societies, where a man usually does not participate as much in child rearing. This is true even though the extended family is more active here. Babies in Tuvalu hardly have their feet touch ground because there is always an auntie, cousin, or grandparent who is delighted to hold them. During my visit to Vanguna's house I watched him carrying his eight-month-old baby while his wife was busy. Suddenly, he had to get something from the garden and without a moment's hesitation walked next door and handed the baby to a woman there. When asked about it, he said, "Oh, that's one of my cousins."

Apparently, the disciplining of the children has not changed much. One long-time observer of the local scene told me that errant children, especially teenagers, are severely scolded and sometimes physically beaten, and they always feel great pressure to fit into their

place in the family and community. If nothing else works with a rebellious teenager, the parent will usually say something like "Well,
if you continue to misbehave and to ignore what I tell you, you
won't get any land from me." In a society where land is almost everything, that final threat usually is effective.

Though discipline is severe, it is tempered by understanding
and even empathy. My informant told me that a young girl found
pregnant before marriage is considered a disgrace here; there is always big trouble in the family because of it. Yet, if you were to talk
to some of the older people, they may have done exactly the same
thing themselves and they might say, "*Mea o te olaga*," or "Oh,
that's just part of life." And, of course, any baby born out of wedlock
is immediately adopted and lovingly reared by the grandparents if
the mother is too young to bring it up. For a while the girl might
find difficulty being accepted, but in almost all cases she eventually
marries, if not the baby's father then someone else. Even in this
most serious of social situations, the family loves and supports their
child. They will not turn away from her.

.

I didn't think that a dugout canoe under sail could skim over
the water in a light breeze, but this one does. Fappiano, the silver-
haired fisherman who built the boat and sails it every day, sits in the
stern with the sheet in his right hand while holding a steering paddle
against the transom with his left. Vanguna sits in front of him,
watching Fappiano and getting a sailing lesson. Since there is no lagoon on Vanguna's home island, he has never been taught to sail
and he is eager to learn. I am in the bow continually asking questions and screwing up the sailing lesson.

We are headed toward Motulalo, the island at the southeast
corner of the lagoon five miles from Savave, where we plan to fish
with the net we have brought. The day is lovely. A wisp of a wind
gently propels the outrigger over the water. Small white powder
puffs, cirrocumulus, dance across the sky, and before us a pair of
crested terns skim the lagoon, easily outdistancing our boat in the
light breeze.

The twenty-foot canoe has only a small sail laced to a sharply raked, thirteen-foot mast benched near the bow. A spar attached to the gunnel near the stern is bound to the mast close to the top. The rig is supported by a rope stay on the other side. When the boat comes about or jibes, the stay and the spar must be reset. Fappiano accomplishes this maneuver quickly and easily by himself, but I wonder how simple this feat would be in a strong wind. I ask him how closely he can sail to the wind, and with only slight shifting of sheet and steering paddle, he brings us up until the boat is only about fifteen degrees off the wind direction. That seems very good indeed.

Sailing canoes, particularly dugout sailing canoes, have nearly disappeared from the South Seas. A few are used on some of Tuvalu's other islands, but only on Nukufetau are they still the predominant form of lagoon transportation. Besides Tuvalu, they are used on a daily basis only on Wallace Island and a few Fijian islands. Although sailing canoes can still be seen in Kiribati, they are built from timber planking. In the rest of the South Pacific they have been relegated to museums.

Fappiano guesses that half of Nukufetau's population, women included, know how to sail. He says that on most days ten or twelve small canoes like this one are taken out by the island's fishermen. Larger canoes, some more than thirty-five feet and with a capacity of fourteen hundred pounds or ten people, are used as translagoon cargo carriers to haul coconuts or pulaka between islands. The children learn to sail in their early teens and soon become skilled enough to be trusted with their own canoes. Though many sailors have been caught in bad storms, no Nukufetau has ever failed to return.

In a little over an hour we are in the shallows near Motulalo. With no keel or fixed rudder, we sail right up to the beach, arriving just in time to miss a torrential downpour. Motulalo is larger than Savave, yet the dozen families here live in very poor and dirty conditions. They share the island only with rats, coconut crabs, and zillions of flies. I have never seen so many flies. They swarm over everything but nobody seems to mind. I am the only one they are driving crazy. We talk to a few of the families, then walk through the bush to look at the overgrown remains of a landing field built by the Seabees in 1942 to launch B-24s against Japanese forces on Tarawa, to the north.

Returning to the boat, we take the net into the shallows and stretch it out parallel to the beach, where we leave it. We wade back to the beach, space ourselves, then head toward the net, driving darting silver flashes before us. In forty-five minutes we have caught nearly twenty pounds of small reef fish, enough to feed seven or eight families. Fappiano will not sell the extra fish. Instead he will give them to neighbors and relatives. They in turn keep him supplied with vegetables, eggs, toddy, and the occasional chicken or piece of pork.

A line squall darkens the horizon to the south, and as we head back it overtakes us. Within a few minutes the light breeze is replaced by a fierce, gusting wind. Fappiano takes it on the port quarter to keep the outrigger down and to prevent the boat from going over. Only six inches of freeboard separate us from the sea, and the wind-driven waves begin sloshing over the side with alarming regularity. Vanguna and I bail continuously using coconut shells but only manage to keep the water in the bottom of the boat from rising. Yet as quickly as the squall came it disappears, taking the last breath of wind with it and making us paddle the final mile back to Savave.

Later in the day Vanguna and I stop at the edge of the village where four men are building a canoe. They have felled and hollowed out a large puka tree (*Hernandia*) using only axes and an adz. Timbers hewn from the tree have been joined to the sides of the hull with coconut-fibre twine and sealed with tar to provide another eight inches of freeboard.

The men are shaping the hull. Wood chips fly as the skilled islanders, using short strokes, carefully reduce the bottom thickness to two inches and the sides to but half an inch. The finished canoe will be nineteen feet long, carry two fishermen, and weigh less than seventy pounds, including the outrigger and mast—also to be made from puka saplings. Except for tar to caulk the few seams, the boat is built entirely with local material. The owner and his three friends will take only two days to build it, and with luck and good care it will last twenty years. The cost? Almost nothing, although there is a shortage of trees from which future canoes can be built.

The canoe owner will not pay his helpers except to supply them with fish or to take them fishing. When they need assistance, however, he will be there. More important, if one of them should become incapacitated or die, it is likely he will play a major part in feeding and caring for that person's family. The spirit of cooperation and sharing still shines brightly here, fostering a camaraderie and unity that are fundamental to the well-being of the society.

Tonight I am to go with Vanguna and his wife, Sunia, to a *fatele* at the maneapa. This afternoon, however, I plan to laze. Though it will feel good, too much lazing would be difficult to take. Most Westerners couldn't adjust to the low level of activity here. In fact, they would go bonkers or become alcoholics. The islanders possess a languidness, a complacency, that seems necessary for survival on a tiny atoll with almost nothing to do. They develop a daily ritual of gardening, cooking, and fishing. But more than that, their lives have a natural rhythm that long ago disappeared in clock-watching societies. This is not a distrustful, neurotic society. On the contrary, the sanity and contentedness here are enviable. True, some inventiveness and individuality are sacrificed. There is a saying that peaceful Switzerland, which has not been involved in a war for four hundred years, in that time produced nothing greater than the cuckoo clock. So it is in Tuvalu. But maybe the lack of those traits we value so highly is no loss but rather a gain for the collective sangfroid. I ponder this as, along with most of the islanders, I lie down for my midday siesta.

At dusk I accompany the Satupas to the maneapa. Since no children are allowed, babysitters watch the small ones left at home. Sunia has left her baby with her cousin. We carry covered plates and bowls filled with food that we three have prepared under Sunia's direction. Besides rice and pulaka—which tastes like hard, flavorless boiled potatoes—we bring tiny reef fish fried whole to a succulent crispiness, a dish made with lau lau (a green-leafed vegetable mixed with onions in coconut milk), and banana blended with coconut milk for dessert. We have also brought a pandanus fruit, which looks like a golden pineapple and breaks into short carrot-shaped segments that even taste like a sweet carrot. People carry this fibrous fruit around and chew on it as if it were sugar cane.

Many adult families are already at the maneapa when we arrive. Kerosene lanterns hanging from the pillars cast an amber glow over the room. We find an unoccupied space along the periphery and seat ourselves on the floor, leaning against the two-foot-high wall. People are packed around the room's edges, leaving the center of the floor open for the eight island dignitaries who sit facing each other. I recognize the eleaki, the minister, the president of the island council, and one or two others. All are busy eating and talking.

When most everyone has finished eating, the president of the island council stands and addresses us. A recently retired seaman, he seems worldly compared to many of the others who have never ventured outside Tuvalu. He tells us that the fatele tonight is the opening contest in the yearly games celebrating Tuvalu independence. The maneapa team will compete against the *aulotu*, or church, team, though the names have no significance except to designate the two dancing and drumming teams drawn from all the islanders. The president wishes both sides luck and ends by saying "May the best team win."

Ten dancers stand in two rows just to one side of the center of the floor. They are dressed in T-shirt and shorts covered by woven pandanus skirts. In front of them six men are seated around a hollow wooden platform, eighteen inches high by about eight feet square. The platform—actually a drum called a *pokisi*—is beaten in unison by the pokisi players. The dancers, called *saka*, move to the beat of the drummers.

The pokisi players start with a fairly slow beat; their dance team moves arms, shoulders, and feet in rhythm to it. There are no hip movements anymore because the church has outlawed them as too suggestive, so the dancing seems hollow and unexciting compared to dances performed in many South Pacific countries. Still, the audience takes great pride in their teams and as the pokisi's tempo increases and the dancers step faster and faster, they become caught up in the competition. The tempo continues to increase until, with a great drumming flourish almost deafening to the spectators, the exhausted players collapse on their drum.

There is polite but enthusiastic applause and the second team takes the floor. It performs a similar piece, or so it seems to me, uneducated in the nuances of both the drumming and dancing, until finally, after ten minutes, these players also fall exhausted on the pokisi. The dancers wipe the sweat from their foreheads and the first team takes the floor again. The two teams alternate, each trying to outdo the other in enthusiasm and rhythm. The tempo continues to increase, the drummers pounding to the limit of their abilities, as the fatele reaches its climax.

With a roar the last team completes its final routine. The eight judges sit together to decide the winner. Finally, the president of the council stands and announces that because the teams were so evenly matched the judges have declared the fatele a tie. Since this is not a competitive society, the spectators and performers both seem satisfied with the outcome. Everyone applauds the two teams, now standing in the center of the room, and all the families pick up their dishes and file out of the maneapa.

We walk back through peaceful, darkened lanes. Only the occasional glow of a lantern or flicker of a candle in a nearby house, or here and there the tiny beam of a flashlight, makes some fleeting penetration into the night. Far above us, though, the sky is filled with light. Brilliant stars, signposts for the navigators, blink reassuringly from their distant domains.

I feel a sense of personal security, of absolute safety, here. It is a blithe, carefree feeling that I had forgotten existed. What a wonderful society that can still provide such lighthearted sanctuary. No wonder foreigners try to get local families to adopt them so that they can become citizens of Tuvalu. This little country, in spite of its various problems, produces a commodity almost unique now on our earth. May these fine people appreciate what they have and continue to nurture those qualities and values that produce it.

My time on Nukufetau ends too quickly. A sailboat that I have arranged for arrives from Funafuti, and early one morning I say good-bye to my new friends. Within an hour, sadly, I watch the little island disappear in the distance—a beautiful dream vanishing over the horizon.

IV

The Solomon Islands

A CANNIBAL'S LIFE

12

TIMOTHY,

ARE'ARE ASSASSIN

After a day at sea in a cramped outboard-powered canoe, the simple thatched village of Houhui looks like
Mecca to a pilgrim. We started at seven that morning
before the wood-fronted shops on Auki's single street
had even opened. Heading down the coast from Malaita's only
town, Edward, the stoic Indian-looking boatman, and I have endured bad weather for almost half of the island's one-hundred-
twenty-mile length. Now, after getting hit in the face with a dozen
waves a minute for nearly seven hours, as our canoe pulls up on the
village beach I am so numb that I can hardly stand up. When I hit
the sand my knees buckle, and only by grabbing the side of the boat
do I keep from falling flat on my face.

I am on my way to a distant village to talk with the only surviving practitioner of cannibalism in the Solomons. My introduction
to this area had been arranged by David Kausumae, a self-made
Solomon Island mogul, politician, and elder statesman, who is also
a local chief. David had tried to set up contacts for me, but owing to
Houhui's remoteness he had been unable to reach Mathew and
Lysander Namo, the two brothers who are to guide me to the interior village where Timothy, formerly a tribal assassin, is still hanging on to life.

My contacts, the Namo brothers, turn out to be thoughtful,
balding men in their forties. They received primary and some secondary education at Auki, the only town on Malaita, and have
worked as clerks, storekeepers, and managers of various small island
enterprises. Naturally, the brothers are astonished to see a white

man popping up in their remote village. It has been two years since they last received a foreign visitor. However, Lysander, Mathew, and both their families are warm and hospitable. I am immediately invited to stay in Mathew's house and share the evening meal. His ten-year-old son is sent out to kill a rooster, a task to which the boy is barely equal. The rooster and some vegetables from the Namo garden, together with food I have brought from Honiara, provide a bountiful dinner.

Mathew's house contains a low-ceilinged main room, two sleeping rooms, and a small kitchen. Like the few dozen other village dwellings, it is thatched with leaves from the sago palm, and its floors are constructed of split trunks of the betel nut palm. Jungle vines lash together all the structural and covering pieces. No nails and little purchased material can be found in the entire village. And short of being hit by a hurricane, the houses usually last ten or fifteen years. The village's water comes from a standpipe connected to an underground spring. The community latrine consists of an exposed seaside hole in the coral shelf over which all and sundry must squat. Under the squatter flows the Pacific Ocean.

The evening of my arrival, a group of the senior men of the village gathers with us in Mathew's house, and we talk in the dancing shadows thrown by a single kerosene lamp. The village elders all agree that their tribe, the Are'are, along with the Kwaio, their neighbors to the north, had been the most bloodthirsty clan in the Solomons. The elders also say that the two tribes had similar attitudes toward women, who were regarded as expendable. In the living hierarchy, women ranked only above the pigs—they had both a monetary and labor value, but no other worth. When there was a reward put forth for a life to be taken in revenge for a past wrong or killing at the hands of another tribe, a woman would always be sacrificed rather than a warrior, who could help to save the entire group. The Are'are were not worried about bearing sufficient numbers of children. The main problem in the mountains, where it was difficult to grow food, was being able to feed those they had. In most other respects, Are'are and Kwaio customs were also similar.

Blood feuds between clans or villages were frequent, not unlike feuds between Scottish clans or perhaps family vendettas in Sicily or American Appalachia. Often a violation of the strict sexual codes against adultery or premarital intercourse precipitated a killing, but theft or putting a curse on your neighbor was also grounds for war. The most common motive, however, was revenge—for the killing of a family member or friend. The aggrieved had three options: to request compensation in pigs and shell money,[1] to avenge the wrong himself, usually by murdering the wrongdoer, or to put up a bounty of pigs and shell money for someone else to commit the act of revenge. In that case, a warrior, called a ramo, by using trickery or surprise, carried out the act of vengeance in return for the agreed-upon bounty. Generally speaking, the first murder led to a spiral of vengeance killings that sometimes went on for years and could claim even distant relatives, such as aunts, uncles, or cousins of the perpetrator as substitute victims.

These tribal practices changed dramatically in the late twenties, however, after the Kwaio massacred District Officer William Bell, his young assistant, and twelve Solomon Island constables (see page 227 for a description of this incident). As a consequence, the colonial government clamped down on intertribal killings. Tribal life changed again in the 1950s, when missionary conversions led many mountain people to surrender their old ways. Houhui and most of the surrounding villages, including the one where Timothy lives, are now predominantly Baha'i. In fact, Mathew claims that the Baha'i faith, which he says asserts the unity of the world's religions and of the human race, is the primary religion for about a third of the Solomon Islands people.[2] This faith is popular, he says,

---

[1] Shell money was, and still is, the most common medium of payment used by the Kwaio and other mountain peoples. Its value is based on the color and type of small rounded shell pieces pierced and strung together. Usually, a certain length of shell money is required for a certain transaction; for example, ten three-meter-long strings of red and white shells would be the average bride price, equal to U.S. $250.

[2] This figure is disputed by the other religions and by government statistics (1976), which show that 34 percent of the population belonged to the Church of Melanesia (Evangelical), 19 percent were Roman Catholics, 17 percent were South Sea Evangelicals, 11 percent belonged to the United Church, 10 percent were Seventh Day Adventists, 5 percent were unknown, 3.6 percent were pagans, and only half of one percent belonged to the Baha'i faith.

because it allows the villagers to retain many of their old pagan beliefs and cultures, whereas the Christian sects force them to give up the old beliefs completely upon accepting Christianity.

.

The following morning, dawn is just breaking as the orange canoe, with Lysander in the bow, heads down the coast toward the Wairaha River. In less than a half hour we are at the river mouth, which is fronted by a sandbar neatly sandwiched between two sandstone cliffs and almost invisible from the sea. A point to the south shelters the entrance to the river, but because of the extreme dry season the water level is so low that everyone must get out and push the canoe over the bar. Just inside, the river becomes deep again, and with a cough the outboard roars to life and the last part of the journey begins. On our left, high up on the sandstone cliff, are two caves, one above the other. The upper cave, which can be reached only by a narrow ledge, was where the local people, an Are'are sect called Ausi, kept the skulls of their ancestors. In the bottom cave pigs were sacrificed by the local priest; the unhappy squealers met their end in the jaws of sharks which, according to Lysander, congregated especially for the occasion when summoned by jungle drums. Five miles upriver is another *tambu* (taboo) area where pigs were sacrificed to resident crocodiles.

While all the people in the area are Are'are, they belong to many subtribes. When asked whether his people belong to the Ausi clan, Lysander replies, "Not really closely, but we have common relations. We don't have the right to sacrifice, but if there is a problem, even within our own tribe, the priest would do the pig [sacrifice] for solving that problem. So if there was a sickness or something, then the priest would make a sacrifice."

Lysander says that an old priest by the name of Jack, who used to perform all the sacrifices, died at the age of eighty, in the early 1960s. The villagers had great faith in his powers, but not long after he died these same villagers shot the remaining crocodiles and sold their skins to a buyer in Honiara. The crocodile buyer is just about out of business now because he has already bought the skin of most of the crocodiles in the Solomon Islands. Unfortunately, neither the government nor the people have yet learned the value of the conservation of species.

The Wairaha River has reached as far as two hundred yards across. It is the largest river in Malaita—in fact, in all of the Solomons—and is fed by dozens of small streams that cascade from the island's mountainous central spine. But now the river is shallow in many places. We have just had to push the canoe a quarter of a mile upstream over another sandbar. Once we are in deep water I hop in again, hot and wet and excited to be in this beautiful, untamed place. We are in a river valley that extends a quarter mile on one side of the river and maybe a half mile on the other.

In front of us tree-covered hills rise sharply until they disappear in a cloud bank. The trees are all broad-leaf evergreen, but instead of the umbrella tops common to many tropical rain forest hardwoods, these have a few large branches with only scraggly foliage at their tips. Most hardwood species have telephone-pole-straight trunks towering up a hundred feet before big branches dart off at crazy, sharp angles, and some have buttresses fanning into the red clay beneath them, but those are slight compared to the enormous eight- and ten-foot-high buttresses at the base of trees in most tropical rain forests.

This, in fact, is not heavy rain forest. Tree trunks are clearly visible, and while some lianas and creepers climb or hang from limbs, they are not abundant. Nor are there many tree ferns or other forms of parasitic foliage. Tree outlines are also very distinct. So rainfall here must be much less than in some of the western Solomons or northern areas of Vanuatu, where hundreds of inches yearly spawn so much plant growth that the entire forest is camouflaged by masses of parasitic growth covering even the tops of all but the tallest trees.

We pass small thatched villages, one every few miles. Usually, one or two inhabitants lounging by the river will wave or call out a greeting and stare incredulously as our orange canoe curves out of sight. Twice, women going about their morning baths in naked splendor hastily snatch a sarong and cover themselves as the canoe flashes past.

We motor past a lovely pool bounded by smooth, giant boulders. Lysander says this was another holy place of sacrifice. Here lived an old crocodile as large as the canoe—more than twenty feet long—which the people used to worship. This crocodile belonged to the village we just passed. Each tribe, it seems, had their own crocodiles. I ask Lysander, for the third time, whether they used to sacrifice people or only pigs. Either he has not heard the question or he has heard it and hasn't wanted to answer it. Finally he says, "No. No people, only pigs."

By now we have stopped eight or ten different times to push the boat over shallows. The river is still a hundred yards across, but there are more and more little islands that will surely be buried by the next rainy season. Judging from driftwood and vegetation along the banks, the river will probably rise ten feet or more when the rains come. For the most part, the water is very clear, swirling cleanly over a gravel and river-rock bottom. Pushing the boat over this riverbed is a chore, since one can easily take a spill or twist an ankle on the round, mossy rocks.

An occasional bittern, fishing from a gravel bank, flies up with slow, powerful wing beats at our approach. Flights of large brown ducks rise into the air, circle above us, and then with a low glide land on another pond downstream. They are Australian gray teal that have made their yearly dry-season migration here and are feeding on plants, insects, and small river fish and prawns. A big snake-eating hawk has also been keeping his eye on us as he makes lazy wheels four or five hundred feet above the cliff tops. As we penetrate farther inland, limestone cliffs crowned with heavy forest rise higher and higher on each side of us.

It is early afternoon when we come around a bend to see children playing in the shallows of a stream where it joins the main river. Ohio (pronounced Oh-hee-oh) is the name of this stream, as well as the village that is our destination. We climb steps dug into a high bluff and at the top find ourselves in a grassy glade. Around its periphery stand neatly thatched huts and the village's two communal buildings—a tin-roofed, open-sided school and meeting room, and what seems to be the men's house. Ohio is an extraordinarily well-kept village, and from its grassy, open center one looks out on the river twisting between verdant ridges and on valleys of unbroken

Malaitan rainforest. To the west lie the jungle-covered mountains forming the island's spine.

.

Lysander has stepped into a nearby hut and presently reappears leading a sinewy, gaunt old man wearing only a faded sarong fastened around his waist by an old belt with a new silvery buckle. Timothy leans heavily on a long walking stick but seems to be exceptionally healthy for a man more than one hundred years old. As he approaches, he looks as though he is crying, and his weeping eyes are covered by a semitransparent film. His near blindness suggests that he has trachoma, a disease caused by an organism that is a cross between a bacterium and a virus. Trachoma is the number-one cause of blindness in Third World countries where people like Timothy do not have access to tetracycline and other antibiotics that can quickly cure it. Since he has had this condition for years, it probably is too late to restore his sight. However, he seems to have found an inner peace, a state of grace in which he is no longer concerned with day-to-day problems, sickness, or worries. If he is blind, so be it. If his nose runs, let it run. Peace, fond memories to savor, and joy from today's simple pleasures: These are the coin of his present realm. He sits on one of the roughly carved schoolroom benches, chatting quietly with Lysander, chuckling at some small joke, while his eyes gaze off at another world.

The room has filled to capacity with villagers of all ages eager to hear Timothy's account of his past. Lysander begins by telling me a little of Timothy's early history. He was a warrior with children and grandchildren at the time of Bell's murder in 1927, and so he is approximately one hundred years old. His original name was Riki-hanua, and he was born in the village of Rokada farther up in the mountains. "He was adopted," Lysander says, "for the reason that his mother was killed when he was two months old, and so the grandmother adopted him and [somehow produced] milk from her breast and became the nursing mother."

"How did his mother die?" I ask.

"She was killed by someone because they suspected her of stealing. But actually she didn't. But any bad reputation has to be blamed [on someone] in their tribe. So anyone who is blamed—for the satisfaction of the other [accusing] side—they [her own tribal members] have to kill her, especially if she is a woman."

"So even her own people would kill her if anyone even *accused* her of stealing? During those times was there much killing of people from within your own tribe?" I ask.

"Was too much," Lysander replies. "Very much."

"Was Timothy one of the leaders of the tribe?" I ask.

"He was not regarded as a chief," Lysander answers. "Through his life he was more highly respected for the rank of warrior."

From this point on, I ask questions of Timothy directly, instructing Lysander to translate as closely as possible the meaning of Timothy's answers.

"How did you become a warrior?" I ask.

"I became a warrior," Timothy answers, "[by] fighting my way up [to] being a warrior, by putting myself into courageousness to fight, and if a man could achieve that, then he is a warrior."

"Were you stronger than most men, or tougher or better with a spear or a knife or whatever you use—a musket? What kind of weapons did you use?"

"During those days," Timothy replies, "we were using bow and arrow mainly to fight, though we were also using the muskets. And we are fighting in an [organized] place because it has to be arranged, and before that [before a battle was to take place] we were building defensive wall around our village."

"Did you also use the spear and the knife or the axe?" I ask.

"Yes, that is known [used], yes," he answers.

"How many warriors would there be in a tribe, in a village? Would the village be the same size as this, or larger?

"Yes, the villages just about this size," he says, "some even smaller."

"So how many people are here?" I ask Lysander.

"About, say, hundred fifty," he answers.

"And so in this size village, Timothy, how many warriors would there be?"

He says, "That can't be graded [computed] because everybody goes to war when there is a war."

"So every man helps to defend the village." I continue, "But if there are special warriors, how many special warriors?"

Timothy says, "In a village, through fighting, [one goes up the ranks]. In those wars, anyone could be called upon to receive a ransom or himself to go to fight. There's no one appointed warrior."

"If there was an argument between your tribe and another tribe close by, and somebody in your village had been offended or killed, the family of that person would put up a reward, would put up money to have you avenge the wrong. How much would it be?"

Timothy and Lysander confer together on this question.

"A ransom would be today over two thousand dollars [Solomon Islands dollars, equivalent to U.S. $1,000]. Shell money, our own money," Lysander answers.

"Over two thousand dollars?" I gasp at the enormity of the amount. Later I reflect that this is what it would cost *now* to buy the amount of shell money that Timothy has mentioned. The barter amount *then* might have been much less, eight or ten pigs, for instance.

"You were using shell money then. So they would pay Timothy to kill someone of another tribe?"

"No," Lysander answers. "That has to be paid *after* he has achieved the purpose. When putting up a ransom, they don't go to any particular warrior, they just send notice that there is a ransom put for anyone [to kill a particular person]. So he was hunting with other warriors, and whoever would get hold of [kill] this guy [would get the ransom]."

"Well, who did he kill when he was a warrior?" I ask. "Ask him to tell us the stories of what he did when he was a warrior."

(I have had to rearrange the following story for coherency. Because of language problems, it came out convoluted and difficult for a reader to follow; it should now reflect Timothy's meaning and intent.)

Timothy had a girlfriend who mated with him at great risk to herself because she would be killed by her relatives if it were discovered that this unmarried girl was having sex—even though they had plans to marry. One day when this girl was still a child, she and her older sister were walking together through the forest on their way to attend a feast. The sister said, "The decision has been made by our people that when we arrive at the feast, they are going to kill me. Even though I proved that I did not do what they accused me of—that I did not steal—still they are going to kill me." Her little sister cried and then told her, "It's hard for me to do anything to avenge you because I am just a little girl. But I will someday avenge your death."

The elder sister was murdered that day by her own uncle, who, in fact, had been her accuser. The little sister vowed her revenge, and upon reaching puberty claimed Timothy as her man. In lieu of a bride price, the girl agreed to marry Timothy if he would avenge her sister's death by murdering the hated uncle. By this means, also, the girl saved the amount that would otherwise have had to be paid to get her uncle killed.

One night the girl let Timothy into her uncle's hut after the old man was asleep. The uncle was curled up on his mat next to the fire, and Timothy crept up on him with an axe. He struck the old man in the neck so hard he almost severed his head. Timothy and his girl ran from the village and later married. Fortunately for Timothy and his girlfriend, it appears that there was no relative or friend who cared enough about the uncle to put up a ransom to avenge *his* killing. This was the first of Timothy's three killings.

"Was there any time when you got in a fight with another warrior, when you were battling with another warrior?" I ask Timothy.

"In a situation where you are face to face," he says, "you usually planned your attack very well, even to the killing of a man. So what happened in another case, I was so kind with another friend [on whom a ransom had been placed]. We were on a trip [together] in the bush along a stream. We were making fire and this friend was sitting close to the fire, so he didn't expect what was in my mind. So he didn't turn around. I surprised him and just knocked the man down with my axe on his neck. So he died. So there has not been any struggling face to face."

"And was that the usual way it was done?" I ask. "So it would not be two people fighting face to face but rather trickery to get the man whose revenge price was on him?"

"That is how it was always done in the case of the revenge—

which is different from when a tribal attack is done. That is very different."

"At that time were there attacks between tribes very often?"

"Yes, wars were [always] going on [in the region]."

So maybe there would be an attack from another village, and for what reasons would that occur?"

"It must be on special purposes that such tribal war could occur, which is not very much [often]. Might happen, say, once in every tribe [village], oh, once a year or twice a year."

"And what would the goal be? What would the tribes try and do? Would they try and kill many warriors? Would they take women? Would they burn houses? What were the attackers' goals?"

"We all [would] burn the houses, attack even women, and even men."

"So you would kill women, not take them to your tribe, but you would kill them, kill the babies, everyone?"

"The women, we don't take the women," Timothy answers. "The children, we do. You know, [if] somebody having [has] a chance to escape with a child, you know, to save a child [to take it] to another tribe, we do."

"The women were killed along with the men? I mean, it was okay to kill the women as well as the men. There was no distinction made?"

"No distinction."

"What would be the conditions under which one village would attack the other village, rather than going after one man?" I ask.

"It depends on the tribe who would make the decisions: Shall we go to war as a tribe or [should] we do it single, by one man. It all depends on the [decision of the] tribe."

"I see. At that time were you still practicing cannibalism? Sometimes would you eat the other people?"

Timothy pauses to reflect on his answer, then says, "Those who died during battle we wouldn't eat, because there is no time to escape with the bodies. Eating is done only on particular killings, on small [revenge] matters, but [not] in tribal wars."

"Okay, so if a taboo, a tambu, was broken, and you killed a man, would you eat him?"

"Yes."

"And why would you eat him—because there was not much meat, or because . . . what was the reason that you would eat him?"

All the village people who have been listening silently up to this point in rapt attention now break into laughter when this question is translated to Timothy. "What happened is that we eat flesh, human flesh, not because of anything, but because it has already been practiced long ago and that we just feel like eating human flesh," he answers.

"What does human flesh taste like? I mean, could you describe it, compare it to chicken or to pig? Was it better than other animals?"

Timothy laughs heartily, as do the other villagers. He explains, "There is no similar type of meat which we would compare it to. It is different altogether and one wouldn't say that it is best. It is not, but it [cannibalism] is done because we feel we should eat part of this [person]. After killing a man, you know, he has to be left for four days. Then we could eat [him]."

"What part did you like the best?" I ask.

"At the time of carcassing, slaughtering, we would make a selection just on the right, from the arms, chop off, or just on the other left, chop off."

"Chop off just below the shoulder?" I ask.

"Yeah, just [cut off the bone at the shoulder on] both sides and even the thighs. Then rip, cut the meat on the thighs off."

"So that you would have pieces of flesh without the bone, and the same with the arms?"

"Without the bone. It has to be taken off. That [fatty] portion of abdomen has to be just thrown into the fire and that is to light the fire up and we all just practice the barbecue."

"So this was barbecued?" I ask.

"Barbecued, yes," Timothy answers. "What is left we put into bamboo. [Meat is stuffed in a section of green bamboo and then smoked over a low fire to preserve it.] But what could be finished [eaten at once], it is in barbecue."

"So the stomach, the fat part of the stomach, was made to bring the fire up and that was cut away from the intestines, the insides, which were thrown away. And then the arms were roasted and the thighs were roasted. What about the buttocks?" I ask.

That question brings a roar of laughter from the crowd. "They [some] eat it," he answers, "but we, it was graded to be very bad taste. I mean [it tastes] like waste matter," he adds.

"Waste matter. So you don't eat it?"

"Not much. Best place is the women, their nipples."

"Yes?" I ask, perplexed.

"Breast."

"Oh, the breast!"

"Very greasy," Timothy adds with relish. He is referring to the amount of fat contained in breast tissue. Because of the very low fat content of their diet, any fat is considered a great delicacy.

"That was considered the best part?" I ask.

"Yeah, we would pick [that as] the first place."

"So would you eat one person over a period of, maybe, days?" I ask. "How many people from the tribe would eat these? Everyone?"

"No, human being doesn't have much meat."

"Doesn't?"

"Yeah, so it does not last long, and it cannot take many people to even eat a man."

"How many people would normally be able to eat a man?"

"Eating of the human being is not a thing which you should invite anybody [everybody]. Those who got hold of this [victim] enjoyed that [themselves]. Depends, maybe, if two or three [warriors were in on the killing they would split up the victim among themselves]."

"When did this practice stop for the Are'are?"

"This particular region here, the killing was stopped during Mr. Bell's days," Lysander adds, "because he [Timothy] was taken, arrested for a killing."

"Timothy was arrested for killing?"

"Yes," Lysander answers, "[for] killing, and took down by the British officers to Auki. And that time it puts an end to such killing and eating of people in this region."

"So this was in the early 1920s?"

"Early 1920s."

"What did he think of Bell?" I ask.

Timothy answers, "Before that [before I was arrested], because Mr. Bell is a government officer and everybody is frightened of him, and I myself am also frightened and I don't feel better [good] about Mr. Bell."

"You don't feel very good? You don't like Mr. Bell?"

"I don't like."

"You wanted the government just to stay away?"

"Yeah, that's right, yeah. But what happen is that my feeling changed after [I was arrested] about Mr. Bell when he make the decision that because there was no boat to take me over to the final judgment in Tulagi, because it was so windy, Mr. Bell made the decision that they have to return me back to my home without any sentence. So that makes me happy again."

"So did Mr. Bell act like the judge and did you convince him that you did not do this?"

"He made the decision, not because of my statement but because no ship ever arrived from Tulagi to Auki to fetch me." Because of a storm the ship was never sent from Tulagi, the island which at that time was the colonial British administration center for the Solomons and where the court and the penitentiary were located.

"It [the ship] was too late, so he has the authority to just say, 'Go back [home],'" Timothy continues.

"What did he tell you when he sent you back?"

"Mr. Bell tell me not to do the same again anytime soon. So I didn't do anymore [kill anyone] since that time."

"And that was all that Bell said?"

"Yeah, that's all, [except] that because now you have much more enemy, because you have killed people, they [will] try to pay revenge on you. So if any such thing happen, I'll give you this statement, this paper."

"That you didn't do it?"

"No, he *knows* that I did it. That is not to clear that [at] all, but just to assure me that if anything happens to me, that has to be dealt with by the police. So no one can take any more revenge on me."

"Or the police would go after that person?"

"[Yes]. That person."

"So that made you very happy. And so when Bell was killed, were the people happy to see Bell killed? Or were the Are'are and the Kwaio enemies? What was the situation?"

"We were not happy when they [the Kwaio] kill Mr. Bell because some of [us], most of us, were trying to live peacefully and [we] accepted his treatment [enforcement] to begin cutting down the tribal wars and killing."

"So you wanted to see Bell succeed in his work with the Kwaio because the Kwaio were doing most of the killing at that time?"

"No, both Are'are and Kwaio do the same [amount of killing], but majority of the people who doesn't do the actual killing, they understand they see that through Bell's work, things are changing into a better life. So when Bell was killed, we were a bit sad to hear [it]."

"What was the feeling about the government going up and killing all the Kwaio? Were the people here happy to see it or did they think that it was too much?"

"Feel happy. I mean, the people around here, they felt that it was better that government has to do that to them [the Kwaio] because for seeing the progress already been [made] and then, just for that reason they support the [government's policies]."

Lysander interrupts. "I think he's getting tired and maybe we should quit."

The interview has been going for nearly an hour and a half.

Timothy's head is nodding and he is having problems now answering the questions. I tell Lysander, "Please tell Timothy he has done very well and I appreciate his help."

After I take some photos, Timothy is led outside back to his hut by his third wife (he has outlived his first two), a pert lady in her early sixties. After a meal with the village elders, we return to the canoe and sail back down the river to Houhui.

·

Timothy died in August 1989.

13

THE STORY OF THE CURSED

FISH: A TRUE PARABLE

 This is the story of Lysander's grandfather, who was a warrior, and of a fish that he caught and how it led to his murder. It took place, apparently, around 1900—before Lysander was born—and was told to him by his father.

"Lysander," I ask him, "would you tell me that story?"

.

"My grandfather, that is, the father of my father, was living in a village with his parents and family in the hills near this Wairaha River. And at that time we have bait fish coming into the river, and this attracted many big fish, so he came to fish for a night. And early in the morning of that night he caught a fish called mamona, a big fish—almost ten feet long. And he caught it by net which he threw into the water. Then, early in the dawn, came a fishing canoe from a neighboring village. They came up the bank from the river, and a youth that was with them, a seven-year-old boy, was so surprised at the fish in his path that he stepped on it by mistake. Because he was so young, he didn't understand that stepping on anything [that someone is going] to eat is a hurting thing to anyone in Malaita. It is taboo because you are putting your dirty foot on what the elders are to eat.

"Because it is just his character that he doesn't talk much, my grandfather didn't say anything. But he was so annoyed he rolled up his fishing net and got the fish and walked down to the canoe belonging to the other group, which was tied to the bank. So he

slapped the canoe with the fish and broke the pointed part of the canoe. The group was so very annoyed of this that they swear at the
fish [made a curse on the fish]."

"What was the curse?" I ask.

"The swear goes that the fish is the waste matter of the worst of
the women in their village. So then he didn't reply to the curse,
though he was very angry, but got the fish and walked away, silently, back to his home in the hills. When he reached there, he
threw the fish to the elders and the priests. The women prepared the
fish even though they wouldn't take part in the meal. When the fish
was cooked, all the men sat to enjoy the fish. My grandfather didn't
say anything to them, and he didn't participate in the meal. He
stood up watching them, and just before they finished eating he told
them that this fish was cursed as being the waste matter of the
women in the other village. The men were very surprised, but they
didn't know what to do because they had already eaten the fish."

"Were they angry at your grandfather?" I ask. "Why did he do
this to people of his own village?"

"Yeah, they were angry. He did this because he wants to have
revenge on the other village. So [his people] must be angry so that
he would gain respect from them for killing on their behalf. So then
he got up and pulled his musket from the house. He told them [his
people], 'Now I'm going to pay the revenge for [your] eating this
fish.' And he went [off] and when he got to the other village, it was
night and the people were asleep. So he climbed up to a flat place
on top of a wall which was used for keeping food, and looking from
this flat place, down, he sees two people were sleeping around a fire.
So he throws the candle match [a small, pitch-filled piece of wood
that flares up when lit] into the fire, and it lit so clear that he could
see on the one mat there is a woman and on the other mat there is a
man. So he shot the man. Then he escape. But before that [before
he entered the village] he tied the doors [of the entry] from outside.
[The village was surrounded by a high fence, probably of palm
trunks, with only a single entry.] So when they tried to chase him,
they were so late in trying to loosen the tying that he escape to his
village. There he tells his parents and the elders [what he has done
and] that he's going off and they have to protect themselves. Then

he went out in the bush, knowing that they are going to raid for him. So he stay out in the bush, and after some months of raiding, they [still] could not get hold of him.

"So this group [from the other village] paid another tribe to do the job for them, putting up ransom. If anyone kills my grandfather, they would receive the ransom."

"Do you have any idea how much ransom?"

"Oh, must be about two thousand [Solomon Island] dollar of shell money. So then he was [still] hiding, and even this other group could not find him, so they paid another one man from our own tribe to show them where he was hiding. This man did that. And so they ambushed him and cut him alive. Then they killed him and slaughter him and eat him."

"And ate him?" I ask.

"And eat him," Lysander replies.

"How do you know they ate him?"

"Oh, because everybody knows and people went there to see the happening and they all witness."

"So was there any more killing after that to avenge your grandfather?"

"Yes. Just on the same day the custom drum was sounded from that next village to tell the information that he has been caught and killed. So then one of his friends wished to pay revenge on the same day. So he did that by going down to the next neighboring house, which was owned by one of the relations of the tribe who caught my grandfather. So [grandfather's friend] was telling this old man, the relative of the murderers, that he was going down to the seacoast. So [he told the old man] that he stopped so they could say good-bye to each other—they know each other very well. So [grandfather's friend] just seat himself at the boundary of the house, pointing the gun at the door. When another drum sounds, [the old man] comes out to listen to the drum, and at that time [the friend] snapped him off with a musket. Yeah, and he died."

"What about the man from your tribe who told them where your grandfather was hiding. Did anything happen to him?"

"No, they didn't know who it was. And when this man killed

the other old man as revenge, then it makes the game not squared up."

"So the murders didn't stop?"

"It didn't stop. It is not squared up. Because another man died. Because my grandfather killed a man, he should be killed. If he dies, then it is squared up. But this man [of the other tribe] didn't think so. He thought this way: 'If [we] people who [the grandfather] was injured by killing [our] man, if [we] would have killed [the grandfather], then it would be all right. But because we are paying another tribe to kill him, I am going to kill one of the grandfather's tribe.' So the other related group ambush a man of my grandfather's village."

"Okay, and then was it square?"

"It was not square."

"Even then it was not square?"

"No."

"So then what?"

"So then one of the friends, relative to this old man [who was killed], promise that he is going to kill someone else in revenge, for our tribe. So he was keeping a beard and he shaves his beard. Then he must kill someone in revenge because he shaved his beard."

"So did he kill someone from the other tribe?"

"No, he never did."

"Lysander, I still don't understand why your grandfather would give the cursed fish to his own people."

"So that he have some witnesses, some support from his own people to kill [a person from the offending village]."

"But I would think his people would be so angry for tricking them that they wouldn't support him."

"Yeah, they were so angry. That is why he is going to kill somebody, so that their angry be finished. They would feel that he has done something not straight if he has not gone to kill somebody. But because he offered himself to die for this, they were pleased."

14

THE MISSIONARIES

OF VANGUNU

This is a land of fable. Mountainous, verdant islands whose names evoke distant jungle drums—Mondomondo, Kolombangara, Ngcatokae, Vonavona, and Vella Lavella—spiral above hundred-mile-long Morovo Lagoon. The islands rise from the sea in a jagged line heading northwest toward New Guinea. On their eastern lee, dozens of coral atolls seal off the lagoon from New Georgia Sound—the famous "Slot," site of some of the fiercest naval battles of World War II—and to the south, the Solomon Sea. Through the lagoon, coral and volcanic islands lay scattered like misplaced stepping stones for a hidden giant.

Lying at the southeast end of the archipelago is a narrow peninsula jutting into the lagoon at the southwest tip of Vangunu Island. There sits the Seventh Day Adventist Batuna Mission Station, consisting of a church, two schools, a sawmill, a small clinic, the missionary's house at which I am staying, and housing for workers and students. From the station one looks south toward Ngcatokae, a tropical Mt. Fuji, in the distance. Between Batuna and the mountain, small palm-covered islands appear to float on the quiet waters, unbroken strips of green save for the infrequent cluster of huts marking an isolated village. Here and there a wooden dugout canoe passes silently, seemingly without destination, in this placid inland sea.

The sun has just disappeared over the forested ridge behind the station. Shy black and brown tykes play in the shallows alongside the mill next to a derelict fishing boat. Parrots and lorakeets chirp in the palms, and beneath them a couple of young German shepherds frolic on the lawn in the cool of the evening. Though the workday has ended, there is still plenty of activity. A soccer game is in progress between the students and the millhands. The field is out of sight behind the school, but the excited voices carry easily to the bluff at the end of the peninsula where the ramshackle missionary house is perched. Perry, the spoiled white cockatoo, hangs upside down from the underside of the missionaries' porch roof, screeching furiously. A black-and-white cat, the resident mouser, scrutinizes the miserable bird with disdain. Leta and Grace can be heard in the kitchen preparing the evening meal. Jill, the mistress of this remote world, is at the clinic. Her husband is down at the mill. Ken's fifteen-hour day still not complete, he supervises the installation of a commercial blast freezer. He hopes this will be the essence of a new fishing program that will bolster the economy of the villages around the lagoon.

One of the German shepherds breaks from the other's grasp and lopes up to an island girl sitting by herself on the grass. The startled girl rocks back on her shoulders to get away from the dog, but not before it plants a wet, sloppy lick on her mouth. She laughs and wipes her face. Perry moves to the nest he has excavated behind a porch rafter. The cries of the playing children peal happily through the tropical evening. This place seems like a peaceful oasis in an otherwise chaotic world.

The missionaries' house, a medium-pitch wooden colonial, was built shortly after the station was established in 1915. Inside it has been remodeled to resemble a 1950 tract home with blond plywood paneling and lots of Formica. The large kitchen where Jill's two helpers are preparing dinner leads to a dining area that is separated from the living room by a slatted room divider. Every table is adorned with storks, porpoises, and other figurines carved locally from ebony or kerosene wood, which resembles Philippine mahogany. All the entertainment amenities are here: phonograph, tape deck, VCR, and accompanying TV to play tapes. (The Solomon Islands do not have a TV station.) Three small bedrooms and a bath complete the main floor; downstairs are two rooms for visitors.

Ken and Jill Hiscox hardly fit the missionary stereotype. Jill, an effervescent, curly-haired Australian in her middle forties, and Ken, who looks as though he could out-crocodile Dundee, represent the modern counterpart of the frontier missionary couples who were among the first Europeans to settle in the South Pacific. The life led by the Hiscoxes, while not subject to the dangers and hardships of their predecessors, is still not easy: Their days are long and their responsibilities often overwhelming.

At six o'clock in the morning it is still dark as Ken huddles over one end of the dining table, facing the wall. His hands, meeting in prayer, press against his chin. Already he seems exhausted and his day has hardly begun. Certainly among his prayers must be a request for Jesus to give him the strength to get through what he knows he must accomplish—the travails and constant demands of the next fifteen hours.

An hour later he is at the sawmill conducting the morning prayer meeting for the millhands. Fifteen island men, most in their forties and fifties, wearing overalls or ragged shorts, sit attentively on piles of sawn lumber facing their pastor. Dressed in shorts and a polo shirt, Ken pulls himself up on a stack of timber until his knees are against his chest. His sockless boat shoes point toward the expectant congregation.

"We can bow our heads," he tells them, "makem once a bit of prayer before we makem a start." Obedient heads are cast down, and reverently, silently, the men pray. Then they sing together:

> God issa good, God issa good,
> God issa good, issa good to me.

The men harmonize beautifully. Their deep voices contrast with the pastor's clear, pleasant tenor.

> He tooka my sins, He tooka my sins,
> He tooka my sins, He'sa good to me.
> Now I am free, now I am free,
> So good to me.
> God is so good, He tooka my sins,
> Now I am free. He'sa so good to me.

"You lookem, remember on this Monday, on breakknee [yesterday's prayer meeting]," Ken begins, "we talkum about the Ten Commandments. Me like go on a little more yet on this one, because me studied on this one. Me like findum inside Exodus 20, verse 12, where we talkum about one fella commandment, inside on this Ten Commandments. Remember on this one me talks, 'Honor thy father and thy mother, that thy day may be longer upon the land which the Lord thy God giveth thee.' God give him fella commandment blong him. He long talkum how good long children me helpa respect him this fella the family circle. Me can feel God, who Him put him Jesus inside on wan fella small family."

Ken continues talking about how Jesus lives in the family. He tells of God accompanying Moses and the Israelites from Egypt. Though it is not clear how this connects with the "honor thy father and mother" theme, the workers seem to get the connection. At least they nod their heads reverently. Ken begins praying, asking God to bless the men and their families, to make them strong, to help them to love, to walk beside them, and to look out for them through the day. He thanks Jesus, their savior, and says amen. A hushed chorus of amens echoes his.

The men disperse. The mill's saws start up. Their harsh whine slices through the morning quiet. Ken climbs the stairs of a building next to the mill where his small cluttered office is located. On the way he is stopped four times by mission employees, each wanting directions or Ken's decision on some pending matter. He answers each question thoughtfully, in pidgin, carefully conveying his meaning and searching the face of the man in front of him to make sure he is understood.

The mission station hums with activity. The dilapidated backwoods mill is at the center of the complex in an open-sided tin-roofed shed. With its antiquated equipment, the operation resembles a small American sawmill of the 1920s. More time seems to be spent repairing equipment than cutting timber, but there is no money to buy new machinery. Lumber is stacked by hand, then moved with a thirty-year-old Cat loader. An old farm tractor pulls logs from the lagoon, where a launch has deposited them after towing small rafts of timber from villages along the coast.

Actually, this is the best, most environmentally beneficial timber operation possible for a developing nation like the Solomons. Individual villagers cut one or two trees as they need money. The logs are floated down the numerous streams until they reach a pickup point. The business puts money directly into villagers' hands instead of foreign corporations' pockets. It also saves the forests. Wherever large-scale mechanized logging has taken place in the South Pacific, the thin layer of topsoil has been washed away in the torrential rains before any replanting can occur—even if someone tries to replant, which is seldom the case in many Third World countries. Because of government ineptitude, lack of funds, political payoffs, or logging company dishonesty, most land is never replanted. Too late do the naive and trusting village people realize the irreversible devastation that is their new legacy. In most tropical countries, if replanting does not occur soon after logging, within a year the topsoil is gone and the land, usually the local peoples' only asset, is destroyed for generations.

Behind the sawmill and planing mill shed, a two-story wood-frame building houses the vocational school. In one upstairs room a bespeckled Ni Vanuatu teacher lectures on the nomenclature and uses of all types of screws, bolts, and other fasteners. In the next room a young woman just graduated from the SDA's Australian Teaching College administers a typing test to thirty island girls. The Australian girl's husband gives a class in outboard engine repair on a lower floor. In a series of adjoining work areas, forty island students in their late teens or early twenties learn woodworking by making furniture that will be used on the mission or sold in Honiara, where the lumber and molding milled at Batuna also go. Unfortunately, there are not enough power tools or hand tools, so half the boys must watch the others work before trading off.

Much of the housing for workers and students built before World War II is close to collapse. Two Australian SDAs who have volunteered their vacation time to come to Batuna are finishing a concrete hundred-bed boys' dormitory to replace the ancient rabbit warren that must still be used. A new thirty-bed girls' dorm is also under construction, to be completed when the next batch of volunteer builders arrives from Australia.

There is always a long waiting list of young people of many religions eager to enter the vocational program, which also includes classes in agriculture, auto and truck repair, business, and bookkeeping, as well as English and math. Between the Batuna school and its counterpart on Malaita, the SDAs provide twenty percent of the eleven hundred vocational training spaces available in the whole country. A primary school for children of mission employees also serves the surrounding villages.

Two women paddle up to the station in a canoe filled with small children. Boats from local villages come and go all day, bringing shoppers to the store or patients to the twelve-bed clinic. This clinic is staffed by two local nurse practitioners who are so capable that Ken says he would trust his life to them. The nurses can handle most emergencies short of major operations and are specially trained in obstetrics.

Jill, also a nurse, often helps at busy times, in addition to handling the administrative and financial work for the clinic. What's more, she supervises the store, is in charge of young people's religious programs, and teaches a course in deportment, self-improvement, and modern living to the secondary and vocational students. This class is her special joy. Kindness and happiness radiate from this woman like the sun on a cold day. With her irrepressible laugh, Jill describes her deportment class:

"I have found it *most* rewarding. When they [the students] asked me, I thought, oh, how am I ever gonna find time, but I have just found it so rewarding. I've got so much closer to these students by being involved with them, and I hope I've won their confidence, and I'm finding they're coming to me with their little confidences. I feel if I can help them in their lives, then to me, that is greatly rewarding. Just to see them now! When we first came and we had [European] visitors, if they were to go out to shake hands, you would not believe, they would put—this is a fellow of twenty, say— he would put one finger out and hide his head like this." Jill tucks her head behind her arm before continuing. "He didn't know how to meet a person. So this has been my pleasure, teaching them in the class. Hilarious classes, you know, all shaking hands, a good firm handshake, look in the eye, and they look so pleased.

When visitors come now, they all line up to shake hands.

"I've taught them how to speak on a microphone. Most of them had never ever touched one. You know, these big lads just falling to the ground in fright, everyone's roaring laughing, and they're just so embarrassed. But now they hold the microphone up and they'll take part, and it's just tremendous. I've taught them all how to talk on the radio. And they all do beautifully. We've learned deportment, we've learned exercise, we've had them out jogging," she says with a laugh.

"How to press their uniforms, how to launder their uniforms, 'cause nobody [in the villages] has irons. They have to so that they look respectable. Oh, what else have we learned? Different health aspects, and now we're learning music. You know, these people love to sing, and it just flows from them. The harmony is absolutely beautiful. So now they're all learning what the notes are, the value of the notes. They're learning to conduct; they're all conducting. All these little things that we take for granted; they are so appreciative. We've learned table manners, how to set a table, although it's not their custom. But it's only not their custom because they're half between two customs. They're in a culture now that has to mingle with the outside world, and a lot of Solomon Islanders are traveling the world, government positions and all. So I've taught them how to use a knife and fork because they wanted to learn how to use them."

Throughout her description of the deportment classes Jill giggles continuously. The trials and tribulations of her students will be cherished memories for her. "One fellow who was with us in New Guinea a long time ago came to us one day," she continues, still laughing, "and he said, 'Look, they're sending me to Australia.' He'd never been overseas. 'Teach me what to do at the table.' Well, we had a hilarious time. Ken was a real tease, teaching him all the wrong things and having a laugh and that. But we taught him what to do. Now, how would he have ever known? That fellow has traveled the world, I think, eight times. He's taken Ken's table manners around the world. We laugh about it, you know. He's dined with the Queen on the *Britannia*, he and his wife. So it's preparing them for the outer world."

Ken has spent his morning meeting with the mission's accountant and bookkeeper. The mission is on precarious financial footing, and expenses must be watched carefully. The meeting is interrupted by a workman who needs Ken's advice about a construction problem that has just cropped up.

Isaiah, a bright young fellow in his early twenties, asks Ken if they should break a recently poured concrete wall of the new freezer room in order to get the freezer motor in. The motor is too large to fit through the doorway. Ken tells him no, that if he does that he will destroy the structural integrity of the building. Instead, he should remove the frame containing a three-by-six-foot window, bring the motor in, and refit the glass and frame. Other workers come in to receive advice or instructions about a variety of other problems.

Ken handles all the interruptions easily, but they wear on him. "It's rather nerve-racking," he admits. "There are decisions that you have to make that are going to affect a large number of people. So, consequently, once you start realizing that you have a role that does affect other people, that's a heavy responsibility, if you weigh it seriously."

The small interruptions are commonly interspersed with more serious problems as well. Ken describes a situation that occurred a few days earlier: "Recently, we were surprised that we were receiving so many babies and children which were having severe diarrhea and gastric problems. All of a sudden babies started turning up at the clinic, and Anessa West [one of the nurses] came to me. 'Ken, we've got another urgent baby case. What are we going to do about it?' Now we have a kind of structure that if there is a medical problem over there, we will assist because, naturally, we feel that life is more important than timber. So, consequently, we dropped everything and went to find out what the problem was. Another baby was seriously ill and the nurse in charge said, 'Well, I can treat the baby, but I'm worried about what's going to happen if we don't do something at where it came from.' So we just jumped into my boat, my wife and I, and went up to the village. It had to be an instant decision, and we started straightaway doing our education program, explaining why babies get sick from dirty surroundings, unhygienic conditions, and so on. In this particular case it was because they just weren't following the hygienic principles that you and I learn when we're small children, like washing your hands, how to clean things and keep flies away, just the basic things, that's what we're talking about. We went up there and did that and then had to come back and jump into our role here again. Well, that took us about two hours. Now, we always have emergencies, medical emergencies, and we are delighted to help, but they all seem to take a major part of your day."

Jill, who has come into the office, has been listening and agrees. Emergencies are time-consuming, and to her they seem to take place when they are most impossible to deal with. "We had one occur last year on our school graduation day," she adds. "This was an extraordinary day in our life here. Fortunately, not all days are like this. Ken got called away early in the morning that day to go down to the lagoon where we are helping to put in a new airstrip. He'd been maintaining the machinery down there, and it was having trouble, so he went down there. He was away and missed all the graduation ceremony in the morning. At lunchtime, I was just saying how some of the huge canoes had come eight hours or more to the graduation to pick up their students. Anyway, I was seeing them off when a call came for me to get to the clinic. One of our clinic sisters had been called to a village up the lagoon. It was her own father actually, and she thought he'd had a stroke or something, so she'd gone and [left] just the one sister here.

"The remaining nurse called me to give her a hand because a week before a little boy had had a stab wound. The children had been playing with knives and he was stabbed in the leg, and he'd hemorrhaged greatly when it happened, but that had been treated. Then, midweek, he was in the clinic and it had hemorrhaged again. Now at the end of the week, it was hemorrhaging again, blood everywhere. Anyway we got it under control, but I couldn't get the father under control. He was most agitated. I thought, I need Ken with his calming influence." She laughs, then continues. "Anyway, I didn't realize that this father had already lost a child through hemorrhaging, previously. If I'd known I could have found a steward, but I just couldn't, you know I'm trying to tell him, 'The emergency's over. Don't worry. We'll get him out on the boat.'

"The boat was going that night and the other sister was going on holiday and she would have traveled with him to Honiara. It wasn't a medical emergency, but he wanted the plane to come to take this child. So I thought, well, I'll do all I can, and I just made him quiet and found out that our plane was too far away. I told him that we couldn't get the plane. But he was very agitated and he wanted the plane to come. I said, 'Well, look, we can't afford a plane. We will have to pay [to charter a commercial aircraft from Honiara]. It will be six hundred, eight hundred dollars, and if it was an emergency, yes, we would, but it's not an emergency. The child can be at the hospital in twenty-four hours' time.' So I just had to leave him, and then Ken arrived back, and I was talking to Ken down here at the wharf when Johnny came running and said, 'Come to the clinic quickly. There's an emergency coming in from the bush.'

"It was a fourteen-year-old girl from one of the villages. They were pushing one of their big canoes from the bush where it had been made, pushing it downhill, and it slid out of control. It caught her against a tree and ripped her leg, simply pulverized all the flesh. The bone was shattered. The artery was still intact, and it had like a balloon on it, just pulsating, and we had no painkiller at that time. We've had a lot of hassles getting medicines. No painkiller, and we couldn't do an intravenous because the blood vessels had just collapsed. She was in such shock. We felt she wouldn't last the night from shock. Our plane was four hours out of Malaita, the other side of Malaita. It was late afternoon by that time. So we called Sol Air. But by the time they got a plane over here it [would be] eight o'clock at night and we'd never had a night landing here, at our little airstrip."

The Batuna airstrip is notorious, even in a country filled with substandard landing strips. Since there is no level ground around the mission station—built long before air service—a tiny landing strip has been bulldozed from the isthmus connecting the station to the steep mountain adjoining it. From the air the landing field looks too small to take a helicopter, and in fact most small planes, using every inch of the field, land with only a few feet to spare before going nose-first into the lagoon. Somehow the pilot coming in that night would have to place his plane on that tiny field in the dark, for of course there is no lighting.

"Fortunately, they brought the Islander,"[1] Jill continues, "and it just drops on sixpence. By now everyone on the station knew what was happening and the entire airstrip was lined with people and children—no way of keeping them off. We could hear the plane circling above us. Oh, I was praying so hard. Anyway, Ken had had the men fill Sunshine milk tins with kerosene or something and put in wicks, you know, made from hessian bagging. And at the right signal, we gave the order for them to be lit up. The pilots were absolutely amazed. They said it was as if someone had just turned a switch on—better than Honiara, it was lit up. They landed all right and loaded the two children. I told the pilot, 'I bet you've never had so many prayers go to heaven for you.' He said, 'Don't worry, I was praying myself!' So the children got off all right but that wasn't the end of the day.

"The ship [to Honiara] had meanwhile come in, and many of our students were leaving on it to go home for holiday. So Ken and the students were all on the dock and our wharf collapsed. Down it went with Ken and the students on it. Fortunately, it was slow collapsing and nobody was hurt. This is now about ten-thirty, getting toward eleven at night, and we thought, that's it, that's enough excitement. But no, that same night we had a death at the station, one of our old retired workers. However, the good news was that the girl was saved, and also the little boy who flew out with her. And so that was a day on the mission station," Jill concludes with a smile, "but one that we don't want ever repeated."

·

The life of the Hiscox family reads like a fifty-year-long pioneer saga. Ken's parents, who were also Australian missionaries, set the standard their son and his wife would follow. In 1937 Ken's father and mother were teaching and nursing in Cambooboo, a primitive area in the wilds of New Britain, the long crescent-shaped island northeast of New Guinea. Ken's mother came out of the bush to the

---

[1] The Britten-Norman Islander, a twin-engine, ten-passenger, high-winged STOL.

coastal clinic at Rabaul to have her first baby, and while she was waiting to deliver, Matapi, the volcano hovering over the town, erupted. Instantly Rabaul was covered with molten lava and a suffocating blanket of ash. Hundreds died within minutes.

Ken's mother ran with a crowd of townspeople to the port, hoping to find boats to take them to safety. Instead, she and the other hapless survivors witnessed a sight that must have horrified them as much as the erupting volcano. All the water suddenly disappeared from the harbor, leaving boats and fish flopping in the sand. Minutes later, with a roar louder than the exploding volcano, an enormous wall of water came hurtling back in. The tidal wave resulting from the eruption engulfed what was left of the town, killing dozens of people who had thought themselves fortunate to have escaped the first catastrophe. June Hiscox, hardly able to walk with her advanced pregnancy, was swept down a steep embankment on her back. Miraculously, neither she nor the baby she was carrying was injured. Later the same day a boat that had escaped destruction carried her and other survivors down the coast, where the following day she gave birth to Lynn, Ken's older brother. Eleven months later, pregnant again, June came back to Rabaul's little hospital, now rebuilt, and gave birth to Ken and Dave, his twin brother. A year later, back in Australia, she gave birth to a girl, bearing four children altogether in slightly more than two years.

After the children were born, Ken's father returned alone to New Britain to do missionary work at an isolated station an hour south of Rabaul. It was planned that when the children were a little older, they and June would join him. One day an Australian Navy flying boat swooped down and landed on the bay in front of his mission. The propellers were still turning as a sailor shouted to him, "Rabaul has fallen. Get on board." The missionary instructed his native parishioners to flee to the bush, then boarded the plane. No sooner had the lumbering PBY taken off than two Japanese Zeros began to pursue it. The pilot just managed to swing the slow-moving PBY into a cloud bank before the Japanese could bring their fighters into firing range. Once in the clouds they were able to elude the Japanese fighters.

After spending World War II in Australia, the Hiscox family

moved to a remote mission station on a small island in the New Hebrides chain, now Vanuatu. With both their parents engaged in establishing a school and hospital, the children were often on their own. Normally they could complete their weekly Australian correspondence courses in one day and then spend all but their Sabbath out on the reef, exploring the island, visiting the native villages, or just having a wonderful time. The children learned self-sufficiency in the bush, skills which Ken would find most valuable later in life.

The older boys were eventually sent back to Australia to complete their education. Ken went to the SDA college at Avondale, where he studied to become a schoolteacher and where he met Jill, who had been brought up in Queensland, the most northeasterly state of Australia. The stoic, blond-haired, blue-eyed Ken melted Jill's heart. But before they could get married they were separated. Jill describes their situation:

"Some people that were self-supporting missionaries, who had a timber mill in the highlands of New Guinea, came to Australia looking for a young fellow to take the place of a man that drove their front-end loaders and, you know, logging machines. This fellow had contracted polio, and so Ken just jumped at the invitation. It was like going home to him. So his teaching just went by the way. He went out to work in their timber mill, working their machinery. I went to our hospital in Sydney, to the Adventist hospital, to train and do my nursing. We were separated three years," she continues. "Ken was in a very isolated place, right up in the western highlands of New Guinea, and there were no telephones, no connection whatsoever, so it was just letter writing for three years. The young people of today say, 'Oh, how could you do it?' But we just accepted it, that that's what we had to do. There was no choice if I was going to be of service to the Lord [which necessitated nurse's training], and so that's just what we did. And [three years later] he came down, we were married, and he took me out there as a bride of a week.

"I was a city girl, and I'd lived a sheltered life, but as a church we're very mission-orientated. We hear lots of stories of the mission field, and when the missionaries would come back, we'd hear their stories, and we'd read stories. So I sort of felt that I knew quite a bit about it. And I feel that I can adjust, can adapt fairly quickly, though I think probably more so when I was younger. Where we went was a very primitive area. It was before the town of Mt. Hagen. It was just a little airstrip, and the government had a patrol post that was of native material, and it might have been about half a dozen native-material homes [thatched huts]. We were in the mountains. We lived at seven thousand five hundred feet above sea level. We were in the clouds more than we were out of the clouds quite often. It got very cold at night, but it was like a perpetual spring: beautiful climate, magnificent. It's just delightful in the highlands.

"There were no stores, nothing. I would have to order my groceries, about a six months' supply, and it would be flown in by DC3 plane. In those days the planes had no lining, and the wind'd whistle right through the cracks in the sides. All the cargo was right along the center of the plane, and sometimes it was so laden up, you couldn't even see the people on the side, and there'd be natives there, you know, primitive natives, in the plane, as well as pigs or some fowls or whatever.

"The DC3 was a very reliable plane, you know, engine-wise, but in the years that we were in the highlands, many planes crashed, many planes. Ken and I, we were first on the spot to one plane crash, a small plane, a Cessna. It had just taken off from the airstrip, and we could tell it was having difficulty as it went over, just couldn't get height, and it crashed into the bush a couple of miles further on. By land that was quite a distance to get. At this stage we had had a little girl, a little baby, and I just threw here in the arms of a bush kanaka, and Ken and I just ran. We ran and ran till we got to the site of the crash, and George Weeks—he was a young English pilot—he was killed instantly. He was the one person. He'd been doubly loaded, which is very sad, but this is what happened, and those sorts of things made a great imprint on one's mind. They did to me. I always felt nervous in a plane. 'Ye of little faith,'" she says, laughing at herself. "But I was always very nervous flying. Perhaps I'm more ready to die or something now," she adds thoughtfully.

"As I said," Jill continues, "the highlands were very primitive. The Kukakuka area was not open [to outsiders] and they were very ferocious little people. They were pygmies, very short, and where we lived they were all around us—bush kanakas, not a stitch of clothing. They had no clothes, they were covered in pig grease, they carried their bows and arrows, their spears, their tomahawks, and their knives with them continually. They were fighting amongst themselves, warring all the time. But we were safe. That's how we felt. It was all tribal fighting, so we were safe. In fact they just loved us to come into their area. They, you know, they would rub your arm to see if the white color on your skin would rub off. We went into a valley where I was the first white woman to ever go, and by way of, you know, surprise, they would go 'Ay, ay, ay,' shaking their heads, and the men and the women would want to see our children and want to touch them. Yes, we were very, very welcome. They would just love us to stop or talk with them or do anything with them. You know, you really felt wanted, really wanted.

"They had formed native police by this time,[2] and they used to have to be called in to stop tribal fighting, and that [provided the tribes some] protection. But we have had natives run to our home to hide. We have had natives fighting in our valley in the area. Bush kanakas are really primitive. Ken is marvelous. Ken is very placid and he has a way with them. He can just talk with them. He's had two different tribes wanting to fight over something, over land, or a pig someone had killed. And Ken would just talk to them by the hour, and he'd listen to this side and listen to that, and calm them down, and they'd just get up and off they'd go home, happy as larks—all settled. If it had been me, they'd probably have killed me and each other as well." Jill laughs. "But that's just Ken's calming influence. He's marvelous, whereas I'm the opposite.

"Then [after they'd been there a few years], Ken decided he'd like to go out on his own, start our own timber mill, and by this time [early 1960s] the township of Mt. Hagen was starting to develop. There was a little welding and engineering works that we established there, and we got my brother-in-law and sister from Australia to come up and look after this for us, because we were go-

---

[2] Prior to achieving its independence in 1975, Papua New Guinea was an Australian territory.

[*208*]

ing out into another valley to set up our own sawmill. We had another young Australian fellow who went into partnership with us in
the mill. We went out into this valley, and where finally the road
ended we had two miles of swamp up to our knees. We lived in a
tent for three months until they built us a native-material home.
We've lived in more native-material homes than we have permanent homes," she adds.

"By this stage we'd lost a little baby, and then our little girl was
born, and there was no hospital in the western highlands. You had
to go fly to the eastern highlands for medical attention. They had a
little four-bed European hospital for the expatriates. When we went
out to establish this mill, I was very pregnant with our son. So you
can picture us going through this swamp with our mattress tied to
poles, bush kanakas carrying it, and little Carrie was sitting on the
shoulders of a fellow just covered in pig grease, and the kerosene
fridge going in on poles, and I had a native on either side of me
helping me through this bog. You had to lift your legs up and we
had two miles of that. And there we lived, you know. We arrived,
there was nothing, absolutely nothing, no water or anything.

"Anyway, I'm just sort of standing there observing everything
as things are arriving and being dumped, and Ken's organizing for
the tent to be put up, and I felt something. I looked down, here's
this old mama, bush Mary, she probably wasn't that old, but they
age so quickly up there. You know, she probably was fifty, but she
certainly looked eighty. She might not've even been fifty. Not a finger on her hands, not a finger! Every time a baby would die, and
many babies died, or every time a pig would die—see, their pigs are
as valuable to them as their babies—off would come a joint. They'd
just chop off a joint on a finger to show how they're sorry. And she
didn't have one finger left on her hand, just the stumps. She was
just so thin and wizened up, poor old soul. But as I said, she probably wasn't very old. And she was just so intrigued. I don't think she'd
seen a white woman, you know, probably ever—or close up. And
there she was feeling my legs, and she's down there bending up,
looking up under my dress.

"So we lived out in that valley. Ken eventually put a road
through that swamp by just digging a drain about six to eight feet on

either side of the swamp, all by hand, no machinery. Yes, two miles of it, and that eventually drained that valley completely. Eventually all that water just ran down these barrets [ditches], and you had to drive on this little strip of a road, you know, otherwise you're down in the barret. Ken pulled in all his machinery for the mill. It was just pulled in by ropes and logs underneath it, pulled it across the rivers, fast-flowing, *freezing* cold rivers, and established the mill. So we lived out there.

"It was while we were out there that we discovered that our little girl had a heart murmur. It was a patent ductus, a valve that had never closed. When you're born, this valve should close, and hers had never closed, and her lungs were receiving too much blood. Otherwise she was a normal little baby. We didn't pick it up. It wasn't until later when she started getting chest infections and would run out of breath, and this sort of thing. There we were, out in this valley with the child like this, but it wasn't a matter of life and death. A heart specialist we had taken her to, who had been visiting in Rabaul, had suggested we wait until she was four years old to have surgery. I mean, you just accepted everything, and me very pregnant. We didn't have any transport other than a motorbike. Ken would sit on the front, the dog on the petrol tank in front of him, little Carrie—and me very pregnant, mind you—and then me at the back, and we would go to the end of the road and then we would have to walk. A couple of times we had to walk out with Carrie, who was so sick. She'd caught malaria, had this fever . . . pouring rain, walking out. I can still see us with me holding the umbrella, wondering if we'd get her to medical care in time.

"Anyway, by this time an expatriate woman doctor was at Mt. Hagen, and she said when we brought Carrie in this time, 'Look, this child must have surgery. There's nothing more I can do for her.' And we didn't have a cent to bless ourselves. To start with, Ken had absolutely no money, but you know he saved all he could. Then we were married, and still we saved. But we were self-supporting missionaries. We worked along with the Church, but they didn't pay our wages. We supported ourselves. We just didn't have a penny in those days. There was no way we could go to Australia.

"We brought Carrie in again, another time, and the doctor said, 'Look, don't bring this child back to me, there's nothing I can do. You're gonna lose her unless she gets surgery.' So we thought, well, we've gotta do something. So this doctor said, 'I'm going to try the government. They should pay for a medical emergency, for the fare to Australia, because we haven't the facilities here.' She was marvelous. She really got rapped over the knuckles we heard later, but she didn't wait for the red tape. She really pushed for us. Ken had parts of two Land Rovers, you know, that didn't fit, just as parts. So he worked on putting them together to make a Land Rover, and then he sold that and he got his fare to go to Australia, and the government paid my fare. Well, we'd had so much trouble with me at labor and birth and that, so it was all worked that I would have our next baby in Australia under very good medical care. So to Australia we went, and that to us was marvelous. The Lord helped Ken to get his vehicle and his fare to Australia. Well, Carrie had her surgery, and Dean was born. Anyway, back to New Guinea we went and then we were blessed marvelously. The more we gave to the Lord's work, the more we were blessed financially, our business just prospered so well."

The Hiscoxes eventually settled in Australia, where their two children could receive a better education and learn about their own culture. The family purchased a forty-acre farm near Brisbane where they set about raising gladiolas commercially, but a disastrous freeze wiped them out the following year. Ken then went into the real estate business, and within a year he had sold more property than anyone in the company. Seeing a real estate slump on the horizon, he began selling surgical instruments and supplies for the Australian subsidiary of a large German company. He was the company's top salesman in Australia, even though he refused to work on Saturday because of his religion.

The family then sold their farm and moved into a luxurious four-bedroom home with a swimming pool, a stable for the Hiscoxes horses, and every amenity. "Yes," Jill says, "it was quite luxurious, a beautiful home, it really was. But we just felt that our lives were lacking. We had all these things. We were so involved in this rat race. We thought, there's more in life, because we had known better days, much more rewarding days in New Guinea where we felt we needed God much more than we did back in Australia. When the children were sick, the doctor was on the end of the phone. When the car broke down, the garage was just down at the corner, whereas when you're in isolated places like this [Vangunu], it's on your knees." She laughs. "There's no other way, it's just, on your knees. We just rely on God the whole time."

The Hiscoxes sold their beautiful house and Ken became the minister at an SDA church camp for children on Lord Howe Island, a lovely island lying opposite Sydney, four hundred miles off the coast of New South Wales. They enjoyed working with children there and had plans to improve the camp, but one day they received a call from Church headquarters asking them to go to the Solomon Islands to manage the Batuna mission. The Hiscoxes had to make a decision, though as Jill tells it, they decided they were not the ones to make it.

"We said, 'God, what do you want us to do?' We said, 'There's no way we're going to make this decision which has just gotta be worked out.' So we prayed very very hard about it, that God would show us what he wanted *us* to do, where he wanted us. We looked at it that anybody could walk in our shoes at that camp and it would be fine. But we felt that, you know, it was hard to get people to come to these isolated islands, and we knew we could adjust to an island situation, and this is where we felt that God meant us to be. So this is why we're here. It hasn't been easy. We miss our family greatly. Nobody would know the heartache I feel for our children. This is the first time we have been separated from them, although our daughter's married and she was away from home in Brisbane. Our son was with us until we came. I used to speak to my daughter every day on the phone. Well, we have none of that whatsoever now."

·

At lunchtime the Australian building volunteers, a visiting church official, an SDA pilot stopping in on his way west to Gizo, and Jill all eat around a big table in the missionaries' house. Most SDAs are vegetarians, and so the midday meal consists of meatless tamale pie, seasoned rice, and fruit salad. Ken is still at the mill. The gang saw has broken down again, and unless it can be repaired quickly, production will come to a standstill. Finally, when everyone else is finished and has left the table, Ken comes in and retrieves his plate, which has been warming in the oven. He looks worn and weary, worse than he had appeared earlier.

The mill was in terrible shape when he and Jill took over, Ken says. And the equipment, much of it forty or fifty years old, continues to break down. Finding parts for ancient sawmill machinery is not easy anywhere. In the Solomon Islands it's nearly impossible. Eventually something is sent from Australia, England, or the United States, but often it is not the correct part and the ordering process must start over again. Even getting staples is a constant worry. Sometimes there is no gasoline, or perhaps lubricating oil, or even rice. Jill's kitchen stove operates on bottled gas. The containers must be shipped to Honiara for refilling. Once, the refilled gas bottles were shipped to Gizo by mistake and the valuable bottles disappeared before they could be returned. The Hiscoxes could not use their stove for months, forced to make do with an old discarded wood stove as substitute. Improvisation is standard fare, but the constant making do just adds to the weight of their responsibilities. How do they manage? It is worse for Ken, Jill says. He is the one who is responsible for the entire mission and all its programs. Though he has capable island lieutenants and tries to delegate as much authority as possible, the islanders are just learning to handle it, and most important decisions still are directed to the man at the top.

When asked why he cannot leave some of the difficult jobs to his assistants and take life a little easier, Ken replies, "We've gotta show by our actions, here in the Solomon Islands, that if we say, 'Do something,' we are prepared to go and do that thing ourselves. If I say I would like that timber to be shifted, and if I cannot shift that timber, then I don't expect them to do it. If I can't go and fix up a machine, then I don't expect them to do it. If I can't go and help somebody, even if it means them weeping on my shoulder, then I can't expect those guys to go and do the same. If I can't go out and talk to people in their villages, then I can't expect them to. So I've got to lead by my action."

[*213*]

Ken agrees that being willing to take on any job at the mission adds another level of stress to his already burdened existence, but he believes he benefits from it. He says, "I feel that too many times in Australia, people rely on experts to come and fix all their problems, instead of being prepared to work out situations with people together and make a mateship or a friendship or a spiritual connection, which is beneficial to both. I feel by me being out here I've become closer to my Creator, my Lord, because I'm facing so many complex problems that I know I can't do it. I can't go and buy my problem solving at the corner shop like the Australian or American does.

"Of course this work can be very stressful," Ken continues. "However, I find that with my religious background and my close relationship with my Lord that I'm able to get through. I rely a great deal on the Good Lord up above. That's where I get my stamina, my batteries charged. I have learned over the years, especially the years that I've been in the South Pacific islands, in New Guinea and its subsidiary islands, and then Vanuatu as a child, I've learned that once I get away from that relationship with my God, things start to fall apart. I've tested it and tried it out, and now when I have a successful day, if you can call it a successful day, it is one of those days when I have my little morning devotions, and if a crisis does turn up, I can say, 'Well, listen, Guv, how the heck am I gonna get out of this one?' It is a kind of a communication as to a friend, and that's how I relate to the whole situation."

Jill says she derives the same satisfactions as Ken from her relation with and dependence on her Lord in a remote area like Batuna. She also gains the pleasure of achievement from her work. "I enjoy life," she says. "I feel life is what you make it, and this is my life, where I'm meant to be. I try to make the very most of my life. I love to be involved and to help people. If I can impart some knowledge that will help them, I receive great satisfaction from that. If I can contribute and help to improve their lives, *that* is the reward. *That* is worth the effort."

The Solomon Islands depend heavily on people like Ken and Jill and the religious groups they represent. The government possesses neither the money nor the human resources to provide universal primary education, let alone secondary or tertiary schooling.

In 1986, only fifty-four percent of primary-age children were receiving an education, and throughout the entire country there were only eight secondary schools, six operated by the churches. There are eleven hospitals nationwide, of which three are mission-run; and throughout the Solomons, where medical care is free, only about twenty doctors work outside the capital. That's not nearly enough to care for the two hundred and fifty thousand people in the bush.

Missionaries educate about twelve percent of Solomons children and provide nearly one-third of the country's health care. The Anglicans, Catholics, and Seventh Day Adventists have been active in both fields. No other religious group, however, has approached the SDAs' efforts to improve the financial well-being of the people. In addition to the two secondary and two vocational schools it operates in the Solomons, the SDA Church provides nurses' training at its hospital in Atoifi, runs a carving and copper crafts factory near Honiara, and operates a fifty-cow dairy, one of the few in the country. The SDAs also run Western Pacific Air Service to augment the facilities of the small national airline, but the main thrust of their economic programs is to enable the villagers to support themselves better. The new fishing program, they hope, will accomplish that goal for the thousands of people living around Marovo Lagoon. While the rich fishing grounds of the lagoon provide food for those living beside it, there has been no means of selling the fish that are caught, even though an unfilled demand exists in Honiara.

The Church believes that its new fishing plan should enable the people to be paid on the spot for their catch, which will then be flash-frozen and airlifted to Honiara on a daily basis by one of Western Pacific's Piper Aztecs. A foreign aid program has already contributed the commercial blast freezer and ice-making equipment now being installed at the mission station. The Church expects that they will be able to ship fifty-five hundred pounds a week, thus providing cash for nearly five thousand local people who presently have no income. If Batuna's fishing scheme succeeds, the promise of similar programs exists around the Solomons. The government is as excited about the possibilities as the village people and the Church.

.

Late in the evening, Ken comes in after working with the technician on the freezer installation. He is exhausted and flops down in a chair, face in hands, almost too tired to eat his dinner, which still sits in the oven. Jill brings him his plate and he seems to recover a bit of energy. While he is eating, three old men from a nearby village come in with small figurines they have carved to sell to the visitors they know are staying with the Hiscoxes. The wood- and black-coral porpoises and sharks they offer are good but not extraordinary. The visitors have been discussing what, if any, of the old culture remains in the local villages. So Ken asks the old men, who have lived in an SDA village most of their lives, if they remember how to do any of the old tribal dances. They shake their heads. What about the old songs? No, they don't know any. Do they remember any of the old tribal stories? No, they shake their heads sadly. Everything has been lost. Ken himself seems shocked that these village patriarchs have already forgotten their entire culture.

In much of the Solomons it is the same. The old cultures have been extinguished, and the Christians—particularly the missionaries—have been responsible for the greatest part of this cultural liquidation, which extends, more or less, across the entire South Pacific. The scope of this loss is almost too enormous to contemplate. Ken, on behalf of his fellow missionaries, accepts some of the blame.

"I may be the odd-bod out here," he says. "My ideas about culture might be a bit different from the norm and what are the stamped ideals for missionaries or our mission in particular. In the past our missionaries have tried to turn the cultural behaviors of the people away from their own culture and into a more Westernized type of culture. We, as a church, have at times said, for instance, 'Right, you Church members, we do not agree that dancing is beneficial for your religious experience.' And so consequently we have put a blanket on *all* types of dancing. We whiteskins have taken away their cultural tendency, and there have been some very good cultural tendencies that they've had.

"I know, for example," he continues, "that there are some expressions that they [the islanders] would find beneficial to convey to others in the form of a cultural dance and which would be meaningful. Now I don't agree with the majority of dances they used because of the connotations of them, but there are one or two that could be left which would be beneficial, as far as their communications or their cultural ideas."

When asked what was wrong with the dances he didn't like, Ken answers, "Well, many cultural dances I am aware of, and that's going through New Guinea and Vanuatu to the Solomons, have sexual, satanic connotations, and those, I say, are not good to continue on. But where there is, for instance, the telling of a story by a dance about how their forefathers arrived or what they saw, I'm saying that should be retained."

Ken is asked about harvest dances, which either ask for or celebrate bountiful harvests, and which were an important part of tribal cultures across most of the Western Pacific before the missionaries arrived.

"Harvest dances are generally okay to a point," he answers, "but there is interwoven in harvest dances quite likely puberty or connotations of a sexual nature, and that's why our forefathers, or I should say the early missionaries, were very, very careful. So they just said, 'Right, all dances out.' Now I might be a little bit more liberal, maybe, in my ideas, but I think there should be some toleration given to people to retain some portions of their cultures which are beneficial. If the missionaries could have been a little bit more tolerant in certain areas instead of just banning everything, that's what I would've liked to have seen."

Ken wants to make sure that his predecessors don't get all the blame, or even most of it. "Now I am blaming a little bit of not being sensitive on the missionaries, but also I'm blaming a large portion of it on the government [the present Solomon Islands government, as well as the old colonial administration], which hasn't been sensitive to the people's feelings about their own culture."

It is true that the Solomon Islands government has done little more than pay lip service to the importance of maintaining or reintroducing the old tribal cultures, but the country has only been independent since 1978, and there are few funds available to promote a national cultural reawakening. Even more to the point, however, is that the government is composed mostly of missionary-educated Christians, who themselves have been raised to believe that their own cultures are at best worthless or at worst evil and satanic. So we are back to the doorstep of the missionaries and religious leaders. What is needed is Church support to change the status quo, and this does not appear to be forthcoming.

According to Kirk Huffman, the director of Vanuatu's cultural center who has monitored the cultural scene in both countries over the past ten years, there is some awakening. "The Presbyterian Church, by the late sixties and early seventies, began to change its attitude," he says, "and by the mid- to late seventies actually came to a sort of general understanding that Christianity and traditional culture can go together, like a canoe and its outrigger."

The Anglicans in both countries have been respectful toward traditional cultures, Kirk says. The Catholics are also beginning to see the importance of the traditional cultures, but the SDAs and the other fundamentalist religions do not at all. Indeed, as Ken Hiscox says, he is the odd-bod in his Church in that he sees *anything* worth preserving from the traditional cultures. His peers in the Church, when questioned on the subject, become most uncomfortable and defensive, and the only example they can cite of a cultural activity worth preserving or reintroducing is the building and sailing of the traditional Western Pacific canoe.

Although the aim of the early missionaries—some of whom sacrificed their lives in Melanesia—was to further their religious beliefs while aiding the native peoples, the fact remains that they gave more to the islanders than any other Europeans in the Pacific. Very few other Occidentals were *at all* concerned about the welfare of the Melanesians. It was largely because of publicity about missionaries' efforts that England passed the Pacific Island Laborers Act in 1901, which eventually ended blackbirding in Melanesia. Subsequently, the missionaries were among the small minority of whites who stood up to protect the rights of the Melanesians from unfair land and labor practices, which were occurring locally at the hands of European plantation owners and managers. So any criticism of the missionaries must be tempered by knowledge of the good they have

done and are still doing. This does not excuse their systematic eradi-
cation of Pacific Island cultures, however.

When asked whether they have the right to change or obliter-
ate another person's culture, some missionaries reply that they do
have the right because they are more knowledgeable about what is
good for the subject people than are the people themselves. Other
missionaries, Ken included, admit that no one has the right to
change anyone's culture. But, they add, if the person himself sees
something better to change to, then it is certainly *his* right to give up
his old culture. What goes unsaid, of course, is that, historically,
threats of fiery death and destruction have often been used to scare
and coerce very naive and unsophisticated peoples into giving up
their heritage.

It is fortunate that more and more religious leaders from many
faiths have changed their thinking on the subject, going so far as to
help the peoples whose cultures they had once denigrated renew
and relearn them.[3] One can only applaud this long-overdue trend
and hope that soon it will be a standard accepted by the clergy of all
religions.

Late in the evening, the faithful are asleep and silence reigns
over Batuna. The palms sway gently. A full moon has risen, and to
the west, from the hill on which the missionary house stands, small
palm-covered islands rest on the placid lagoon. Across the entire
horizon not one light mars the serenity of the night. The world
seems at peace.

---

[3] For an example, see appendix B.

V

The Solomon Islands

THE "I WILL KILL YOU" PEOPLE

15

MARCH TO THE KWAIO

For two hours our group has been walking toward the mountains, skirting small farms with one or two thatched huts bordered by patches of pawpaw, some spindly cocoa trees, yams, and a few other sad vegetables that poke meekly out of the infertile red dirt. We have cut up a steep hillside and now drop into a lush, verdant, jungled valley, a steamy cauldron of humidity, where the native trees—fata, baula, kwae, and ngali—intermingle with broad-leaf ferns and dozens of different palms, all thrust upward in an amorphous mass. An enormous black butterfly with brilliant yellow-orange spots flutters above us, pointing our way—the most gorgeous of fairy guides.

In the suffocating heat the ten of us pause to catch our breath and wipe perspiration from our eyes. Accompanying me and acting as my assistant is Jo Ann, an athletic forty-year-old teacher taking her sabbatical. The rest include five porters hired in a nearby coastal village, each with a large pack balanced on his head; a man and his son who live in a village in the general direction we are heading and who prefer to accompany us, rather than travel alone in a dangerous land; and Paul, our good-natured Kwaio guide and translator who, with hair like a rusty Brillo pad bobbing before us, deftly breaks the trail by using his machete to sever tendrils and thorny branches jutting across our path.

We are heading into the mountains of central Malaita to visit a tribe many of whose members have never seen an outsider, much less a pair of Caucasians. The Kwaio live in one of the least accessible areas in the South Pacific, and they are the only people, outside of a few Small Nambas in Vanuatu and a few tribes in the two New Guineas, who still exist almost completely untouched by modern civilization. The Kwaio, more than any other tribe, have resisted the message of the missionaries and shunned their presence, as well as that of all outsiders. Even government soldiers and police seldom venture into the Kwaio mountain domain, where the only laws are centuries-old tribal precepts and where an outlander in trouble is on his own.

In the 1920s, Malaita and the Kwaio were looked upon as the most dangerous place and the most savage native population in all of the British Empire. Their reputation for violence and treachery spread around the world to such an extent that they were regarded with fear even in the capitals of Europe. In fact, it was the Europeans who began calling them *Kwaio*, which in their language means "I will kill you," and indeed the Kwaio themselves confirm that their reputation has been well deserved. Their hierarchy resembled that of many other tribes in the western Pacific; it was led by the triumvirate of priest, the Big Man or feast-giver, and the warrior leaders and professional assassins they called *lamo* and neighboring tribes called *ramo*.

Before European law arrived in Malaita, the Kwaio warred incessantly with neighboring villages of their own people, as well as with the Are'are to the south and the Kwara'ae to the north, two tribes closely allied culturally but who speak slightly different languages. The handful of Europeans—mostly missionaries and traders living in a few scattered settlements on the coast—were also subject to their attacks. No one escaped their wrath.

As early as the 1870s, Malaita was supplying manpower for the plantations of Australia and Fiji, usually in return for payments made not only to the workers themselves, but also to big men and family elders who served as labor brokers or procurers. The rub was that one in four Malaitamen who sailed away as laborers died in transit or on the plantations, and their kin never heard of them again. The Kwaio regarded these disappearances as murders and, in accordance with their tribal beliefs, they exacted revenge on white labor recruiters, missionaries, or any other European they might chance upon. This is how Malaita gained its reputation as one of the most dangerous places in the world for Europeans.

Even as late as 1909, when the British, who had ruled the Solomons as a protectorate since 1877, established a district officer in Auki, he neither retaliated against attacks on Europeans nor sent patrols into the Malaitan hinterlands. Indeed, the security efforts of this zealous young Englishman, T. E. Edge-Partington, centered on trying to protect his own administrative outpost against attack. His thirty poorly trained Solomon Islands policemen would most likely have been massacred if they had ventured into Kwaio territory. As it was, a massacre did not occur until nearly two decades later, on October 4, 1927. The murder of District Officer William Bell, his young English assistant, K. C. Lillies, and thirteen Solomon Islands constables still reverberates throughout the Kwaio mountains. More than any other historical factor, this act influences the present lives of thousands of Kwaio struggling to survive outside the twentieth century.

William Robert Bell certainly looked the part of a jungle explorer-policeman. Solid, big boned, and barrel-chested, he would have been right at home in the center of a rugby scrum, no doubt as a fearless but sportsmanlike competitor. Indeed, throughout his life he was respected by Europeans and Malaitans alike for both his bravery and his fairness. Born in 1876 into a poor migrant farm family on the colonial frontier of southern Australia, Bell was forced early on to abandon his education when his father died prematurely. He and his brothers worked as their father had, tilling the soil of their wealthier neighbors until in 1899 they enlisted to fight in the Boer War. After some bloody fighting in Witwatersrand, William was commissioned a lieutenant in the 6th Commonwealth Horse and then, in rapid succession, was court-martialed for cowardice, acquitted, and finally given a medal for bravery. He returned to Australia after the war. When a farming accident mangled his right hand, he drifted north to Fiji, where he was employed as an accountant for a large trading company, then as a government labor inspector on vessels enlisting and carrying native laborers to plantations on Fiji. This work introduced him to Malaita and the Kwaio people.

Conversations with the Cannibals

In 1915, at age thirty-nine, William Bell became district officer for Malaita. The island's interior had hardly been penetrated by Europeans, and the mountain tribes continued to kill each other and anyone else they chose with impunity, in spite of the police post at Auki. Bell viewed the ramos and lamos as criminals, gangsters motivated by financial gain and not by some traditional necessity to preserve their culture. He believed there were *no* extenuating circumstances for their murders, and he pursued and captured them to stand trial for their crimes; if found guilty, they went to jail in the district capital on the island of Tulagi—or were hanged. Naturally, the Kwaio lamos, some of whom had become very wealthy and powerful as a result of their bounty killings, feared and hated Bell with a vengeance.

In 1917 the American adventurers Martin and Osa Johnson visited Bell. They thought he was brusque and cool to their presence, though he did share with them what comforts his frontier lifestyle could offer, including listening to his favorite Gilbert and Sullivan on a windup Victrola. Osa Johnson, in her book *Bride in the Solomons*, said that Bell felt he was in constant danger. One day when Osa, against Bell's warnings, wandered into a taboo area away from the post, he screamed at her, "You bloody little fool. Do you know that hundreds, probably thousands of people have been murdered within sight of where you are sitting at this moment? And that I spend every hour here at my peril? I have expected the house to be rushed any night and have had special guards posted. Why, this place reeks with murder and headcutting. And I wouldn't be surprised if they have my head one day."[1] The Johnsons, it seems, were as upset by Bell's unmannerly outburst as by the prospect of losing their heads. At any rate, they left immediately on a schooner that had propitiously stopped at the remote outpost.

Another visitor, W. E. Mann, an American entomologist who was in Malaita on a collecting trip, described witnessing a trial conducted by Bell:

---

[1] *Bride in the Solomons*, Osa Johnson. Harrap Co., 1946, p. 143. Martin & Osa Johnson Safari Museum, Chanute, Kansas.

I sat crosslegged near Bell and listened to evidence from Filia, who had shot Ramafuna, and to about fifty natives representing both factions. . . . I wondered how Bell could decide it. There had definitely been a murder, but it had been occasioned by another, and that by still another, and that by still another, and it all went back to a witchcraft [i.e., sorcery] case. It seemed hardly fair to hang the latest in a series of murderers when the others had gone unharmed. Shaking his fist at the accused, Bell demanded that he and his village give four pigs and six fathoms of shell money to the other group; then, still shaking his fist, and raising his voice, he promised both sides that the next time there was a killing he would bring his soldiers in and shoot the murderer. Both parties seemed satisfied with Bell's judgment. . . . We heard later that the pigs were duly turned over, and that both groups had a big feast together . . . terminating . . . a long feud.[2]

The rule of European law began to squeeze the Kwaio king-dom harder and harder. By 1924 six Kwaio lamos convicted of mur-der had already swung on the gallows of Tulagi. In that same year, Bell started collecting a head tax, five shillings per male adult. This was a great imposition on the Kwaio, most of whom had no foreign money and no prospects for getting any unless they defied the pre-cepts of their religion and went down to work on the coastal planta-tions. The European plantation owners, desperate for labor, had convinced the Crown that a tax should be levied, and now Bell was administering the law even in this last stronghold of native domi-nance. The penalty for defaulting on the tax was either three En-glish pounds, which only the richest Kwaio could afford to pay, or three months' imprisonment.

The last straw fell in 1927. Bell planned to confiscate all the Kwaio's rifles while he collected taxes for the year. Perhaps he thought their rifles represented greater firepower and a more sub-stantial threat than they actually did, or perhaps he wanted to sub-ject the Kwaio to his utter domination. In any case, it was the first of

[2] *Anthill Odyssey*, Boston: Little-Brown, 1948, p. 284.

two major errors in judgment Bell was to make that would cost him his life. The rifles posed almost no threat to anyone. For the most part they were outdated muzzle-loaders and breech-loading Snider rifles left over from the last century, and more importantly the Kwaio had few bullets for the rifles and no possibility of obtaining more. Yet these rifles were a symbol of Kwaio pride and manhood and were carried everywhere. They had been paid for in overseas labor and in some cases by the blood of their ancestors. To willingly surrender these to Bell would be to surrender to complete domination by the white man. Certain Kwaio lamo determined that this would not happen.

The harbor of Sinalagu on the east coast of Malaita is nearly landlocked. Roughly rectangular and about three miles long by a mile and a half wide, it faces sheer rock cliffs shooting straight up more than two thousand feet. It is one of the few eastern entries to the Kwaio kingdom. On a small spit of land jutting into the harbor, Bell had decided to conduct the tax- and gun-collecting drive for the adjacent Kwaio territory. The bushmen had been told to assemble there with their guns and their shillings, and assemble they did. On Tuesday, October 4, 1927, two hundred warriors armed with bows and arrows, battle axes, war clubs, and lances—besides their muskets—milled around the thatched tax house located in the middle of a large glade. Inside the tax house were nine Solomon Islands constables; another four constables and a police clerk stood on each side of two tables set in front of the house, all armed with repeating rifles. Bell sat at one table, Lillies, his assistant, at the other, with loaded revolvers placed in front of them. Rumors and warnings of a plot to murder Bell had been buzzing around even before he arrived at Sinalagu. Already many Kwaio bounties had been placed on his head, and now, upon his arrival, the rumors of an attack were confirmed. Local missionaries and Christianized Kwaio begged him to leave, not to hold the tax collection. Bell ignored the warnings, error number two. No doubt he felt that even though his men were greatly outnumbered, the prospect of superior firepower from their repeating rifles would cow the Kwaio into submission.

Two long lines of Kwaio warriors formed in front of the tax tables. As each man handed over his musket and shillings, his name was entered in one of two ledgers. A small, thin Kwaio in his forties edged forward, a rifle concealed in his lavalava. Basiana was one of the most feared of all the Kwaio lamos. His reputation for ferocity and cunning was known to all the Kwaio as well as to Bell, the man Basiana had vowed to kill. With him were thirty other lamos and male relatives who had also vowed to their ancestors to kill this hated symbol of European oppression. Some of the attackers grouped around the tax house with their weapons concealed. Others edged forward in the two lines behind Basiana.

When Basiana reached the front of the tax line, Bell was bent over as he made a notation in the ledger. He looked up to see Basiana's heavy old rifle raised high above his head. Before Bell could make the slightest move, the barrel came crashing down, splitting Bell's skull in two and splattering his brains over both his assailant and the table. Another lamo, Fuufu'e, tried to decapitate Lillies with a machete, but his blow was partially deflected by a constable. With a gaping wound in his head and covered in his own blood, young Lillies grabbed his revolver and staggered into the tax house. Behind him stormed the Kwaio, charging the tax house from all sides. The fragile thatched walls instantly collapsed, and most of the unfortunate constables inside were killed in vicious hand-to-hand fighting. Only one constable, foreseeing what was about to occur, had prepared himself. He had taken off his uniform and cartridge belt so that he would be indistinguishable from his attackers, and as soon as the walls of the tax house fell he leapt out and escaped into the throng of milling Kwaio. He then swam to a nearby boat. All told, in addition to Bell and Lillies, twelve constables and the clerk were killed. Only one Kwaio died, but six were seriously wounded.

The news of the massacre rocked the small European colony in the Solomons. The English and Australian planters living alone or with their families on isolated trading and copra stations in the middle of the jungle, surrounded by thousands of potentially hostile bushmen, felt particularly vulnerable. Once they realized that the outbreak was confined to Kwaio territory, however, fear gave way to cries for vengeance. Planters from all over the islands gathered at Tulagi and formed a civilian force to lead local constables on a punitive expedition into Kwaio territory. The three-stack Australian navy destroyer A.M.A.S. *Adelaide* sailed from Sydney to bolster the attacking force.

Three weeks after the massacre the punitive expedition set forth. The group included twenty-eight planters, many of whom were in such poor physical condition that they were called the "breathless army," forty native constables, and a detachment of marines from the *Adelaide,* along with more than a hundred porters and guides. They formed a human chain that scaled the cliffs leading to the Kwaio kingdom. Indeed, many of the planters were capable of little more than raising one of an impressive number of accompanying whiskey bottles to their lips and actually had to be carried up the mountain on the backs of their porters. All in all, the Europeans were inept at moving through the jungle, and their single contribution was to machine-gun some harmless pigs and destroy a few of the natives' vegetable gardens left by the terrified fleeing Kwaio.

The Kwaio had felt that their mountains were impregnable to attack from the Europeans, and largely they were correct. The punitive expedition ended with almost no concrete results. However, the Kwaio did not reckon with the animosity that their killings had fueled in their neighbors, the Kwara'ae and the Are'are, and in the Christian Kwaio living on the coast, some of whom had lost relatives in the massacre. Very capable Malaitan constables, well armed and well trained by Bell, raised in the jungle themselves, and every bit as strong and cunning as their adversaries, conducted subsequent forays of their own throughout the Kwaio mountains. Ruthlessly they tracked down men, women, and children, burned village after village, desecrated the holy shrines, and eliminated every pig and vegetable garden that could provide food for their enemy. Not only the perpetrators of the massacre but *all* the Kwaio suffered. Nearly two hundred were shot or arrested, and the reprisals left other completely innocent Kwaio on the verge of starvation. Many left the mountains to accept Christianity in return for food and safety.

Sixty years after the massacre, the entire Kwaio society still suffers for the deeds committed by only thirty of its members. Less than half the pre-massacre population now lives in the mountains. Those remaining still cling to their old ways, fighting off the advances of the multitude of missionaries who pray for their God's assistance each morning in converting the bushmen. The Kwaio are poor and powerless to combat the intrusion of a twentieth century they barely comprehend. They fiercely maintain their independence, however, bowing to no outsider. They still carry their rifles and they still rule their own territory, allowing in their midst only those they choose. In 1965 they killed the last missionary interloper, a South Seas Evangelical from New Zealand. In 1985 a Malaitan constable who ventured into their realm was shot and killed. To this day the police obtain permission before entering the Kwaio kingdom, and most often it is denied. There are also substantive but unproven rumors that in 1987 ten Eieisils, a small neighboring tribe on Malaita's east coast, were murdered by Kwaio from adjacent villages over a land dispute. The Solomon Islands government admits to being aware of only one killing. It also has declared the entire Kwaio area closed to tourism, and foreigners apprehended have been jailed and deported.

.

Fortunately, I have not yet heard about the latest intertribal killing. Still, I have heard enough, and I ponder the Kwaio's reputation for violence and hostility to strangers, wondering nervously what kind of a reception we will receive. I stumble laboriously after Paul's hacking machete and his rubiginous Afro bouncing along the slit of a jungle trail as we begin walking uphill again. Jo Ann and I are dripping with sweat, the Solomon Islanders less so. Above us on a low branch, a brown fantail, a white-breasted, grayish bird about the size of a crow, provocatively swishes its tail at us. The bird accordions its pleated tail, thrusting it from one side to the other, opening and closing it like a Japanese courtesan using her fan. I ask Paul about the common bird species in the area. He tells me about a bird that is awake only in the night and sleeps during the day. He calls it an owo.

"And that's the English name?" I ask.

"Oh yes," Paul responds, "it is called owo."

Still mystified, I ask him to spell it for me.

"O-W-L" comes the slow, carefully spelled response.

"Oh, of course." I feel a little stupid, but while Paul's English is fairly good, his pronunciation is often difficult to understand. "So what does it look like, Paul? It's face, I mean?"

Paul makes sure there is no misunderstanding this time. With great seriousness he says, "He look like a cat, C-A-T, cat."

I try unsuccessfully to keep from laughing. "Okay, it's a type of owl, and it has a face that looks like a cat, and it eats birds or mice? What does it eat, Paul?"

Now Paul is perplexed. "You mean the mice?"

"No, the owl."

"He sleep and during the night it looks for its food and during the day it sleeps."

"Okay, and it makes a noise like? Let's see, who can do the noise?" I address the question to the young porters, most of whom are still in their teens. They speak little English, so Paul translates into pidgin. Immediately comes a fountain of giggles mixed with a variety of coo-coo-coos and other wild-owl imitations.

"You try it, David," I suggest to the youngest porter, a stocky, muscular sixteen-year-old who is the group's jester. Between laughing and maintaining the balance of his pack, David has a hard time replying, but finally he comes out with a credible high staccato ooh-ooh-ooh that draws further laughter from the other porters.

High in the dense forest canopy above us more fantails chatter to each other. Our party wades through a river, low in this dry season, that we have already crossed twice and will cross four more times. Eventually, we leave the valley and begin climbing a steep mountainside. We are no longer walking but crawling, grabbing roots, plants, and whatever else will give us a handhold. But we must carefully watch what we grasp. Many of these plants and vines have thorns or razor edges. Particularly troublesome is the laurkin, one of the many species of palm from which rattan is made. The laurkin sends out hundreds of small branches that look like vines. Some grow upward, others horizontally, but all are covered with long, needle-sharp thorns that pierce the skin like miniature arrows and then break off, causing serious infections. The thorns must be cut out, as generally they can't be pulled out of the skin. Frequently, Jo Ann or I instinctively reach out for a laurkin branch, only to recognize it a split second before wrapping a hand around it. The result is that we lose our upward momentum and have nothing holding us. Unless, in an instant, we can find a substitute hand-hold, we go crashing back down the trail into the porters behind us. Miraculously the porters, with one hand steadying their packs and the other maintaining a handhold of their own, somehow manage to break our runaway descent. In any case, the foliage on each side of the trail is so thick that there is no danger of falling a great distance. It is more a question of what kind of plant will eventually act as the backstop.

We must also be vigilant to avoid wrapping a hand around either of two venomous vipers common to the Solomons: The Guppy's *(Boiga irregularis)*, a light brown snake that reaches lengths of six feet, may be aggressive, striking repeatedly if aroused. The Woodford's *(Salomonelaps McDowell)*, reddish-brown with a pale underside, is more docile, though highly venomous. Its bite can be fatal, and the nearest antitoxin, which must be kept refrigerated, is at least three days away, back in Auki.

We reach the top of the mountain and, chests heaving, stop to look around. Far to the west the sun glitters on the sea. In every direction there are only jungle-covered peaks. After an all-too-short pause to catch our breath, we start down the other side, heading northeast for our trek through dense rainforest. The trail is a mere chink, only the width of a human foot in the ten-foot-high foliage. The oil palms of the coast have disappeared, and in their place, large broad-leaf evergreen trees, most with the same branch and leaf structure, form a partial canopy over us. They are interspersed with thorn, sago, and dozens of other varieties of palms, all covered in a crawling profusion of creepers, climbers, epiphytes, and vines. Enough sunlight filters through the canopy to encourage tree ferns, however. Some grow ten to fifteen feet high, and along with masses of smaller ferns and vegetation, they cover every inch of the forest floor.

Going down the mountain is more difficult than going up. The trail is exceedingly steep and is covered with roots and creepers that hurl me to the ground every third step, sometimes head first. It helps to have staffs that Paul has hacked from bamboo or saplings with a few whacks of his machete, but they do not solve the problem. I am plagued more than Jo Ann, but neither Paul nor the Kwaio porters, who are all barefoot, seem troubled in the least. Their wide feet splay into the soil, their toes gripping the roots like fingers, and they seldom fall or stumble. Eventually we reach the bottom of the mountain. We cross another river and crawl halfway up a second mountain. By this time it is early evening. As the sun slides out of sight beyond an endless jumble of mountains, we stop and make camp on a narrow plateau. Sleep is not a problem. Exhaustion is our blanket.

The next morning we are out on the trail early, soon after daylight. We have just reached the top of the second mountain and are sitting in the ferns, panting, when three Kwaio men appear from nowhere. One is armed with a small-bore rifle of World War I vintage. Another has a long lance. The third, a smaller, younger man, carries no weapons. The older man with the rifle wears ragged short pants; the others are in cotton sulus or lavalavas. There is a guarded greeting between parties. Paul later says that the youngest, who is unarmed, fortunately, has a reputation for being very dangerous and unpredictable. The Kwaio do not seem surprised to see what to them must be an extraordinary sight in their secluded mountains. They are coming from a village far to the east on their way to a mortuary feast at another village near the coast. After glancing at us briefly, they disappear in an instant, like puffs of smoke, over the mountain trail we have so laboriously ascended.

The mountain trail we must now descend drops almost vertically for more than half a mile. At every step creepers grab at our feet, and vines reach out to trip us. It is as if all the vegetables were conspiring to prevent us from reaching the bottom of the mountain upright. For a while we follow a mostly dry stream bed, lowering ourselves over moss-covered boulders and hanging from ferns to drop down, one level after another, after another. I slip on a slimy boulder and plunge ten feet off the edge. I am in the air an eternity and wonder what bone-bashing projection I will crash into. Fortunately, my fall is broken by a pool of water, where I lie for a minute blissfully luxuriating in its coolness. The others, after seeing that I am not injured, look a little envious.

At the bottom of the mountain we stop for lunch alongside a river. Jo Ann and I find we must force ourselves to eat, as the intense heat seems to have robbed us of any desire for food. We have been eating very lightly, and the consequent reduction in energy is noticeable. The porters cook some rice, and we pass around a large jar of peanut butter, along with crackers. For most of the Kwaio boys this is their first taste of peanut butter, and unanimously they decide that they would like it at every meal. In a flash the entire jar is gone. After a short rest our group, now numbering eight since the departure the previous afternoon of the man and his son, begins walking again.

A half hour along the trail brings us to the base of a cliff. We must wade up the river that flows alongside it. All afternoon we wade in knee-deep water through the narrow canyon. On each side, steep granite walls rise hundreds of feet into the air. Paralleling the river a hundred and fifty feet up, a trail only a few inches wide hugs the cliff face. If we weren't traveling in the driest month of a drought year, the river would be a roaring cascade, impossible to traverse, and we would be digging our fingernails into every crevice, inching our way along the towering cliffs above us. Even during most dry seasons there is too much water in the river for it to be waded. Paul says that some years ago his father died here. Heading back to his village, he was edging his way along the narrow cliffside path when he lost his grip and plunged into the torrent below. His body could not be recovered until the following dry season. I ask Paul if there are any other routes that would take us where we want to go. He shakes his head. This is the only one.

Late in the afternoon we stop on the side of a mountain. On an arm of a neighboring peak across a high valley from where we're standing, through a break in the trees, lies our destination: a small village of thatched huts. It seems hidden and desolate. We trudge onward. High above, two large white Solomon cockatoos, the aerial king and queen of the jungle, wheel and glide while shrieking at each other. Then, one cockatoo follows the other in a diving, swooning, fluttering, controlled crash, sideslipping, first on one wing, then on another, until finally they light in some trees a few hundred yards down the slope, where they continue to shriek. Their ear-splitting calls echo over the forest.

It is almost dark when we come to the village we saw across the canyon. We are expected. Word of our approach has preceded us, whispered by an unheard voice or announced by an unseen spirit. All the Kwaio know of our presence, our path, and our number, but not of our purpose.

16

IN THE LAND OF

CENTURIES PAST

The jungle parts to reveal a shallow clearing from which all plants and even grass have been removed. A tiny village stands in the clearing surrounded by a four-foot-high wall of piled boulders and palm trunks embedded in the ground. Peeking out between thatched huts, a group of Kwaio women and children study us intently—silently. There are no men to be seen. A few pigs root in the bare dirt, and three sickly, half-starved little mongrels yip at our heels, then scurry for safety. Young women carrying machetes, all bare-breasted, and with infants or small children either in their arms or clinging to them, stare frankly now, open-mouthed. We are the first Caucasians they have ever seen, although an Iranian Baha'i leader some years ago visited a few of the nearby villages. They are particularly fascinated by Jo Ann and appear as if they long to touch her blonde hair, but dare not.

Packs are set down, and Paul leads us to a seven-foot-high raised dais built from rocks and packed dirt. On top of the stone platform is a well-thatched hut; in front of it sit the men of the village solemnly peering down at us. The dozen Kwaio range in age from boys just into their teens to a pair of old men, one of whom looks ill and leans weakly against the front wall of the hut. Jo Ann and I feel like defendants standing meekly before a panel of judges scrutinizing us prior to passing sentence—and, of course, this is the intended purpose of the elevated men's platform.

This village is called Muilage. One of the elders, a lean-faced, wizened old man by the name of Anifanaia, asks why we have come. I tell him, via Paul's translation, that the Kwaio are the last tribe in the South Pacific who have still not accepted the missionaries and Christianity. People hear many bad stories about the Kwaio from the missionaries, the Christians on the coast, and the government, but no one hears the Kwaio people's story. We have come to hear from the Kwaio what *they* think, and to tell people about the Kwaio's problems.

Old Anifanaia lowers his head in agreement. He and Paul begin an animated conversation that seems to go on for an eternity. Finally Paul turns to me and says, "Anifanaia agree to talk with you about these things. First, though, I must tell you, Mike, my people don't beg except for one thing: medicine. The other old man is very sick. These people have prayed to their ancestors for him. They have sacrificed pigs for him. Still he is sick. These people think he will die. They ask if you can give some medicine for him."

The request is not unexpected. With the advice of an American expert on tropical medicine, I had acquired a substantial array of antibiotics, fungicides, and antimalarials before leaving the States. Then, after deciding to visit the Kwaio and realizing that they would have unmet medical needs, I added to our supply in Honiara. But diagnosis, not supply, is the problem. Many tropical diseases show similar symptoms, and without blood testing, even a trained physician must guess at both disease and treatment. The stark reality is that if we give this old man the wrong medicine or one that has no effect, we may witness his death instead of curing him. Not good news for either him or us.

I ask what is wrong with the old man. There is a lengthy consultation between Anifanaia and the others. By this time the old fellow has been assisted back into the men's hut, where he lies on a mat, wheezing and breathing with great difficulty through his mouth. He has not been able to swallow food of any kind and is now having difficulty swallowing even water. He is very weak and seems to have a high fever. How long has he been like this? Four or five days is the answer, each day getting worse and worse. The old man's illness seems to have arisen too rapidly to be cancer or any sort of diverticular disease. The old man has nothing caught in his throat, and his fever seems to indicate an infection. So with fingers crossed,

I empty the contents of two penicillin capsules into half a cup of water, which I have Paul give the old man as soon as he has sucked on a throat lozenge.

Hardly have we finished with the old man when another villager asks if he can have some medicine for his small daughter who has a very bad case of malaria. He had made the five-day round-trip to the little clinic on the coast to bring the child some medicine, but it has done her no good. The understocked clinic probably gave out only chloroquine, to which almost half the local malaria strains are resistant. I tell the father that the drug that might help his daughter might also do her great harm—might be more dangerous than her malaria. Does he want to take the chance? Yes, he does. Apparently the girl is delirious and, besides having the usual fever interspersed with chills, is on the verge of unconsciousness. I look through my notes on tropical diseases. The symptoms seem to indicate falciparum, the most serious form of malaria, which often affects the brain and may cause death in untreated sufferers. With great trepidation, I cut two Fansidar pills in half and make sure that the father knows that the girl must not have more than one piece for each seven days. There is a substantial question in my mind whether the man can count to seven or keep track of the days. But Paul translates carefully, and the man seems to understand. I hope so. I instruct him to report any changes in his daughter's condition to us.

When we have finished with the second man, Jo Ann whispers that she has to go to the latrine. I ask Paul if one of the women could guide her. "Yes, of course," Paul replies, and tells an older woman sitting back in the shadows to do this. But the women of the village decide that one guide is not enough. They all troop out, leading their white visitor to the latrine.

While Jo Ann is gone, I ask Anifanaia how often doctors come to the village. Through Paul the old man replies, "Since I am a baby I never meet [have never seen] a doctor from the government or from anywhere to visit [our villages] or to give us medicine. Never has been a doctor in the village."

"What about the other mountain villages?" I ask.

"No doctor [ever] come to these mountains" is Anifanaia's angry reply. With the exception of Seventh Day Adventist doctors nervously climbing the peaks to visit a few villages closest to their hospital at Atoifi on the eastern seacoast, near where Bell was killed, and two Catholic priests who made a few medical visits on the western slopes, almost no medical aid has come to any of the Kwaio mountain villages. Most of the nearly twenty-five hundred mountain Kwaio, living in more than a hundred villages, have never even seen a doctor. Amazingly, as is soon evident, many of them have never seen outsiders either.

Jo Ann presently returns, trailed by the village women. She looks white, shaken. I ask her what the matter is. "They made me take off all my clothes before they would take me to the latrine," she answers. "Then when we got there, all of them started feeling me, all over. Feeling me *everywhere*, and giggling. They couldn't believe that I had the same parts as they do. And when they did realize it, they wanted to compare, to see who had the biggest, or in my case, I guess, the littlest. They thought it was a great joke. Have you ever tried to go to the toilet when a dozen people are feeling every part of you?" I shake my head. Indeed, I have not. "So anyway," Jo Ann adds dejectedly, "I still have to go."

I don't have the same experience as Jo Ann, fortunately. However, the men's latrine, on the opposite side of the village from the women's, is situated so that pigs won't root through the feces. That is to say, it is on the edge of a cliff. When I get there, craning my neck and peering over, I can hardly see bottom. There is also absolutely nothing to hang onto. Using the latrine is like trying to relieve yourself while balanced on top of a two-hundred-foot ladder. One misstep and you are in for a nasty fall. I decide that finding another latrine site is a top priority.

In the dark Jo Ann and I put up our small tent, and as soon as the scrutinizing Kwaio have left, we take a flashlight and head into the night. A few minutes' walk brings us to a suitable latrine place off the trail that is both private and not on the edge of a precipice. Adapting to village life suddenly becomes more tolerable.

·

The Kwaio believe that a woman's body is impure, particularly when she is menstruating or giving birth. Even a small baby is impure because it recently was in contact with the mother's blood. When a woman is having her period, she must stay in the menstrual hut outside the village. Whenever she goes to the latrine, she must take off her clothes—usually just a tiny bark or cotton "apron," if she is married. Unmarried women and all men usually are naked, but because of our presence, most of them have wrapped an old piece of cotton cloth around themselves. Any clothes or ornaments a woman wears to the latrine could contaminate the entire village. The effect might be twofold: enraging the spirits of the (male) ancestors, who could retaliate against the villagers, or causing disease or death for some male relatives. If a woman ever urinates near a man's hut, the Kwaio believe it would cause his death, and before the 1920s any woman even *suspected* of transgressing these pollution taboos would be put to death. As with the Are'are, a woman would also be killed not only if she committed adultery or had premarital sex but even if she was accused of having sex, whether in fact she did or not. If a man did not like a woman—any woman over the age of puberty—all he had to do was announce that he had propositioned her. The uncorroborated statement alone would be her death warrant unless she could escape to relatives in another village who might save her life by paying a ransom of pigs and shell money.

The existence of Kwaio women, never secure, was also one of continual drudgery. Even today, although a woman no longer has to fear for her life, she has little to smile about. She may walk only on certain trails and in specified areas of the village. She may not enter the men's house or even mingle with the men except under certain prescribed conditions. She must continually tend the gardens, which supply almost all the Kwaio's food, and daily she must carry on her back the heavy bamboo water containers, the yams, and all the firewood, often over miles of steep and narrow mountain trails. Because there is so little flat or terraced ground on which to plant a garden, and because the ravines down which the streams tumble are devastated by flash floods in the wet season, the village may be located an hour's strenuous hike away from the nearest stream or vegetable garden. Consequently, Kwaio women climb three or four hours a day, and their arms and legs are like bands of steel. Owing to their low status—just above the village pigs—and to generations of subservience, the women, for the most part, are like shy, overgrown children. Most have babies clinging to them. Besides rearing the children and all their other jobs, the women are also responsible for caring for the Kwaios' most prized possessions, their pigs. The pigs are either sold or sacrificed and eaten in male-only ceremonies, and so the women generally don't get to eat their charges. In spite of the sexual inequities to which the women are subjected, they seem to harbor no rancor or resentment.

Since most of the women have never been out of the mountains and don't realize a different life might exist, their choices are tightly circumscribed. Some, however, do flee with their babies to the Christian communities on the coast, where their lives are easier but where they are displaced persons, having no land or families of their own. Because they have no medical care, particularly during childbirth, and lead such hard lives, one sees few old women in the mountain villages. Most Kwaio women die early, probably in their thirties or forties.

The Kwaio men's lives are much easier. They control everything, make all the decisions, enforce all the tribal laws, and do relatively little physical labor. In the past their primary role was to provide security for the village, warding off enemies and punishing transgressions of tribal taboos—usually by killing the offenders. Now that most of their old roles are unnecessary or no longer practiced, adult males are usually involved with religious and tribal ceremonies, though they still do the heavy work of felling trees and clearing new areas for vegetable gardens, as well as some hut building. From their perspective, their most important duties are accumulating pig- and shell-money wealth and placating ancestral spirits by prayer, sacrifices, and enforcement of correct behavior within the tribe.

The Kwaio believe that pleasing the spirits of their ancestors is vital to their welfare—a matter of life and death. The wrath of their most powerful ancestral spirits can bring upon them every catastrophe that is within the realm of their experience, from poor crops and sickly pigs to devastating cyclones, disease, and death. Conversely, happy ancestors, pacified by offerings of pigs and prayers, and satisfied with the correct behavior of the living, may offer their protection and, even better, bestow their blessings in the form of mana. This supernatural power manifests itself in very concrete ways: It allows the blessed to accumulate wealth in the form of pigs and bountiful harvest; it prevents disease, or assures a rapid recovery; and it guarantees superiority over one's enemies. Essentially, by Kwaio standards, mana enables one to succeed in life.

If the pragmatic Kwaio observe one of their men to be successful, he must carry mana in him, and therefore it is certain that he has been blessed by the spirits. He then will be followed, since his success will ripple down to those around him, and he may become a big man or feast-giver. Since the feast-giver always receives more valuables than he expends on his feasts, attended by gift-bearing adults from all the nearby villages, this role, together with continued mana, will enable him to gather even greater wealth and power.

.

It is early morning. Wearily I leave my air mattress, open the tent flap, and back out. Practically on top of me stands a Kwaio with an enormous warted war club raised above his shoulder. He looks at me intently. There is no expression on his face—none. I can't tell in the slightest what he is thinking. He is middle-aged and powerfully built, with sinuous biceps, a strong-looking face, and a wrinkled forehead. The club he hefts so lightly is, at the business end, four times the size of a baseball bat; eight or nine squared, carved knots protrude more than a half inch each from the cylinder, just enough to put some big holes in my skull. This weapon is meant for one purpose only—to kill men—and it may be a split-second away from killing *me*. I can feel the shock permeate my body.

The Kwaio makes no move but simply stares at me. I am in a Neanderthal time warp. Should a brontosaurus lumber by right now, I would not be more surprised. Very very slowly, I gradually ease around a corner of the tent to put even a little insubstantial nylon between him and me. My mouth is frozen shut. It would like to say something, but what? Possibilities scamper like terrified rabbits through my mind and disappear in a fog of frustration. I can neither outrun nor outfight him, I can't talk to him, and there is no one close enough to call out to. Jo Ann is still asleep, and the others are nowhere in sight. What I must not do is show fear. Am I showing fear? I can't tell. Probably he smells it. Each second drags like an hour. Suddenly he turns on his heel and trots off into the jungle. Wham! I take a couple of deep, gasping breaths and start the new day.

The women and children are already having their morning meal. They sit around a pile of cooked yam pieces on a banana leaf in the center of the dilapidated, smoky cooking hut. They eat silently, stuffing pieces of cooked yams into their mouths with dispatch. Small mongrels, salivating hungrily, edge forward between the humans, hoping to catch a scrap. Fear of their masters is offset by their near-starvation. The Kwaio ignore the dogs completely except to cuff one that boldly darts out to gobble a dropped bit of yam. The men eat separately in their own house from a pile of yams brought by one of the women. The Kwaio will repeat this same meal in the evening, consuming four or five yams at each sitting. They may carry a few pieces with them as they go out to forage in the jungle or, in the case of the women, to work in the vegetable garden, but essentially the eight or ten yams constitute nearly their entire diet. When they can, they will eat ngali and other wild nuts, as well as wild breadfruit and berries, grubs, and the occasional rat or flying fox. But these and pork are only occasional supplements. Neither coconuts nor edible pandanus, both coastal dwellers, will grow this high in the mountains. Thus, the Kwaio must derive nearly ninety percent of both calories and nutrients solely from sweet potatoes. Although this diet approaches the nutritional minimum of 1350 to 1650 calories a day for inactive adults, it lacks by one-third the number required by active people. What's more, because a sweet potato contains only two grams of protein and one gram of fat, their diet is dangerously deficient in each category, as well as in many vitamins and minerals.

Nutritional deficiencies are most easily seen in the distended, worm-filled bellies of the children, who also suffer from running ulcers, hemorrhages, and the infected craters of yaws. Because of their inadequate diet, the children are more than normally susceptible to diseases—severe respiratory infections, diarrhea, and kwashiorkor. Then, when they contract a disease, they have great difficulty overcoming it. There are no statistics on infant and child mortality among the Kwaio, but they must be very high. Adults, too, suffer with open and running sores, but premature loss of teeth seems to be the primary indicator of their poor diet.

All the adults and nearly all the children from the age of eight or nine smoke a strain of wild tobacco that they also cultivate. They puff constantly on graceful pipes that they have carefully crafted by pounding, shaping, and scraping small pieces of metal removed from the remains of a Japanese fighter that crashed on a nearby mountain during World War II. The adults also chew betel, a product of the palm *Areca catechu*. The pulverized nut is wrapped in a leaf along with a small amount of lime paste, then chewed to produce a flavorful appetite suppressant. The chewer's teeth turn black and his saliva becomes a bright red, an effect that the bush people do not seem to consider unattractive, since it is a common practice throughout the Solomons. Both betel and tobacco are commonly used by many Third World peoples who would otherwise be subject to the nearly constant muscular contractions of an empty stomach.

With their babies in slings, the women leave for the vegetable garden carrying their machetes. Some of the small children trail after them; others stay in the village in the nominal care of the only old woman we have seen. I learn that she is, in fact, only in her fifties, since she was a small girl at the time of World War II. The men sit on their dais, smoking their pipes and dipping into small bamboo sections for the lime paste to accompany their betel nut.

Earlier this morning, one of the dogs gave birth to a tiny black-and-white spotted pup. The little thing, still unable to open its eyes, was feebly trying to crawl away from where its mother dropped it— right in the center of the most heavily trafficked area of the village. The bitch attempted to carry it into the quiet sanctity of one of the huts but was chased out. The struggling puppy is now ignored completely by everyone in the village. Conversation goes on around it. People barely miss stepping on it. One of the male dogs tries to snatch it, but the female snarls, baring her sharp teeth, and chases the male off. Then she, too, ignores the puppy. Probably she has no milk with which to nurse it. Later that day, mercifully, the little thing dies.

Aside from dogs and pigs, the village has no animals. The

Kwaio do not raise chickens, they say, because it is too difficult finding food for them. This is hard to believe with a lush jungle, brim-
ful of insects, surrounding every village. The pigs seem to do fine
rooting and foraging for much of their food, though they do get
yams and wild greens from their owners.

Muilage's site has been carefully chosen, no doubt in prayerful
consultation with the ancestors. Located on the only gently sloping
spine of the mountain, it encompasses about an acre of relatively
flat land if its immediate surroundings are included. In a country
where it is nearly impossible to find ten square feet of level ground,
this in itself is extraordinary. On the jungle-covered mountain
above and below the village, wild hibiscus grow in profusion. On
the other two sides of the village, the mountain falls away sharply,
crashing down almost vertically for more than one thousand feet
into a narrow valley totally hidden by jungle. Pacific swallows glide
below us, avian roller coasters, riding the hot currents upward,
looping over, then plunging down again through the silent
mountain-facing thermals. On a tree branch at the edge of the forest, an iridescent-blue dwarf kingfisher sits pensively, as if contem-
plating its long bill. Then with a shrill chree-ee, he too disappears
into the abyss.

The men are still sitting, smoking and chewing betel, in front
of their hut. I join them and ask Anifanaia why the Kwaio choose to
remain in the mountains when life might be easier for them down
on the seacoast.

The old man replies, "Our grandfathers give us this land and
also our culture and they say [to us] that you will not go down to the
seacoast and not become a Christian because already you have your
own god to worship. So that's why we don't. Our forefathers forbidden us to join the Christians or to go down to the seacoast. Our fathers told us that we will stay in our own land and keep our customs,
and from fathers to sons we teach the children to know about our
culture. So that's why we are not feel good to go down to the seacoast, to become Christian. And our land, nobody can take from
us. If we go to the seacoast we wouldn't have any land. Most of our
people from the mountains [who] went down to live on the seacoast
and become Christians, they have no land. The people, there they
start to push them away because they don't [own] any land and it's

very hard for them to come back to the mountain again because they are Christians."

"What about when the Christian missionaries come up here," I ask. "Do you want the missionaries to come up here or to stay down on the seacoast"?

There is no question in Anifanaia's mind about what he wants. Vehemently he says, "For the missionaries, we don't need them to come here and to build a mission place here. We stop them. We forbid them and say, 'Only place allowed for you to build the churches and the other religion is on the seacoast, but not in our land.'"

Anifanaia goes on to explain that if the Christianized Kwaio on the coast wish to resume their old lives in the mountains, they must first give up Christianity and return to the customs of their ancestors. Apparently, very few of the Christians have done that.

"How do the Christian Kwaio feel about the Kwaio people in the mountains?," I ask Anifanaia.

"The Kwaio people on the seacoast, they hate us people in the mountains keeping our customs, because they say that we are worshipping devils. They don't believe their [old] customs because of [what] missionaries tell them."

"So, what do your Kwaio people have to say about this? Do the Kwaio worship the devil?"

"We believe from our ancestors that when a thing wrong, [for example], like yesterday, there's a thing gone wrong with this old man and he ready to die, but is very helpful the medicine that you give to the old man last night and now he's coming better. But also, what we believe from our custom, that we take a pig and shell money to give over to the devil and suddenly the man['s] life comes back again. So that's what we believe."

"Now wait a minute. You sacrificed the pig and some shell money to the devil?" I ask.

"To the devil," he replies with assurance.

"So who is the devil?" I ask.

"The devil is our ancestors, like our fathers' fathers. When we offer the pig, we mention their names, of our forefathers and their fathers."

"The sacred names that you don't say any other time?"

"Yes, they're the sacred names. And that's [what] keeps them, their customs powerful."

"And you hope that the ancestor will save the life of the man?"

"Save the life of the man, or any people in [his] family."

For the Kwaio, Western medicine would present a valuable backup remedy in case sacrifices and prayers to their "devils" are not effective. At least it could be an effective backup if they had regular access to it. What is truly fascinating, however, is that they have co-opted the Christian concept of the devil and applied it to their own ancestors. In 1977 some of the few remaining Are'are priests, to the south of the Kwaio, were seeking to end the weekly flights of the Seventh Day Adventist airplane that flew over their mountain territory on its way to supply the SDA hospital at Atoifi. The Are'are priests had Christians on the coast write the following letter for them and present it to the SDA.

Dear Director of S.D.A. and the pilot of S. Steck [Piper Aztec] Plain.

I just want to let you know that I don't want your plain to fly over my village including Are are area from now on. I stop in [ask you to stop it] for the following reasonable reasons:

1. The plain carry women with bloody babies.
2. He always fly over our most Holy Alters where we burnt offering to our devil.
3. It always cause death to our people because the devil get angry and kill people.
4. Many pigs are kill [sacrificed because] to mean [to many] the plains fly over our devil.

On behave of majority of headen [heathen] people who are living here, if you are Christians please don't set your flyth over our area for it cause us death.

Thank you.

Yours sincerely Are are Devil Priests

1. Timikooliu
2. Maerora
3. Maealea

Certainly the Kwaio ancestor worship has no connection with the Christian concept of Satan, the devil, the evil fallen angel. But for most fundamentalist Christians, pagan worship of *any* kind *is* devil worship. So, most likely, converted Kwaio or missionaries convinced the mountain people that worshipping their ancestors was tantamount to worshipping the devil. Bum rap.

One old Kwaio, knowledgeable about his people's religion, explained most succinctly the parallels between his beliefs and those of Christians. He said, "We are worshipping the spirit and we are worshipping a similar god as those people [Christians are] worshipping. Only they are worshipping Jesus, the European ancestor. But we are worshipping our ancestor."

The Christians' desire to convert the Kwaio, whom they consider to be the South Pacific's last major heathen tribe outside New Guinea, is almost overwhelming. Only fear of the mountain people has kept most missionaries out of their realm. The Kwaio, though, so badly need medical help that they have accepted the presence of the few missionary doctors who have ventured to their villages, even though the mountain people distrust their visitors.

The Kwaio's suspicion of missionary doctors is frequently well founded. Too often the bush people have discovered there are strings attached to the medical aid they receive. Silas, a young Kwaio raised on the coast, returned to help his mountain brethren in spite of being the son of an SDA minister. When I met him in Malaita, he explained what had happened to make the mountain Kwaio fear receiving medical treatment, particularly at the hospital and clinic on the coast:

"When the custom people are sick," Silas says, "and they cannot be healed by sacrifice, sometimes they go down on coast and doctor heal them. When the doctor heal them, then the Christians come and visit them [in the hospital or clinic], and they pray for them and they tell them, 'We offered several prayer for you and God and Jesus healed you.' They tell them, 'Jesus saved your life, not the medicine, so you must accept Jesus. If not, you die.' And of course these mountain people are not educated," Silas continues, "and they believe the Christians about the prayer and they forget about the medicine, so they forced to become Christian. And Christians make mountain people say forbidden names of his ancestors so then he can never go home again. And the Christians tell him that if you go back to mountains, you die."

No doubt the Christian Kwaio believe what they are telling their mountain brethren, but this religious badgering has only made the Kwaio more suspicious of the Christians, and rightly so.

·

Early in the afternoon the women return from the vegetable garden carrying large baskets of yams. To keep off the rain that has begun to fall, they cover their backs with sheets of woven matting. It provides effective protection under normal rainy conditions, but for the torrential, ravine-filling downpours frequent in these mountains, there is no portable protection. The women stay in the village only long enough to deposit their yams. Some go out again to gather firewood; others carry off four-foot-long bamboo water containers to be refilled. The hollow bamboo sections each hold more than a gallon of water. Once filled, they are plugged, and when a thirsty Kwaio wants a drink, the plug is removed, a banana leaf spout is inserted, and the drinker simply tilts the bamboo up in the air. My first attempt at using a bamboo canteen resulted in a long, cool stream of water hitting me in the left eye.

The bamboo water containers are indicative of the Kwaio's level of self-sufficiency and their independence from the products of Western civilization. Indeed, the only manufactured items widely used are machetes, a few axes, some ancient rifles, and cast-iron cooking pots (one for each extended family), as well as an occasional pair of cotton pants with singlet for a few of the men and some pieces of cloth for women's and men's sarongs. Sharpened sticks are still used for digging in the gardens, flint for striking fires, and rattan for all manner of baskets, mats, and carriers. In fact, nearly everything the Kwaio use—their huts, most weapons, and even their musical instruments—are made from native materials and are usually carefully crafted with only the most rudimentary of tools. Sharp rocks file and shape, bamboo needles poke small holes, and various natural fibers are carefully woven to make twine, bow strings, and rope. Few Kwaio have ever seen—much less used—a cigarette lighter or matches, which would not last long in the greenhouse humidity of Malaita anyway. Almost no Kwaio has ever worn shoes, and only a few of the men have ever seen an automobile. In this age of motorized transportation, there are few corners of the world so untouched. Were it not for the inaccessibility of their mountain strongholds, their fierce reputation, and their total devotion to maintaining their culture, the Kwaio would long ago have joined their Third World cousins around the globe selling trinkets to the tourists.

I ask the men what changes have taken place for the Kwaio since the Bell massacre. They say, immediately, that there are very few killings anymore, either of outsiders or of their own people. Then Anifanaia explains that they have become very poor. "Since when the soldiers destroyed the tambu [sacred/taboo] places of our people," he says, "the result of that even today [is that] our crops is not grown well. If we feed the pig, there's few big pigs. [It is] not as before, when people have power with their ancestors and they grow things well in the garden and they feed pig and there are more pigs. But since then, when they [soldiers] destroy all our tambu places, all our foods not grow well anymore. And when we feed the pigs— mainly the pigs is what we earns money from, shell money from it [trading to the people on the coast]—pigs not grow big. Now we very poor because these tambu places now [are] no good."

There are other factors that have adversely affected the Kwaio's crops. Taro used to be a staple of their diet until the 1950s when a taro blight swept through certain areas of the western Pacific, not only destroying the crop but contaminating the soil wherever it was grown. No one on those western islands has been successful at rais- ing taro since. The Kwaio are vaguely aware of this and of their lack of modern agricultural techniques for dealing with the poor jungle soil on which they must depend. They have long asked for medical aid from their government (and anyone else who did not wish to convert them), as well as for agricultural assistance. Neither has been forthcoming from any source. Still, the Kwaio feel that it is the desecration of their holy places that has been largely responsible for putting them in disfavor with their ancestors. The spirits have withheld the mana which previously had nourished their crops and provided large and healthy pig herds. Now they are poor and are struggling just to survive.

Late that evening a ceremony takes place in our honor. We are invited into the smoky cooking hut, which is packed to overflowing with villagers. Men congregate on a split-bamboo shelf that extends along the rear wall, and women and children wherever they can find dirt floor space around the two fires. In the flickering light, two lines of men and boys sit facing each other on the floor. Each holds two twelve-inch sections of bamboo, which they clack rhythmically on flat rocks in front of them. The men and women in the background set up a moaning chant, sometimes a slow aye-yie-yie, sometimes an ahh-haa-haa, rising and falling in a set pattern. Now a group of women begins singing a rapid dialogue, welcoming us and expressing their hospitality. Not far into the concert, the smoke inside the hut overwhelms us and drives us out. We sit by the door enjoying both the concert and the cool evening air. The chanting and clacking go on, varying slightly in tempo and melody with each new song. Suddenly the clacking instruments are joined by a mountain-clear melody, the lyrical rise and fall of a pair of pan-pipes. They soon dominate completely, projecting a glass-fragile clarity above the background humming, singing, and clacking. Babies sleep in their mothers' arms and larger children are propped against any surface, as late into the night the music continues. Finally, hardly able to hold our heads up, we thank the Kwaio for honoring us and drop exhausted into our tent. Soon thereafter the concert breaks up.

The following morning we leave some penicillin for the old man, now well on his way to recovery. The young girl's father tells us that the Fansidar has checked his daughter's fever and delirium, too. So with high spirits and a feeling of at least a little accomplishment, we thank the Kwaio for their hospitality and, with our small procession of porters, march out of Muilage.

17

LAMEUKA,

PRINCE OF THE KWAIO

The march from Muilage soon turns into a crawl—literally. For the last twenty-four hours it has been raining and the summer picnic is over. What started as a little drizzle grows into a drumming, roaring downpour. Now everything is sodden. The mountainside trails have turned into slimy, ochery ooze, and walking on them is like trying to walk on oil. Before the trip Paul suggested that Jo Ann and I buy some spike-soled, rubber jungle boots. Since our tennis shoes were in decent shape, we neglected to take his advice. Big mistake. Jo Ann has rubber cleats on the soles of her tennies, but mine have worn down and I pay the price repeatedly, falling head over heels, crashing into the undergrowth at each third step. Staffs are cut for me, but since they are covered with slippery red mud, they are impossible to hang onto and go shooting down the mountainside like runaway javelins. Fortunately, no one gets speared. The porters decide that I should lead on mountainside descents. They regard me as the alpine equivalent of the drunken driver.

We have a new guide accompanying us. His name is Lameuka. He is about fifty years old, handsome, with fine sensitive features, a slight build, and an inquisitive but regal demeanor. Lameuka's father, who died only a few years ago, was a chief, and according to Paul, Lameuka will soon be one himself. Even at first glance he appears more aware of the world and more intelligent than most of the village men. Compared to the dull-ash composure of the others, his curiosity radiates like a bright flame. Of the dozen men at Muilage, Lameuka was the only one who seemed to want to

[*253*]

know about us and the outside world. Whereas the others exhibited a haughtiness that barely concealed their insecurity with outsiders, Lameuka seemed open, happy, and sure of himself. He watched while I ambled around photographing the village. I had two cameras around my neck, one with a wide-angle lens and the other with a telephoto. Lameuka was aware of a camera's function, but he didn't understand why I used two, and made signs to indicate the reason for his curiosity. Taking the strap of one camera at a time from around my neck, I focused them on two pigs rooting in front of a nearby hut and had him look through the viewfinders. The first camera showed him a scene of the pigs and hut, the second only the much-magnified pigs' heads. As he took the second camera from his eye Lameuka beamed in wonder.

Lameuka was in the village when we arrived, and so we naturally assumed that he and his family lived there, but they didn't. Lameuka's wife was a lovely woman in her thirties with short-cropped hair and an intense, confident gaze. Mamani was the only Kwaio woman wearing a dress, a worn but eyecatching red, green, and blue paisley shift that Lameuka must have purchased for her in Auki and that, unlike the clumsy cotton wraparounds worn by the other women, showed off her muscled curves. Both Jo Ann and I longed to get to know Mamani. She seemed intelligent and more worldly than any of the other women, and we felt she could give us many insights into a woman's life in the Kwaio kingdom. In spite of her confident appearance, however, Mamani was too shy to speak with us. It might have taken weeks before she opened up to us, and that was time we did not have. Paul had made a commitment to return to the coast in a week for an important festival, and without him the nearly impenetrable barrier of language would have severely limited our ability to understand Lameuka or the other Kwaio people.

Mamani was accompanied by Lumale, her engaging and very attractive thirteen- or fourteen-year old daughter, who closely followed her mother's lead in all social situations. Lumale was one of the few unmarried girls we saw and she certainly must have been in great demand as a prospective wife. No doubt she would fetch Lameuka a good number of pigs and many fathoms of shell money.

Lameuka and Mamani's other child was a boy of perhaps ten or eleven. Ata'obo was proud and curious and exhibited the unabashed superiority and aloof demeanor common to his peers. The Kwaio boys had few responsibilities. They did not help with village chores, though they did on occasion scamper up a tall palm or other large tree to gather wild fruits or nuts as easily and as confidently as squirrels. Mostly they played, or practiced using the various weapons available to them. They seemed to share the bonds of a rich camaraderie, independent of everyone else in the village. Ata'obo did understudy his father, however, learning the rights, rituals, and skills that would allow him to take his place as a male leader of his people. We witnessed a combined panpipe concert and music lesson performed by father and son. Lameuka led, using body language to help convey rhythm. When Ata'obo stumbled, Lameuka would stop, then hum the notes in rhythm, "Huh, huh, hunh hunh, hunh, hunh," until Ata'obo caught on. The boy was very quick and usually was able to play a skillful imitation of his father's melody on the first or second attempt.

Paul informs us that Lameuka has invited us to stop at his home, which is on our route to the next village. Eagerly we accept the invitation. But after a morning on the "trail" we are already so exhausted that we have no energy to think about that pleasant prospect. Digging our fingernails into the ocher muck, we crawl one foot at a time up the next mountainside. At times there are no roots or trees to grab, and after incredible efforts to crawl upwards, gaining only twenty or thirty inches, we slowly but inexorably slide, fighting, grasping and scratching, back down the mountain, four, five or six feet—or until we crash into whoever is behind us, often bowling them over, too. In the worst places Paul uses the machete to cut handholds in the bank, but they give us little extra purchase. The exertion is taking its toll. We are sweating buckets. Every fifteen minutes, for hours on end, I wring a half-pint of perspiration from the loose-fitting shirt that now is plastered to my skin like a soggy bandage. In the week that we trek through the mountains I will lose nearly twenty pounds; Jo Ann, to her dismay, loses only one.

All our energy and concentration is required for each step in this nightmarish journey. And, worse, every ounce of stamina already seems expended. We fall into each passing brook and greedily lap the water like dogs, oblivious in our exhaustion to what organisms it might contain. In one of the packs we have a pump-type water purifier, but our fatigue is so complete that both the purifier and any thoughts of disease are completely out of mind. Fortunately, the sparkling streams are unpolluted, and with the beginning of the rains, in particular, there is no danger of disease.

The frustration of our extreme exertion and lack of progress is compounded by watching how easily the Kwaio surmount the same obstacles. On one mud-covered mountainside that we have been alternately crawling up and tumbling down, an old lady—at least sixty years old—goes effortlessly past us, charging up the mountain, her double-wide feet splayed out and her ample toenails gripping the mud like a fly's suction pads. The amazing part is that strapped to her back is an enormous load of firewood. In a few minutes she clears the summit, three hundred feet above us, and disappears. I am thankful she has gone on her way. Emotionally I could not have endured it if, gaily, she had stayed to help us while almost totally obscured by her mountain of firewood.

At last we reach a more heavily wooded area where the going is easier, only to be confronted by new dangers. A series of very deep and almost impenetrable, thickly grown ravines are directly in our path. Perhaps the result of centuries of flash floods, the ravines extend for miles, thus forcing us to choose either a long and difficult detour or some method of crossing. The Kwaio, of course, have solved the problem by felling trees to provide narrow bridges in the directions they wished to follow. Only now, with the rains, the tree-bridges have become as slime-covered and slippery as the mountainsides we have just climbed. We stop at the end of a log spanning a fifty-foot-wide ravine that is nearly as deep. From the ravine bottom, jagged boulders jut up at us, just waiting for a misstep. Lameuka, his wife, and son cross the log without a care. Even some of the porters carrying packs on their heads stride easily across. "Oh, no. Not a chance," we tell Paul. He spends half an hour cutting through the undergrowth on the ravine bottom before we and the rest of the porters are able to get through. Some of the ravines, though, are either filled with water or for other reasons are impossible to cross except on the slippery logs. Then we take one little sliding step at a time. Eyes half closed or glued on some imaginary star, with breath held tightly and *disaster* firmly fixed in our minds, and sometimes even holding onto Paul's outstretched hand, we edge across, certain of bone-crunching catastrophe.

Finally, leaving the ravines we climb a barren ridge and stagger into Lameuka's compound. Utterly exhausted, Jo Ann and I drop on a log serving as a bench in front of one of the huts. Mamani brings us a bamboo canteen and we nearly empty it, letting a little of the precious water splash over our heads and down our necks. Lameuka and his family look on sympathetically. Their compound is a miniature replica of Muilage and, in fact, of all Kwaio villages. It perches precariously on a tiny mountain shoulder that drops off steeply on three sides. I would hate to be here in a hurricane. The ridge is completely unprotected and the three little huts, though carefully crafted, look as if they would fly to Timbuktu in a big wind. Just outside the bamboo-ringed compound is a two-woman-size menstrual hut that is somehow attached to the almost vertical mountainside. Below it is oblivion.

On a shelf over the doorway of the men's hut rests a lance and a long narrow bow. Observing the direction of my gaze, Lameuka smiles and fetches the objects for my inspection. The graceful five-foot bow, light and smooth to the touch, is made from a reddish-tan, close-grained wood that I have never heard of. With it he hands me four eight-inch bamboo arrows that are like feathers, almost weightless. The heads and shafts of the arrows are one piece, and in place of feathers on the rail are micron-thin flukes cut from some species of palm. Lameuka beckons. We follow him outside the compound. Where the ridge arm joins the mountain there is a slight fold, and in it stand a few dozen skinny saplings, at least three hundred feet from us. Quickly Lameuka fits an arrow to the finely woven fiber bowstring, then in one fluid motion raises the bow and fires the arrow, thwack, dead center in a six-inch sapling. The arrow is so far away that if it weren't a different color from the tree we couldn't even see it. A lucky shot? Nonchalantly, Lameuka sends a second arrow that lands about two inches below and only slightly to the right of the first one. Almost as amazing as his skill is his aplomb. Casually he picks up his lance, instantly finds its balance, and with two quick steps whips it toward the distant tree. This, apparently, is the maximum range for a javelin. But it arcs through the air in a gentle parabola and spears into the dirt barely a foot from the target tree. Lameuka shakes his head ruefully; bad shot.

We return to the log bench and Lameuka sits on a flat rock opposite us. His bright-eyed son squats alongside him. I ask Lameuka if it is difficult to keep the children, as they get older, from wanting to leave their people to work down on the seacoast. He nods. "We need schools among the peoples in the mountains," he says, "so that same time the childrens learn English and other things, we teach them our culture."

Just as most of the Kwaio have never seen a doctor, neither have they had any teachers or schools in the mountains. Generation after generation of Kwaio has grown up without any education whatsoever.

"What about trying to find some means of making money so that your people don't have to go to the coast to work on the plantations to earn money to pay their taxes?" I ask.

Lameuka says, "We are asking the government to give us some assistance, some agriculture people to come and train us here how to plant crops, and mainly because in the mountain only things that we can earn money is like taro, sweet potato, or how to feed pigs. We do it as our old grandfathers did, but we couldn't earn enough money because we don't know how to feed the pigs in proper way or plant taros in a proper way and other things that we can earn money. So we needs the help from the government so we know [how] to grow good crops and earn more money and our people [don't need] to go out into other parts of the Solomon Islands to get money."

"Are there trees or bushes here that do not grow on the coast which the Kwaio people could use to make things or to provide medicines you could sell? Do you know of anything that you could sell? I guess if you knew of anything you'd be selling it," I add, weakly.

"[There are a] few things we can sell to the seacoast because they don't have those vines or those plants or those trees on the sea-coast. Only we in the mountain have it. Some kind[s] of plant are used for making the [traditional] combs and some kind of vines that we can make medicine for curing people when they sick."

"What kind of sickness?" I ask.

"Well, if there's [a boil] on their body, or if their back is very pain and things like that," he answers.

"They rub this on."

"They rub on or they can put the leaf and burn the leaf in the fire. Then they take out and they put in a pipe and smoke [it]."

Who knows how many other medicinal secrets are hidden in these isolated mountains and in the medicinal repertoire of the Kwaio. What this tribe needs is an altruistic ethnobiologist to explore the potential of the native herbs and medicines. Perhaps there are plants growing here with important properties that the Kwaio themselves could harvest or even raise.

I decide to broach a subject that has been intriguing me. Relations between the Kwaio mountain villages in the east and those in the west have been fraught with difficulty. "Are the east Kwaio people coming over here and causing trouble?" I ask him.

"The east Kwaio people are very dangerous," Lameuka answers. "Even though we are related to them, but when they come over to west Kwaio side, then they found out that people here have many pigs and have lot of shell money. Then second time when they come over they will steal all of the pigs that they can and they steal the shell moneys."

Of course the eastern Kwaio deny these accusations and instead insist that it is their more westerly brethren who are actually the pig stealers and troublemakers. This suspicion and mutual distrust exists even though the "eastern" and "western" villages are often as little as five or six miles apart. If someone stole your pig fifty or sixty years ago, you took revenge by killing him. But since capital punishment has largely ended in the Kwaio kingdom, what punishment is meted out today to the convicted pig stealers? And how and by whom are they convicted? I ask my two Kwaio friends.

"At the moment we have twenty-six chiefs from main villages in western Kwaio," Paul answers. "And they are making the rules

for the custom. Yes, and eastern Kwaio have the same," he continues. "Now if somebody steal a pig and they [the chiefs] found out
that he is the one that steal the pig, instead of killing him, they say
to him to pay a lot of compensation to the owner of the pig."

"How can they make him do that?" I ask.

"If they find out that he's the one that steal the pig and they
say, 'Okay, you steal my pig, you give [so much] shell money
then.'"

"Why will he do that? Why won't he just say, 'No, I'm not going to pay? It wasn't me, I'm not going to pay.'"

"Well, but if he's deny that he's stealing that pig, then they [the
chiefs] will say, 'You swear by the name of your ancestors.' Because
this swearing is a very big thing in our custom. But if you really do
that [crime] and if is true that you steal that pig and if you swear by
the name of your ancestors or your grandfather, then your ancestors
will kill you for that, because you tell lie."

"Have you ever seen anybody die from this?" I ask.

"When I was in [another] village, a man was swearing by the
name of his ancestors and his forefathers," Paul says. "But he did
the [crime], so he died suddenly after swearing this."

"This is something that you saw?"

"Yes."

"And you were about how old?"

"Ten years old."

"And this man, what was he accused of, that he denied?"

"He denied that he stealed that shell money, so the old chief
say, 'Okay. You say that you are not the one that stolen this shell
money. Okay, you swear by the name of your ancestors.' Then he
did. Then they say, 'Okay, if after a month that you will not [be]
sick and die, then we believe you, that you did not do that.'"

"And so what happened to him?"

"After a month, before a month, he died."

"How?"

"He got sick."

"But I mean, what kind of sickness? What did it appear like?"

"It's appear like, you know, his body was getting smaller,
smaller, smaller. Then he suddenly he died."

"Was he in pain?"

"Yes, of course, he's in pain!"

"But I mean did he vomit? Did he have a fever? What was the matter with him?"

"I can remember that all of the joining [joints] of his body were, you know, all pained."

"The joints of his body hurt?"

"As well as his head and he cannot walk, you know, cannot go around. He just stay in the house until he die."

"Did he say, 'I'm sorry that I lied.' Did he admit the crime? Did he think that this was causing his death?"

"No, he denied until he died."

"And this was a story that you heard or you actually saw this man?"

"I actually saw that man. He was related me."

"He was related to you? How was he related?"

"Because, you see, he's the brother of my father that this happen to."

"And this happened in the mountains?"

"In the mountains. In the village near that mountain where I was born," Paul concludes.

"Too bad this doesn't work in the United States," I muse.

Actually, this phenomenon, closely related to what is termed "voodoo death," is more common and widespread than most Westerners realize. Ethnobotanist Wade Davis, who researched the causes of voodoo death in Haiti, cites another example of it in his book *The Serpent and the Rainbow:*

In Australia, for example, aborigine sorcerers carry bones extracted from the flesh of giant lizards, and when these slivers are pointed at a person while a death spell is recited, the individual invariably sickens and almost dies. According to one scientific report the victim stands aghast, with his eyes staring at the treacherous pointer, and with his hands lifted as though to ward off the lethal medium which he imagines is pouring into his body. His cheeks blanch and his eyes become glassy and the expression on his face becomes horribly distorted. . . . [H]e attempts to shriek but usually the sound chokes in his throat, and all that one might see is froth at his mouth. His body begins to tremble . . . he sways backwards and falls to the ground . . . writhing as if in mortal agony. After awhile he becomes very composed and crawls to his [shelter]. From this time onwards he sickens and frets, refusing to eat and keeping aloof from the daily affairs of the tribe.

At this point only the nangarri, or medicine man, may save him by initiating a complex ritual. But should the nangarri refuse to cooperate, the victim will almost certainly die.[1]

Davis goes on to explain that European physicians in World War I saw traumatized but physically untouched soldiers keel over and die for no known reason. The doctors later became familiar with voodoo death in other cultures and saw a definite resemblance. They postulated that terrified individuals suffered from a sudden and overwhelming stimulation of the sympathetic-adrenal system, which led to a critical drop in blood pressure and subsequent death. This phenomenon, usually stemming from curses or hexes put on a victim, still occurs in some parts of Africa and Latin America, as well as in the western Pacific. In many instances, the impact on the victim seems to be as effective as any other form of execution.

"What happens if someone kills a person?" I ask Paul and Lameuka. "Do the Kwaio chiefs decide on compensation or does the killer go to jail?"

"Well, for example," Paul says, "in village near here [were] a woman and her husband. This husband went to work on a plantation. So when he return, his brother was committing adultery with her. When he heard the story, suddenly he took a knife and cut off his brother's head and as well as the woman. Killed both of them."

"Did he go to jail for that?"

"He go to jail and the [other] brothers [of the dead man] ask the government that they can fix it, on the custom side of the Kwaio peoples."

[1] *The Serpent and the Rainbow*, Wade Davis. New York: Simon & Schuster, 1985, p. 399.

"And what did the government say?"

"The government said, 'Oh, it's all right.' So they allowed him to come back and they fix it with the custom."

"So he paid compensation?"

"He paid a compensation of hundred grade shell money and a hundred pigs."[2]

"So his family paid that to the families of the woman and the brother?"

"Yes."

"How long was he in jail before they would let him go back to his family?"

"He was sent to prison just one month before the government release him from the prison."

"And this happened in 1981?"

"1981."

"Do the police ever come up in the mountains?" I ask.

"You mean to the village?" Paul says.

"Yeah, not just to that village. Do they ever come if somebody's stealing or there's trouble? Do they ever come up here?"

"Well, but if they [the Kwaio people] ask the police, why, of course, the police will."

"So when you ask for the police, do they always come?"

"Sometimes, but sometimes they don't come."

"How many times have they been up here in, let's say, the last few years?"

"In these western Kwaio area, the lastest policeman that came in the mountain area is during my own time when I was area constable for the western Kwaio area council in 1976. That's the last time that I came with the police for special case between a woman and with her child. She kill her child and just buried it in the swamp and they ask police to take her down to Auki for court."

"You were the constable, Paul?"

---

[2] The shell money is the equivalent of U.S. $125 and the pigs' total value would be about $375. This penalty is so large in terms of Kwaio living standards that the defendant and his entire extended family would likely have to toil most of their lives to pay it. With the close family structure that still exists, such a penalty provides a deterrent to major crime.

"I was constable during that time."

"And that was eleven years ago. That's the last time a police-man has been up here?"

"Yes."

"Okay. Do your people like to see the policemen come up here or not?"

Paul does his best to dodge this one. "Well, at the moment they are twenty-six chiefs form in a council and they are making their own rules for the custom."

Paul refuses to admit that his people don't want outsiders mak-ing their rules and meting out penalties for crimes. Apparently, the Kwaio have been successful in convincing the central government, which does not have the resources to provide adequate police pro-tection anyway in these desolate mountains, that they are capable of governing themselves.

It is getting late, and we still have a long way to go to reach the next village before nightfall. Reluctantly we say good-bye to Lameuka's family, although Lameuka himself will accompany us, since Paul is not familiar with this particular route. We start down the east side of the ridge, cursing every foot of the descent because it means a corresponding long crawl up the next soggy mountain. We are now heading southeast, making a big loop that eventually will return us to the coast. Late in the day, after climbing up and down uncounted slimy mountains and crossing too many slithery log bridges, we arrive at the next village.

Aakon, another impoverished ridge-top village, seems totally deserted. We tiptoe past empty huts. Both Paul and Lameuka call out and receive no answer. Suddenly, coming around a hut, we al-most stumble over a naked old lady sitting on a rock tending three little babies. They are guarded by a ferocious, snarling black and white dog. The porters look startle-eyed for trees to climb. This dog is known far and wide for biting strangers, and it sure looks as though it wants to bite us. Fortunately, a little girl standing nearby, carrying a tiny baby, grabs the dog by the scruff of its neck, allowing us to pass unbitten: eight big adults saved by a five-year-old girl. Most of the villagers have gone to the same mortuary feast as the travelers we passed on the mountaintop on our second day. We are assured, however, that the chief of the area is somewhere close by and will soon be here to greet us.

We set up camp a few hundred yards downslope in an area where the village had once stood and been partly destroyed in a hurricane. Paul and the porters repair an old hut while Jo Ann and I put together our tent. No sooner do we get it set up than we are invaded by an army of small children and huge-breasted mothers. They plop themselves down alongside the hut facing our tent and stare incredulously, unabashedly, at us alien beings in their midst. The babies nurse or play in their mothers' arms. Everyone else stares. We and the porters heat up some dehydrated soup-stew and mix it with rice. We don't have enough to share with the village people, and guiltily Jo Ann and I crawl into the tent to consume our dinner so that at least these hungry people won't have to watch us eat and we won't have to watch them watching us. When we again crawl into the tent that evening to go to sleep, the mothers and children are still sitting, staring at the tent. The following morning when we get up, they are sitting in exactly the same spot, still staring at the tent. We feel like the first intergalactic visitors to Earth, just landed in our spaceship—a somewhat disquieting experience for us, and heaven knows what it is for the Kwaio.

Our campsite is alive with the babble of small voices, the cries of babies disturbed by the hot morning sun. This could be Abyssinia, the Congo, or the farthest reaches of the Amazon. Giant butterflies flutter, some black with dozens of yellow spots, some black with white spots, others blue, green, black, and yellow. They flutter sometimes singly, other times in pairs, like gentle wisps of an ocean breeze. One, as large as a big saucer, comes to rest on my old white handkerchief laid out in the sun to dry. Then realizing its error, that it has not landed on a delicious white blossom, it flips and flops away again.

Insects. There are so many types of insects here, one could spend years just counting them. Lameuka found a "giant walking stick" in a riverbed yesterday. Brown, five inches long, with a bright green thorax, it was a remarkable-looking creature perched atop fragile, long, iridescent-blue legs. Equally large and much more numerous are the grasshoppers, some species of which the people eat. Last night, in another heavy rain, a joyful chorus of insects all came out of their hiding places to dance in the wetness. Centipedes headed everywhere, making determined little trails up the walls of the tent, down trees, and all across the ground. The most common centipede is about two inches long, black, and a fairly rapid mover, its little legs carrying it along at a brisk pace. Apparently it is not poisonous like some of its larger cousins, but emits a very obnoxious odor when squashed. A beautiful red arachnid marked with black balls and white stripes on its back is also busily engaged nearby, spinning its web between two branches of low bush. Paul warns us that this spider is very venomous and to stay clear of it. Nonetheless, I am fascinated by its beauty and move as close as possible, without touching, to photograph it. The spider seems to take no notice but busily goes on about its business.

For some reason the chief is staying away. Perhaps he doesn't wish to present himself without the moral support of the other village men who, with the exception of one aloof, middle-aged fellow squatting off to one side with his grandchild, are still at the mortuary feast. While we are waiting for the chief, we open up our medical kit and do what little we can for the people. There are twenty-six children. Almost all have the distended bellies of malnutrition, as well as running, open sores, the constant Third World evidence of vitamin-deficient diets. Jo Ann dabs neomycin sulphate on the open sores. The futility of it all is disheartening, but doing something is better than doing nothing.

We try, through Paul, to talk to the women, but mostly they just giggle, hide their heads, or even run away in response to a question. One shriveled woman, who looks eighty-five and probably is no more than fifty, is holding a sickly, anemic-looking child covered with big discolored sores. I tell her that green vegetables might help her granddaughter. The Kwaio seem to include no greens in their diet. I ask her if she could feed the children more green vegetables—though I confess that I don't know the local plants well enough to recommend any particular ones. She replies that green vegetables don't grow well in the mountains. This may be true for certain varieties, but surely there have to be some that, with proper cultivation, would grow even in this thin, infertile soil. Along with eagerly accepted bars of soap, we have brought vegetable seeds, mostly different kinds of beans, to give to the village people. Paul carefully explains to the women how they should be planted and cultivated. Somehow, in spite of the women's interest, I don't anticipate that the vegetable growing will succeed.

From behind us a plinking melody titillates the noonday air: Beethoven's *Moonlight* Sonata. Jo Ann and her digital wristwatch with its "Beethoven alarm" are surrounded by a ring of beguiled women and children. In open-mouthed astonishment they listen to this impossibility: music without anyone playing it and coming from nothing that they can see but this tiny box tied to the white woman's hand.

Lameuka and I join the crowd. He is as delighted as the smallest child. Soon Jo Ann is explaining the movement of the second hand to him and showing him how to count the seconds. Lameuka is fascinated. He already knows how to count in English up to ten, from the time he worked at a plantation on the coast. Now he and some of the children are learning how to count to one hundred. Jo Ann makes a sequential chart for them and they count over and over, the chief-to-be and the smallest children helping each other to solve this new puzzle. Two of the porters—Jimmy, a rebellious, bright teenager, and tall, personable John, an intelligent but reserved fellow in his early twenties—join in. They each have had some primary schooling on the coast and eagerly they help the new learners. Lameuka is excited about conquering the numbers and his enthusiasm sweeps the others along. Soon they are all working on simple arithmetic. Jo Ann, using sticks and shells—and even moving the children as examples—has them adding and subtracting to five.

Paul has gone to get water, so there is no one to translate, but Jo Ann, an experienced educator, has no difficulty in getting her points across. And the Kwaio, who have never even seen a teacher, are deliriously eager to learn. After seeing that they understand the basics, Jo Ann leaves them to practice on their own. Jimmy and Lameuka sit with the chart Jo Ann has made. Pointing to the figure 1, they animatedly discuss it in Kwaio. Then they look at the plus sign and compare it to all the other plus signs. Next they tackle the meaning of the minus signs. Lameuka points to all the 2s on the paper, verifying his understanding of what they represent. John joins them and suggests that Lameuka write the numbers. They borrow my pen. On the back of the chart Lameuka, for the first time in his life, begins writing numerals from 1 to 20. At first some of them come out backwards and the 3s look like Ms, but clearly they resemble the numbers he is trying to make. Laboriously, he continues to practice, striving to do his best. He is so filled with pleasure at learning that everyone around him has become excited.

John asks Jo Ann to teach Lameuka the ABCs, and so they work together on the alphabet. Then Jo Ann shows him the letters that spell his name. She tells him that l-a stand for *la*. He repeats it. She puts the m-e-u in and he pronounces *lu*. Shaking her head, she corrects him. He says the *meu*, and seeing how it fits, Lameuka becomes very excited and immediately wants Jo Ann to fill in the *ka* sound, which she does. Carefully copying her characters, this fifty-year-old man writes his name for the first time. When he is finished he sits beaming; he has never seen his name before. With great pride, he writes it again and again. There is one more thing he must see written. With almost imperial insistence he demands that Jo Ann write the word Kwaio for him. Then he sits and stares at the two words next to each other. Worlds revolve before his eyes. Lameuka doesn't say what he is thinking and we don't ask him.

Adobo, chief of the area around Aakon village, finally appears in the middle of our second afternoon there. He is a vain, pompous little man, about fifty-five, with a shrewd, calculating demeanor. We guess that he did not deign to come and greet us earlier in order to give evidence of his superiority and rank. This needless delay is not appreciated because we need his permission to interview and photograph, and we have less than two days to spend in the village. When Adobo finally does arrive, he makes various unconvincing excuses for his tardiness and then begins berating the women and children for their poor manners in not coming to greet us. Of course, they were the only ones who *did* greet us.

Informed that Jo Ann is teaching the children how to count, Adobo immediately presents us with evidence of his superiority. He takes a banana leaf and with the edge of his machete slices it into a large number of slivers. Lining up his obedient but unruly little battalion of women and children, he hands each of them a banana-leaf sliver and begins counting them in English: one, two, three, four, until he gets to twelve, jumps to fourteen, fifteen, thirteen, eighteen, nineteen, and in order to twenty-three. After twenty-three the chief hops a little to thirty-one, skips to thirty-four, dodges a bit through the rest of the thirties, then proceeds to forty-nine, forty-ten and forty-eleven, where he gets stuck. "Forty-twelve," I prompt, helpfully. The chief continues on a bit, but trails off at forty-fourteen, having made a remarkable impression, not only on his villagers, but on us as well.

As soon as Paul tells Adobo our purpose in visiting the Kwaio, he reiterates their need for medical and agricultural assistance, as well as a school for the children. I ask him why they can't go to schools on the coast.

"Because they [would] need [to] live there," he answers. "And who [would] feed them and take care of them? And [there] they need clothes and also school fees: forty dollars pay for one children. So for us mountain people it's very hard for us to get that money. Also, if childrens go to school on coast they forget us, forget their parents, forget their culture, and don't want come back and live in dirty place, rock place, here."

"And yet the Kwaio people pay taxes to the government, don't you?" I ask him.

"Yes," Adobo answers, "we pay tax, one time each year, for whole of our life. Four dollar per person [per adult male]. We thinking government help us with doctor, with school, so that's why we paying tax for so long. And the government didn't do anything for our needs."

According to Paul, more than one thousand Kwaio children are affected. He shakes his head in sadness.

"Why doesn't the government help you?" I ask Adobo.

"Well, I explain you about that," he answers. "Solomon Islands is Christian country and the Christian peoples are trying to take Kwaio peoples and lose their culture. The government don't help the Kwaio people. We don't find out why. Maybe they hate the custom people," he adds with emphasis.

Conversations with the Cannibals

All the Kwaio I spoke with felt that they were hated and discriminated against by the central government, which is largely composed of fundamentalist Christians. Certainly they have few supporters in the government and it has made no effort to help them. However, the Kwaio do not realize how poor and how large their country is. The average family income for the ninety percent of the country's three hundred thousand people who still live in the villages is only U.S. $250 per year. The government struggles to run the country on a minuscule budget. In 1985, the last year for which figures were available, government revenue was less than $28 million and the development funds available, mostly from foreign aid, totaled less than $15 million. This was not enough to begin to address health, education, and social needs in the thousands of villages with significant populations on the country's thirty-six islands. So it is not surprising that the remote and feared Kwaio receive no assistance, even though they have been paying taxes. While underestimating the available largess, the Kwaio are surely justified in believing that the government does not value their culture, for it has done nothing to help them preserve it. Probably only an upwelling of international support will make the Solomon Islands government realize there is value in the now-unique Kwaio culture.

We talk a while longer but it is getting late. The setting sun breaks through the clouds and casts a golden-green glow over the surrounding mountains. The air takes on a cool edge, like a late afternoon in autumn. The raised voices of small children engrossed in their games ebb and flow, babbling and arguing like children everywhere. The women talk quietly among themselves, smoking their pipes as they gather firewood or cut up yams for dinner. Doves settle in the trees around the village, their peaceful coos floating like bubbles in the fading light. The falling shade of evening comes quickly in these forlorn mountains. The setting sun is a fleeting red and yellow ember that seems to disappear in an instant. Then the blueness of dusk envelops the Kwaio peaks as the night creatures come alive, overtaking the jungle village with amphibian and insect sounds. The Kwaio quietly sit by their cookfires, eating their yams.

At about ten that night, Adobo orders the obligatory greeting ceremony of singing and clacking bamboos. It is lackluster but goes on long into the evening, finally ending at one or two in the morning. Even then the young boys are up and making noise. Finally there is silence except for the insect concertos. Again at four-thirty the boys are calling to each other, laughing and shouting. While they are endearing with their bright smiles and easy laughter, the free-spirited little beasts lack any consideration for others.

The next morning we stumble out of the tent bleary-eyed. Paul greets us looking even worse. "Didn't you sleep?" I ask him. He doesn't want to answer. Finally, with great reluctance, he says, "Well some men from east Kwaio villages were coming past here. So I sit next to tent so they know you are guarded." Paul is wonderful—an exceptional person.

Later that morning we continue our journey back to the coast. Aside from my near free-fall down an almost vertical mountainside, the trek back is fairly easy, mostly wading through riverbeds drier, according to Paul, than they have ever been.

As we leave the mountains and descend to civilization, my thoughts turn to Lameuka, the bright, shining, friendly chief-to-be. To me he personifies the finest qualities of the Kwaio people. On the trip from his village I asked him, "Lameuka, the outside world is coming closer and closer. Each year more of your people go to the coast. How can you preserve your culture?"

His answer was a simple one. "We must make our custom grow on to our children," he said. "We must learn them how to do things in our custom life, learn them about tambus and learn them how to sacrifice a pig for our ancestors. So when we die we believe that our sons, they will keep on holding these things of our culture."

"What about the missionaries and the government?" I asked him. "They want to change the Kwaios. If they and foreigners come in, do you think they will change your people?"

We were sitting on two rocks next to a brook. Lameuka seemed lost watching the endless stream of water. Finally he said, "There will be thing[s] changing if foreigners or government come in. Things like wearing of clothes; that will be very new to our mountain people. But the main thing[s] like our tambus, our customs, what we believe from our ancestors, that will *never* change. *Nobody* will change it."

Before we part from Lameuka, we search for something we can give him in appreciation for his kindness and his help. We consider giving him our collapsible shovel, the modern counterpart to the old army trenching tool. It is strong and compact, and along one side of the blade are serrations that can be used for cutting and grinding. Yet we hesitate. All gifts from civilization seem to contribute to the destruction of the culture as much as they help the recipient. Then our thoughts wander to the mountainside vegetable gardens where Lameuka's wife and the other women still dig laboriously in the hard clay soil with nothing more than sharpened sticks and rocks. Of course it is the right gift. Lameuka receives it gingerly, gently, as if it were a fine piece of china. The benefit to his wife and family is evident on his face. It is as if we were giving his wife five more years of life. Tears fill his eyes. He does not know how to thank us. Nor does he know, and we cannot find the words to tell him, that we have much more to thank him for than he us. We put an arm around him and wish him well.

And as we wade through the rivers back to Western civilization, we wish these people who have almost nothing except their slender physical stamina, their pride, and the strength of their beliefs, who ask little of the outside world and who receive nothing from it—we also wish them well.

Appendix A

REVEREND BILL'S SERMON

(July 12, 1987)

Our text for this service comes from the passage we have read from the New Testament. The Acts of the Apostles, chapter nine, verse four. Last part of that verse: "Saul, Saul why persecutest thou me?" "Saul, Saul, why persecutest thou me?" Since Pentecost we have been studying the activities of the Holy Spirit among men. The activities of God the Father through the Spirit, among the different conditions of mankind, and today I want us to look at this story of Saul of Tarsus. To me this is the first stage to preserve the best in man, for the development of mankind. The first stage to preserve what is good in man. The best qualities within man must be preserved.

Now this is one of the activities of the Holy Spirit as I see it. In society we have people who's looked down upon as rebels, as criminals. In our hearts, in our hearts, in our human hearts, in our human understanding, we treat them as criminals and we look down upon those people. We don't see any good in them. We look at the bad in those people. And often it is common that the attitude is always to destroy such, get rid of such.

Now this is part of the human weakness, as I see it, as we study this portion of the activities of the Holy Spirit. In the eyes of God, He sees the good in a person, and if God sees the good in a person he sees the good in that person for the development of other people, for the development of mankind as a whole. The story of Saul of Tarsus. Saul wasn't a criminal. He wasn't a bad man in the eyes of the world of his time. He was a righteous man. He was a good man. He was a believer in God. And because he was a believer in God he was a righteous man, he took it upon himself to destroy anyone who opposes his belief, the belief of his church. He took it upon himself to do away with any person who objects to the belief of his church. They were treated as criminals in the eyes of the church of the day, in the eyes of Saul of Tarsus.

As we read in the first verse in the ninth chapter, he was still breathing slaughter and persecution for those people who followed Jesus, whom the church at that time looked down on, treated them as enemies of God's people, of God's children. And he was out on the road to Damascus with a letter of authority from the chief priest to arrest anybody that he finds in Damascus who follows this new religion or this new line of faith that opposes the established church of Judas.

He was an honest man. He didn't realize that he was doing the wrong thing. Now this is the church of the young man. To him he was doing the right thing in the eyes of God. He was doing the perfect thing for the restoration of his people. He was doing completely the right thing. But he was evil. He was evil to the core. He was evil to the heart, simply because he was out to destroy other people that's created the image of God.

Those he were out to destroy were not famous. They were persons created in the image of God. And because he was out to do that, he was committing a crime, a serious crime in the eyes of God. But the pleasing thing about his whole episode is that God did not look upon Saul as a criminal. God did not look upon Saul to see the bad side of his life. God looked at the good that lies in this man, Saul.

Saul, why are you doing this to me? Saul wasn't doing anything to him. Saul was doing it to the people. But the voice said to him, 'You are persecuting me. You are doing me harm, Saul. Why are you doing that?' Saul became conscious of himself, but there was something tragic in his life, in his behavior as a man of God. He said, 'God, what do you want me to do?' It was the confession of his life. 'Lord, what you want me to do.' Before this Saul said, 'No, I know what I want to do. I know the will of God. I'm out to fulfill the will of God by destroying those people in Damascus who follow Jesus. I'm out to destroy them because I know the will of God.'

But now he says, 'I don't know the will of God. Lord, what do you want me to do?' Now this is the joy that we find in prayer at the adored knee of God. It's looking at the good in the other person for the future development of mankind. How great though the sins there are in another person as we might think, we must always, and at all times, look at the little good there is in a man, in a person. Because that's what God looks for.

Saul, Saul, why do you persecute me? Why do you do this evil thing to me? To our people? Why are you spoiling other people? Why are you spoiling other people in their life? Why do you do it? Let this be a voice for you, and for me, at all times. This attitude of Saul is a weak man's status in you and me at all times. We like to be the good people. We like to be the best people. It's human weakness. Let us put ourselves before God in His hands.

Lord, what do you want me to do? Let this be our prayer at all times. And I'm quite sure it will be shown. He will do it for you and for me. For the benefit of the people around us. For the benefit of the world. And for the glory of God. Amen.

Appendix B

A PUBLIC APOLOGY DUE

THE INDIGENOUS PEOPLES

OF THE SOUTH PACIFIC

The following is a signed public apology from Northwest (United States) religious leaders of ten Christian faiths to the Native American tribes for destroying their traditional spiritual practices and cultures and pledging support to right past wrongs. This same apology and pledge is due the indigenous peoples of the South Pacific.

A PUBLIC DECLARATION TO THE TRIBAL COUNCILS AND TRADITIONAL SPIRITUAL LEADERS OF THE INDIAN AND ESKIMO PEOPLES OF THE PACIFIC NORTHWEST
In care of Jewell Praying Wolf James, Lummi

Seattle, Washington
November 21, 1987
Dear Brothers and Sisters,

This is a formal apology on behalf of our churches for their long-standing participation in the destruction of traditional Native American spiritual practices. We call upon our pepole for recognition of and respect for your traditional ways of life and for protection of your sacred places and ceremonial objects. We have frequently been unconscious and insensitive and have not come to your aid when you have been victimized by unjust Federal policies and practices. In many other circumstances we reflected the rampant racism and prejudice of the dominant culture with which we too willingly identified. During the 200th Anniversary year of the United States Constitution we, as leaders of our churches in the Pacific Northwest, extend our apology. We ask for your forgiveness and blessing.

As the Creator continues to renew the earth, the plants, the animals and all living things, we call upon the people of our denominations and fellowships to a commitment of mutual support in your efforts to reclaim and protect the legacy of your own traditional spiritual teachings. To that end we pledge our support and assistance in upholding the American Religious Freedom Act (P. L. 95-134, 1978), and within that legal precedent affirm the following:

1) The rights of the Native Peoples to practice and participate in traditional ceremonies and rituals with the same protection offered all religions under the Constitution.
2) Access to and protection of sacred sites and public lands for ceremonial purposes.
3) The use of religious symbols (feathers, tobacco, sweet grass, bones, etc.) for use in traditional ceremonies and rituals.

The spiritual power of the land and the ancient wisdom of your indigenous religions can be, we believe, great gifts to the Christian churches. We offer our commitment to support you in the righting of previous wrongs: To protect your peoples' efforts to enhance Native spiritual teachings; to encourage the members of our churches to stand in solidarity with you on these important religious issues; to provide advocacy and mediation, when appropriate, for ongoing negotiations with State agencies and Federal officials regarding these matters.

May the promises of this day go on public record with all the congregations of our communions and be communicated to the Native American Peoples of the Pacific Northwest. May the God of Abraham and Sarah, and the Spirit who lives in both the cedar and Salmon People be honored and celebrated.

Sincerely,

The Rev. Thomas L. Blevins, Bishop
Pacific Northwest Synod—Lutheran Church in America

The Rev. Dr. Robert Bradford, Executive Minister
American Baptist Churches of the Northwest

The Rev. Robert Brock
N.W. Regional Christian Church

The Right Rev. Robert H. Cochrane,
Bishop, Episcopal Diocese of Olympia

The Rev. W. James Halfaker Conference Minister
Washington North Idaho Conference United Church of Christ

Appendix B

[signature: R. G. Hunthausen]

The Most Rev. Raymond G. Hunthausen Archbishop of Seattle
Roman Catholic Archdiocese of Seattle

[signature: Elizabeth B. Knott]

The Rev. Elizabeth Knott, Synod Executive
Presbyterian Church Synod Alaska-Northwest

[signature: Lowell E. Knutson]

The Rev. Lowell Knutson, Bishop
North Pacific District American Lutheran Church

[signature: Thomas J Murphy]

The Most Rev. Thomas Murphy Coadjutor Archbishop
Roman Catholic Archdiocese of Seattle

[signature: Melvin G. Talbert]

The Rev. Melvin G. Talbert, Bishop
United Methodist Church—Pacific Northwest Conference

Appendix C

ASSISTANCE FOR THE KWAIO

Health for Humanity is a charitable organization sponsored by the Baha'i Faith and is based on the following principles: The inherent nobility of humanity; Respect for the diversity of cultures and their unique circumstances; The need for unified action in a spirit of service while using a multidisciplinary approach to comprehensive health care in accordance with locally determined objectives.

At the author's request a fund has been created to receive donations for the development of health services for the Kwaio people. The fund would be used for projects that local Kwaio communities would themselves devise in consultation with Health for Humanity representatives and in conformity with the proceeding principles. Since respect for local cultures is a fundamental principle of the organization, proselytizing or imposing foreign cultural or religious beliefs upon the Kwaio would violate the very precepts on which Health for Humanity is based.

Health for Humanity is a nonprofit charitable organization. Anyone who wishes to contribute or who is interested in learning more can write to: Health for Humanity, Kwaio Project, 467 Jackson St. Glencoe, IL 60022. Interested parties with medical backgrounds are also needed. Donations should be marked "For the Kwaio."

Index

Index

Index

Index

Index